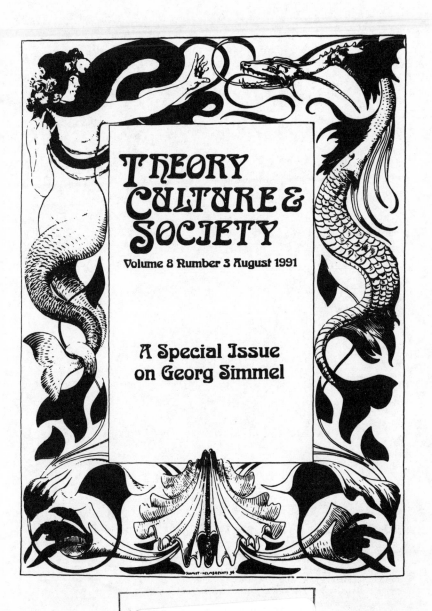

Theory Culture & Society

Volume 8 Number 3 August 1991

A Special Issue
on Georg Simmel

D1510323

THEORY CULTURE & SOCIETY

Explorations in Critical Social Science
Volume 8 Number 3 August 1991

A Special Issue on Georg Simmel

CONTENTS

Book Reviews

Georg Simmel: An Introduction

Mike Featherstone

The work of Georg Simmel has often been depicted in English-speaking circles as a contribution to formal sociology. Jennifer Wood (1983: 354), for example, observes in her entry on Simmel in an encyclopaedia of sociology that he is 'the principal figure in the "formal" school of sociology'. This view of Simmel as the sociologist who laid the foundations for the analysis of social forms such as the dyad, triad and mass, the miser, stranger and the poor, competition, sociability and conflict, has long been the conventional wisdom which has dominated the Anglo-Saxon reception of his work. With some notable exceptions, sociological theory textbooks in Britain and the United States often give only a passing reference to his writings or treat his work merely as a preparatory foundation for conflict theory, exchange theory and interactionism.[1] The reception of Simmel's work in post-war Germany was initially dominated by American sociology with the key influence being Talcott Parsons's estimation of what he regarded as the classic figures of sociology (Dahme, 1990). It was only when conflict theory and exchange theory were developed as an alternative to functionalism in the late 1950s and 1960s that Simmel's sociology was brought back to Germany from the United States.[2] This prepared the way for the more nuanced reception of his work in Germany in the late 1970s and 1980s in which his more strictly sociological writings were placed in the context of his other writings on philosophy, metaphysics, aesthetics and culture. A fuller appreciation of his overall contribution will also be aided by the availability of his collected works which are projected in a twenty-four volume German edition, of which three volumes have been published to date. The possibility of a more informed understanding of the scope of his work has also been aided by the translation into English of two of the works which Simmel considered to be amongst

Theory, Culture & Society (SAGE, London, Newbury Park and New Delhi), Vol. 8 (1991), 1–16

his finest *The Philosophy of Money* (1990) and *Schopenhauer and Nietzsche* (1986). These can be added to recently available translations of *The Problems of the Philosophy of History* (1977), *Essays on Interpretation and Social Science* (1980) and *On Women, Sexuality and Love* (1984).[3] David Frisby's 'Bibliographical Note on Simmel's Writings Available in Translation' in this issue (pp. 235–41) provides a useful update on Simmel's writings available in English.

Simmel's ability to range across disciplinary boundaries and to employ a variety of theoretical perspectives has helped to make his work relevant to those in the social sciences and humanities that are working towards the lowering of the barriers between disciplines. As we have mentioned before in the pages of this journal the rise of interest in culture since the 1980s is one symptom of this, and of all the major social theorists it is fitting that Simmel's stock should rise on the general tide of a resurgence of interest in culture and transdisciplinary theorizing. We are therefore pleased to be able to publish translations of some shorter pieces which give some of the flavour of the many-sided insights he could generate on practically any topic. The scope of his talent for handling a wide range of cultural phenomena is evident in his pieces on 'The Alpine Journey', 'The Berlin Trade Exhibition', 'The Problem of Style', and 'Money in Modern Culture' which are published in this issue, as well as in his well-known brilliant essays on topics such as 'The Ruin', 'The Adventure', 'The Handle', 'Love', 'Flirtation', 'The Picture Frame' and portraits of intellectual and artistic figures such as Goethe, Kant, Nietzsche, Rodin and Rembrandt. But, the problem has been that the brilliant many-sided insights which Simmel generated have been used against him to suggest that he lacked a capacity for systematic scientific thought. Hence we find references — some of them with patronizing and dismissive undertones — to his 'charming observations', 'brilliant insights'; that he writes as if 'overwhelmed by an avalanche of ideas', that his 'overabundance of associations' means he seems to 'take five steps sideways for every one forwards', that his work is 'the sociology of the aesthete', 'the sociology of the literary salon', and that he is a 'kind of philosophical squirrel'.

One of the key sources of this persistent image of Simmel has been the assessment which Georg Lukács wrote for a German Hungarian newspaper at the time of his death in 1918. In this article, a translation of which appears in this issue, Lukács refers to Simmel as 'the genuine philosopher of impressionism', 'the greatest representative of methodological pluralism', who displays 'a marvelling recognition of the endless diversity of the possibility of philosophical approaches and topics'. The weakness of every impressionist movement is that it is merely a protest of life against forms which have become too rigid, and hence for Lukács Simmel is a Monet of philosophy who awaits a Cezanne. This ability to differentiate what others saw as undivided unity through his sensitivity to manifold and intricate connections, in Lukács's view entailed the problem that this 'net of interrelationships must remain a labyrinth and cannot become a system'. Consequently, for Lukács Simmel's *Philosophy of Money* and *The Problems of the Philosophy of History* must be considered in the manner of fragments.

The unsystematic and fragmentary nature of Simmel's work is the central assumption of David Frisby's (1981) book *Sociological Impressionism: A Reassessment of Georg Simmel's Social Theory*. In their contribution to this collection Deena and Michael Weinstein argue that it is mistaken to depict Simmel as a sociological *flâneur* who drifts through modern life and provides fragmentary impressions; rather it is more accurate to see him as a *bricoleur*. For the Weinsteins the term *flâneur*, which Walter Benjamin used in his discussion of Baudelaire in his *Passagenwerk* (1982), is mistaken because the *flâneur* does not seek to understand society, but only to wander through it. The term *bricoleur* is regarded as much more appropriate, precisely because it does not suggest passive strolling, rather it points to the mission of active cultural mapping, which entails 'tracing the affinities and ruptures among the cultural complexes of the modern/postmodern metropolis'.[4]

There is a further related controversy concerning whether Simmel should be regarded as 'the first sociologist of modernity' as proposed by Frisby (1985) or 'the first sociologist of postmodernity ahead of his time' as argued by the Weinsteins (1990a).[5] For Simmel modernity must be understood against the premodern forms of social relations which occupied and dominated the whole human being to provide 'a form of unification englobing the total person' (Simmel, 1908: 412; quoted in Coser, 1965: 14). In modernity individuals necessarily move between a great number of social circles each of which only involves part of his personality. This segmentation of allegiances and associations provides the individual with a greater sense of his uniqueness and freedom, a self-consciousness which favours individualism. Experience, then in modernity is necessarily more fragmented and the capacity to reach some satisfying and lasting meaningful unification of the myriad of cultural objectifications that surround the individual becomes more problematic as Simmel (1968a, b) outlines in his discussions of the dominance of objective culture over subjective culture. Whether or not one wishes to attribute this process of cultural fragmentation to modernity or postmodernity depends, of course, on the definition of these terms, which are by no means unproblematic (see Featherstone, 1991).

The use of the terms *flâneur* and *bricoleur* would seem to suggest a struggle to find an appropriate metaphor to express the problem of the extent and specific nature of the unity and systematism of Simmel's work. The term 'work' itself needs qualifying as it should be differentiated to point to the questions of the unity and systematism of: a) specific works, b) Simmel's oeuvre as a whole, c) Simmel's work in relation to his life and d) the various ways in which all these relate to the particular nature of the times and the specific social relations and cultural complexes within which Simmel moved and which he sought to elucidate. There is not the space to enter into these questions here, save to indicate a few possible lines of enquiry. With regard to specific works, in the first chapter of *Soziologie* Simmel tells us that given the infinite complexity of social life and the initial crudeness of our methods it would be 'sheer megalomania to expect, at this juncture, complete clarity in the posing of questions and absolute correctness in answering them'. He stresses 'the wholly fragmentary and incomplete character' of his book and the way in which he is laying down elements as widely apart as possible in the hope that the future perfection of sociology will be able to connect them (Simmel, 1959: 335–6).[6] In the preface to the *The Philosophy of Money* he remarks that his intention is to go beyond the abstract construction of a system with its great distance from individual phenomena. Rather the unity of the work lies in 'finding in each of life's details the totality of its meaning' (Simmel, 1990: 55). It is this anti-system purpose which can be related to interpretations of Simmel's work which emphasize its affinity to deconstruction. Deena and Michael Weinstein (1990a, 1990b), for example, emphasize the 'deconstruction or de-objectivization of objective form' which is the essence of modernism and the ways in which Simmel anticipates many of the major moves in Derrida's deconstructionism. Likewise, Bryan S. Green (1988: Ch. 5) remarks that *The Philosophy of Money* is a conscious attempt to deconstruct identity and bivalence, to show that money cannot be understood via either/or modes of classification associated with realism. Rather, Simmel's expressed intention 'to build a storey beneath historical materialism' entails a deconstruction of standard narrative and causal forms of explanation in favour of allegoresis.[7]

We are pleased to be able to present for the first time in English his essay 'Money in Modern Culture' which was first published in 1896, four years before the publication of *The Philosophy of Money*, and which contains the kernel of many of the arguments which were worked into the book. His article on 'The Berlin Trade Exhibition', incidentally was also written in 1896, the same year that his important piece on 'Sociological Aesthetics' appeared (Simmel, 1968c). It betrays traces of the latter in his focus upon the richness of the 'shopwindow quality' of things designed to provide fleeting impressions to excite overstimulated and tired nerves. In a passage which anticipates much of the recent writings on consumer culture and the aesthetic aspects of commodities he remarks

> The striving to make the merely useful visually stimulating — something that was completely natural for the Orientals and Romans — for us comes from the struggle to render the graceless graceful for consumers. The exhibition with its emphasis on amusement attempts a new synthesis between the principles of external stimulus and the practical functions of objects, and thereby takes the aesthetic superadditum to its highest level. The banal attempt to put things in their best light, as in the cries of the street trader, is transformed in the interesting attempt to confer a new aesthetic significance from displaying objects together — something already happening in the relationship between advertising and poster art.

This oft remarked fine-tuned sensitivity to the nuances of the many-sided facets of phenomena and ability to illuminate them via analogies and comparisons with opposites Simmel displays in his essays, is also evident in his short piece on 'The Alpine Journey', initially published in 1895, which we are pleased to present in English translation. If Simmel's essays frequently play with unresolved paradoxes, antinomies and ambiguities they also seek to disclose unexpected unities, which bring together the most diverse and fragmentary phenomena into some more underlying coherence. One constantly comes across the term 'unity' throughout Simmel's writings down to his last writings such as 'The Conflict in Modern Culture' (1918; English trans. 1968a). This term has Kantian overtones in the ways he refers to the unifying impulse which we find, for example, in the formation of religious and aesthetic culture as well as in the attempts to make a part of our lives into an integrated whole, a system out of life's lack of system, to make a 'world' which is something beyond the immediacy of everyday life, as in the case of the adventure. At the same time there are also Hegelian overtones in his emphasis upon the transitory nature of such unities when understood in terms of the process of cultural formation and deformation, of the triumph of form over life and the destruction of form by life and the search for new cultural forms. We can also relate this to Simmel's (1959: 326ff.) previously quoted statement in *Soziologie*, which helps to elaborate his remarks that eventually sociology might be able to connect the isolated points into a systematic whole mentioned above. Simmel emphasizes that we should endeavour to move beyond the conceptualization of the central matter of sociology as the analysis of the great organs and systems which already present themselves in the form of conceptual unities such as states, unions, classes, guilds, communities, families, etc. Rather we should focus upon the immeasurable number of minor forms of interaction (*Wechselwirkung*) which flow in and out of them, between, through and around them, the less obvious and visible interactions which tie people together. These fluctuating unpretentious interactions constitute the principle of social unity, a unity which in the empirical sense is nothing but the interaction of elements.[8]

As Klaus Lichtblau points out in his contribution to this issue, for many sociologist Simmel's concept of interaction (*Wechselwirkung*) is deeply ambiguous. Max Weber, for example, found it too abstract, speculative and ultimately metaphysical in its focus upon subjectively intended meaning to the occlusion of objectively valid meaning and consequent neglect of the need for causal analysis in the cultural sciences. Nevertheless, Lichtblau argues, Simmel's concept of interaction should not be dismissed as inferior to Weber's approach, rather it was very much in tune with the contemporary relativistic world view of modern physics of Planck and Einstein, which called into question mechanistic notions of cause and effect in favour of the assumption of the fundamental relativity manifest in the dependence of phenomena on each other within a field. This focus upon the interactions between elements could also be connected to the Aristotelian tradition with its emphasis upon the context of the structural totality. Simmel was therefore opposed to diachronic causal analysis with its stress upon temporal succession in favour of the focus on the synchronic interactions which connected events.[9] The categories of cause and effect were replaced by the logical form of a mutual relationship, or interaction, in which 'the present has an effect on the past at the same time as the past on the present' (Simmel, 1980).

With regard to the question of whether an overall unity is discernible in Simmel's life work we can note that the case for unity is argued by Adler (1919, see Frisby, 1981: 5), Weingartner (1960) and Lechner (1990). Weingartner is particularly concerned to argue that it is wrong to see Simmel as an impressionist or to see his writings as merely unified through an artistic style. Despite Simmel's style, wide interests and alleged inability to sustain a systematic discussion, Weingartner (1960: 10ff.) argues there is a discernible structure in everything he wrote, and a reconstructible structure to his work as a whole which emerges in the *Lebensphilosophie* he sketched out towards the end of his life, a position which he argues was already implicit from the beginning in his various analyses of culture. For his own part Simmel argued in a later work *Grundfragen der Soziologie* (1917) that his entire oeuvre revolved around one basic question: the limits of individuality in modern society (Schnabel, 1985: 751). A theme which, incidentally, is none too far from what recent critics see as Weber's central question: the type of human being which will replace the Protestant type in the modern world. Here a number of commentators seem to be in agreement that there is an overall unity, an inner logic and coherence to Weber's work (Tenbruck, 1980; Hennis, 1988; Jaspers, 1989; Albrow, 1990).[10]

In his article 'Simmel as Educator' in this issue Donald Levine endorses Simmel's own assessment of his basic question when he remarks that 'Simmel's writings reveal a consistent commitment to the value of human individuality and personal integrity.' This again brings us back to his concern with the struggle between life and form and the need to illuminate and conceptualize the various processes which lead to the perception of unities from fragments and the fragmentation or destabilization of unities. Tendencies which cannot be regarded as having a unidirectional effect because one of the basic features of the modern order, as Levine reminds us, is its capacity to differentiate and promote opposed characteristics. For example, the fragmentation of social life can be liberating and gratifying, while the fragmentation of our experience of culture can be frustrating. Levine (1971: xliii) tells us this is 'because social fragmentation promotes the conditions for the developing individuality, whereas cultural fragmentation both hinders and assists man's self-development.' It is this capacity to separate cultural forms from social forms and to detect different modes of unification and fragmentation within them, and then to move between them in ways which at times blur the boundaries, that can be frustrating for commentators determined to extract an ordered and systematic analytical coherence from his work. For example, at the end of the first chapter of his *Soziologie* on 'The Problem of Sociology' he remarks that social science is surrounded by two philosophical areas, epistemology and metaphysics. The latter, which as we would expect, interests Simmel the most, is concerned with 'overcoming the disconnection and inner heterogeneity of individual fragments by the unity of a total picture' and at the same time it is concerned with the question of the meaning or purpose of human existence which takes us into questions of value and religious significance (Simmel, 1959: 333–4). It is, as Klaus Lichtblau emphasizes in his article, this metaphysical need for the unity of an overall view and the need to consider the value of forms of social life which made Simmel dissatisfied with the fragmentary character of detailed knowledge and pointed him 'away from sociology in favour of a more intense concern with the fundamental problems of metaphysics, aesthetics and the philosophy of religion and life'.

In his piece on 'The Aesthetics of Modern Life', David Frisby remarks on the similarity between Simmel's emphasis upon the *forms* of interaction and sociation, which point to an aesthetic dimension to all social interaction, and the way in which the Kantian theory of art (which Simmel followed) indicates the way in which art forms a unity or totality out of the fragmentary. While the aesthetic judgement for Simmel has its origins in symmetry in which harmony and organic unity are emphasized, it can lead with more refinement to the enhancement of the irregular in which the asymmetrical is taken as the highest aesthetic judgement. Frisby remarks that

> With the asymmetrical we return again to the fragment, to the aesthetic appeal of that which 'almost exclusively bears on individualistic character', to the 'rhapsodic fortuitousness' of the individual element. . . . 'Hence . . . the nowadays enjoyment of the fragment, the mere impression, the aphorism, the symbol, the underdeveloped aesthetic style'. (quotations from Simmel, 1968c)

A similar emphasis is to be found in Simmel's short piece 'Momentbilder . . . Gegensatz' which appeared in *Jugend* in 1899 in which he asks 'Have not purity and unity become an unattainable ideal for even our deepest joys, because all our feeling is a feeling of differences?' As Otthein Rammstedt informs us in his article in this issue, this piece signed with the initials G.S., was one of thirty contributions which included poems, collections of aphorisms, fairy-tales, short stories and reflections which appeared in a Munich-based *Jugendstil* illustrated artistic review entitled *Jugend* founded in 1896. Rammstedt provides an interesting overview of the decade of contributions Simmel made, a phase which incidentally he was later to deny having lived through in his unfinished auto-biography. We are also pleased to be able to reproduce some of the motifs and illustrations which appeared with Simmel's articles in this issue.

It is possible to detect in Simmel's work a further variant of this modern tendency to seek to play with more complex aesthetic unities and syncretisms in the paradoxical acceptance of form's absence as itself a form — in the sense that there have been impulses in artistic modernism which have sought not to flee from life into another totality of objective culture, but have sought to capture the sense of the formlessness of life itself in a form. Simmel (1917) in his last essay on Rodin argued that the goal of art should not merely be salvation from 'the confusion and turmoil of life' but could entail a movement in the opposite direction via 'the most perfect styliza-tion and enhanced refinement of life's own contents'. Hence Rodin is seen to 'redeem us from just that which we experience in the sphere of actuality, because he allows us to experience our deepest sense of life once again in the sphere of art' (Simmel, 1983: 153; quoted in Scaff, 1989: 103).

Simmel was concerned to distinguish *art*, which followed the principle of individuality, from *style*, which followed the principle of generality, as is argued in the English translation of his piece 'The Problem of Style' which appears in this issue. For Simmel problems occurred with the cross-overs between the forms which the develop-ment of applied art and consumer culture encouraged. Objects of craft should observe the principle of generality and follow a style, they have a practical function, a chair is to sit upon, a glass to drink from. If they become excessively aestheticized it deprives them of their immediate use-value and encourages an exaggerated subjec-tivism and adds to the tendency towards 'stylessness' which is a characteristic tendency of the modern age. Simmel argues that we need to have things around us which are stylized, for style appeals to broad emotional categories and we feel calm, secure and at home in domestic surroundings which provide a synthesis of a range of styles. Stylization then provides an important counterweight to the exaggerated subjectivism of the times and Simmel adds cryptically 'and if you can't become a unity yourself, then join a unity as a serving partner'.

To become a 'cultivated individuality' requires a balanced absorption of culture as Birgitta Nedelmann reminds us in her contribution, in which she cites an oft quoted passage from Simmel's essay 'On the Concept and Tragedy of Culture', originally published in 1911: 'Culture is the way that leads from the closed unity through the unfolding multiplicity to the unfolded unity.' This is the process whereby we move from life (closed unity) through increasing differentiation as we assimilate a wide range of cultural objects (unfolding multiplicity) to eventually attain a particular unique blend of these developmental lines (unfolded multiplicity). The process of cultivation which is the development of subjective culture, then, entails the successful appropriation, absorption and integration of various elements of objective culture into the personality. Yet as Simmel points out at many places throughout his writings the massive accumulation of objective culture in modernity confronts the individual with an impossible task for it is no longer feasible to attempt to assimilate within the course of a life an adequate synthesis of the vast range of cultural objects which confront and create desires in the subject. As Simmel remarks

> Thus, the typically problematic situation of modern man comes into being: his sense of being surrounded by an innumerable number of cultural elements which are neither meaningless to him nor, in the final analysis, meaningful. In their mass they depress him, since after all, they do belong *potentially* within the sphere of his cultural development. (Simmel, 1968b: 44)

The result is an overstimulation through 'the adornment and overloading of our lives with a thousand superfluous items, from which, however we cannot liberate ourselves'. In contrast to earlier times 'culture no longer had a concrete unity of form for its contents' and as 'each creator places his product as if in an unbounded space next to that of the other, the mass character of phenomena comes into existence' so that 'everything claims with a certain right to be of cultural value' (Simmel, 1968b: 46). These remarks written in 1911 clearly have affinities with some of the characteristics now labelled as postmodernism. Three years later in 1914 Simmel had to address with characteristic openness and detachment the historical possibility which these remarks apparently ruled out, the possibility of a unification of culture in the wave of collective enthusiasm following the outbreak of the Great War, which Patrick Watier recounts in his piece on Simmel's wartime writings.

The struggle between life and form, which on one level form seemed to be winning with the piling up of objective cultural forms which the individual could not assimilate and which seemed reluctant to dissolve and give way to the vitalism of life which would set off a new upsurge of energy to complete the eternal cycle of life and 'more than life' (form), led also to reactions which entailed an immersion in life and rejection of form. Albeit that these reactions had to be represented in form and in the case of artistic modernism, as we have mentioned in discussing Simmel's depiction of Rodin, this entailed the attempt to move away from formal symmetries and unities to find some more flexible mode of form which could represent the formlessness of life. That this is not merely a tendency in art and can be found in other cultural modalities is clear from Simmel's (1968a: 23) remarks towards the end of his paper 'The Conflict in Modern Culture' (1918) written near the end of his life, where he reminds us that there is also 'a tendency for religious *beliefs* to dissolve into modes of religious *life*'.

It should also be emphasized that this tension between lived experience and forms of objective culture was regarded by Simmel as more closely linked to the nature of men. As Lieteke van Vucht Tijssen argues in her contribution to this issue Simmel (1984) developed a metaphysical argument to assert that women's nature provided them with a greater sense of the unity of life which gave them an affinity with morality and the 'beautiful soul'. Assumptions, which as van Vucht Tijssen points out, were strongly contested in his day by Marianne Weber who argued that Simmel's theory could be used to exclude women from participation in objective culture. Nevertheless of all the major sociological theorists, Simmel was the only one to relate the development of modern culture to the domination of men and to appeal to the essentially different qualities of women as a possible compensation.

It is to be hoped that the articles in this issue by Georg Simmel and the other contributors will give *Theory, Culture & Society* readers the stimulus to explore further the writings of a man whose interests so centrally encapsulate the range of issues we have sought to develop in the journal. That Simmel's writings are difficult and demanding cannot be contested, yet they provide a vital example of the conceptual richness which can be achieved when we attempt to understand the manifold ramifications of the process of the formation and deformation of culture. I would like to give special thanks to David Frisby for his advice and encouragement which has been manifest at every stage of the planning of the issue. I would also like to thank Roy Boyne, Mike Hepworth, Frank Lechner, Donald Levine, Birgitta Nedelmann, Mark Ritter, Roland Robertson, Ralph Schroeder, Bryan S. Turner, Sam Whimster and Kurt H. Wolff who have helped in various ways in the preparation of this issue.

Notes

1. At the same time the reception of Simmel's work in the United States has been much more positive than in Britain. Simmel contributed to early issues of the *American Journal of Sociology* and his writings were actively promoted by founders of the Chicago School of Sociology such as Albion Small and Robert Park (who had attended Simmel's lectures in Berlin) and incorporated into the teaching via Park and Burgess's influential *Introduction to the Science of Sociology* (1921). Park and Burgess's book proved to be the key theoretical text until Parsons's (1937) *The Structure of Social Action*. Incidentally Parsons wrote a chapter on Simmel and Tonnies which was discarded from the final printed version (for a discussion of the disavowals of Simmel by Parsons, Park, Weber, Lukács and Durkheim, see Levine, 1985: Ch. 6). Alexander's (1982) four-volume reinterpretation of classical sociological theory follows the Parsonian underestimation of Simmel. Theory books from the United States which have maintained a more positive attitude to Simmel include Nisbet (1967), a book which unusually includes broader discussions of Simmel's writings on religion and aesthetics, Abel (1970), Coser (1971), Turner (1991), Johnson (1981) (the latter gives equal space to chapters on Simmel and Weber), and Robertson (1978), who makes strong connections between Simmel and other classical theorists. In Britain apart from conventional 'formal sociological' treatments of Simmel by Fletcher (1971) theory textbooks such as Rex (1961), Cohen (1968), Mennell (1980), Keat and Urry (1975), Hawthorne (1976), Cashmore and Mullan (1983), Johnson et al. (1984) either completely ignore Simmel or merely make a cursory passing reference to his work. This is also the case with Britain's most influential contemporary theorist, Anthony Giddens (1971, 1976, 1977, 1979, 1984). Incidentally, one of Giddens earliest publications had been an assessment of Simmel in a magazine series on the founding fathers of social science (Giddens, 1969). Even Margaret Archer's (1988) important *Culture and Agency*, which argued for a return to the theorization of culture within sociological theory has no place for Simmel.

2. Conflict theory which was developed by Lewis Coser (1956) drew heavily on the translation of Simmel's (1955) work in *Conflict and the Web of Group Affiliations*. The main proponent of exchange theory was Peter Blau (1964).

3. Earlier important collections while focusing on his sociological writings also provide examples of his writings on aesthetics, culture, philosophy and metaphysics and give some sense of the range of his work have been edited by Kurt H. Wolff (1950; Simmel et al., 1959), Donald Levine (1971), Peter Lawrence (1976) and K. Peter Etzkorn (1968).

4. It is worth mentioning that a further meaning of the term *flâneur* which is addressed in Frisby's interpretation, is the way Benjamin presented the *flâneur* as 'an unwilling detective' (Frisby, 1981: 78); this clearly suggests some synthetic purpose to find some pattern to the fragments. It should also be mentioned that Simmel is cited a good deal in Benjamin's *Passagenwerk* and similar controveries exist over whether there exists an underlying order, plan or unity to the massive collection of unpublished writings and drafts which make up Benjamin's 'Paris Arcades Project'.

5. Weinstein and Weinstein (1990a: 760) observe that this depiction was first proposed by Stauth and Turner (1988: 16).

6. Against Simmel's stated views on the fragmentary nature of *Soziologie* it should be mentioned that a number of commentators have detected key structural principles and central themes to the work (for a discussion see Frisby, 1984: 119ff.). Incidentally in this book, which focuses upon the development of Simmel's sociological writings, Frisby delivers an open verdict on the question of the unity of Simmel's work which can be compared to his earlier position in *Sociological Impressionism* (1981).

7. Green (1988: 128ff.) states that the term 'allegoresis' is a method of interpretive commentary which refers to the allegorical interpretation of something written in another genre. For Green there are strong continuities here with the tradition of Jewish mysticism and similarities between Benjamin's use of allegory in his *Passagenwerk* and Simmel's writings.

8. A unity can only occur when the elements actually interact. To take the example of the global level, Simmel (1959: 314) writes 'In fact, the whole world could not be called *one* if each other part, or if at any one point the reciprocity of effects, however indirect it may be, were cut off.' A sense of the globe as one place therefore depends upon the increased interrelation of the various elements (nation-states, commercial, military, religious plus other non-institutional flows of people information, images and goods) to the extent that the other cannot be ignored. Needless to say this is not to imply equality of exchange effects, but 'reciprocal determination'. Nor is it intended to imply the world is, or forseeably could be, an integrated homogeneous coherent social or cultural entity (these arguments should be familiar to readers of our special issue on Global Culture, *TCS* 7 (2-3) 1990; Featherstone, 1990). These issues of the various blends and gradations of unity also have implications for discussions of 'the end of the social' and postmodernism.

9. It has often been remarked that the contemporary prioritization of spatial over historical forms of analysis is a key feature of postmodern theories. As Frank Lechner argues in his contribution to this issue 'Simmel on Social Space', Simmel alone of the classic sociologists provided a sustained treatment of space. Here we think not only of his well-known essay 'The Metropolis and Mental Life' (1903) (see Levine, 1971), but his lesser known piece on 'The Sociology of Space' which was published in the same year and then reprinted and retitled as a chapter of his

Soziologie. We had intended to include an English translation of this piece in this issue but could not do so because of constraints on space. This translation will now appear in the selection of his writings being prepared: *Simmel on Culture* (Frisby and Featherstone, forthcoming).

10. For a discussion of the range of possible blends of unity in the personality and life orders see Featherstone (forthcoming). It is sufficient in this context to refer to two possible responses to the alleged lack of cultural unity and the de-centring of the self associated with postmodernism. The first is Maffesoli's (1991) use of the medieval concept of *unicity* to refer to a more complex and syncretic unity which allows greater differentiation amongst its elements. The second is Culler's (1983: 199–200) remark that while deconstruction is hostile to what de Man refers to as 'organic unity' and 'the intent at totality of the interpretive process' in favour of a celebration of multivocality, heterogeneity and intertextuality, to highlight the variety of incompatible arguments that inhabit a text, this does not mean that unity can be dispensed with altogether.

References

Abel, T. (1970) *The Foundation of Sociological Theory*. New York: Random House.

Adler, M. (1919) *Georg Simmels Bedeutung fur die Geistgeschichte*. Vienna/Leipzig.

Albrow, M. (1990) *Max Weber's Construction of Social Theory*. London: Macmillan.

Alexander, J. (1982) *Theoretical Logic in Sociology, 4 Volumes*. London: Routledge.

Archer, M. (1988) *Culture and Agency*. Cambridge: Cambridge University Press.

Benjamin, W. (1982) *Das Passagenwerk*. Frankfurt: Suhrkamp.

Blau, P. (1964) *Exchange and Power in Social Life*. New York: Wiley.

Cashmore, E.E. and B. Mullan, (1983) *Approaching Social Theory*. London: Heinemann.

Cohen, P.S. (1968) *Modern Social Theory*. London: Heinemann.

Coser, L. (1956) *The Functions of Social Conflict*. London: Routledge.

Coser, L. (1965) 'Introduction', in L. Coser (ed.), *Georg Simmel*. Englewood Cliffs, NJ: Prentice-Hall.

Coser, L. (1971) *Masters of Sociological Thought*. New York: Harcourt, Brace and Jovanovich.

Culler, J. (1983) *On Deconstruction*. London: Routledge.

Dahme, H.-J. (1990) 'On the Current Rediscovery of Georg Simmel's Sociology — a European Point of View', in M. Kaern, B.S. Phillips and R.S. Cohen (eds), *Georg Simmel and Contemporary Sociology*. Dordrecht: Kluwer.

Etzkorn, P.K. (ed.) (1968) *Georg Simmel, On the Conflict in Modern Culture and Other Essays*. New York: The Teachers' College Press.

Featherstone, M. (ed.) (1990) *Global Culture*. London: Sage. (Also a *Theory, Culture & Society* special issue, 7 (2–3), 1990).

Featherstone, M. (1991) *Consumer Culture and Postmodernism*. London: Sage.

Featherstone, M. (forthcoming) 'Personality, Unity and the Ordered Life', in H. Martins (ed.), *Essays for John Rex*.

Fletcher, R. (1971) *The Making of Sociology: A Study in Sociological Theory. Volume 2, Developments*. London: Nelson.

Frisby, D. (1981) *Sociological Impressionism: A Reassessment of Georg Simmel's Social Theory*. London: Heinemann.

Frisby, D. (1984) *Georg Simmel*. London: Tavistock/Ellis Horwood.

Frisby, D. (1985) 'Georg Simmel: First Sociologist of Modernity', *Theory Culture & Society* 2(3): 49–67.

Frisby, D. and M. Featherstone (eds) (forthcoming) *Simmel on Culture*. London: Sage.

Giddens, A. (1969) 'Georg Simmel', in T. Raison (ed.), *Founding Fathers of Social Science*. Harmondsworth: Penguin.

Giddens, A. (1971) *Capitalism and Modern Social Theory*. Cambridge: Cambridge University Press.

Giddens, A. (1976) *New Rules of Sociological Method*. London: Hutchinson.

Giddens, A. (1977) *Studies in Social and Political Theory*. London: Hutchinson.

Giddens, A. (1979) *Central Problems in Social Theory*. London: Macmillan.

Giddens, A. (1984) *The Constitution of Society*. Oxford: Polity Press.

Green, B.S. (1988) *Literary Methods and Sociological Theory. Case Studies of Weber and Simmel*. Chicago: University of Chicago Press.

Hawthorne, G. (1976) *Enlightenment and Despair: A History of Sociology*. Cambridge: Cambridge University Press.

Hennis, W. (1988) *Max Weber: Essays in Reconstruction*. London: Allen and Unwin.

Jaspers, K. (1989) *Karl Jaspers on Max Weber*. New York: Paragon House.

Johnson, D.P. (1981) *Sociological Theory*. New York: Wiley.

Johnson, T., C. Dandeker and C. Ashworth (1984) *The Structure of Social Theory*. London: Macmillan.

Keat, R. and J. Urry (1975) *Social Theory as Science*. London: Routledge.

Lawrence, P.A. (ed.) (1976) *Georg Simmel: Sociologist and European*. London: Nelson.

Lechner, F. (1990) 'Social Differentiation and Modernity: On Simmel's Macro-sociology', in M. Kaern et al. (eds), *Georg Simmel and Contemporary Sociology*. Dordrecht: Kluwer.

Levine, D.N. (ed.) (1971) *Georg Simmel: On Individuality and Social Forms*. Chicago: University of Chicago Press.

Levine, D.N. (1985) *The Flight From Ambiguity*. Chicago: University of Chicago Press.

Maffesoli, M. (1991) 'The Ethic of Aesthetics', *Theory, Culture & Society* 8(1): 7–20.

Mennell, A. (1980) *Sociological Theory: Uses and Unities* (second edition). London: Nelson.

Nisbet, R.A. (1967) *The Sociological Tradition*. London: Heinemann.

Park, R.E. and E.W. Burgess (1921) *Introduction to the Science of Sociology*. Chicago, IL: Chicago University Press.

Parsons, T. (1937) *The Structure of Social Action*. New York: Free Press.

Rex, J. (1961) *Key Problems of Sociological Theory*. London: Routledge.

Robertson, R. (1978) *Meaning and Change: Explorations in the Cultural Sociology of Modern Societies*. Oxford: Oxford University Press.

Scaff, L.A. (1989) *Fleeing the Iron Cage: Culture, Politics and Modernity in the Thought of Max Weber*. Berkeley: California University Press.

Schnabel, P.-E. (1985) 'Georg Simmel', in A. Kuper and J. Kuper (eds), *The Social Science Encyclopedia*. London: Routledge.

Simmel, G. (1899) 'Momentbilder . . . Gegensatz', *Jugend*.

Simmel, G. (1908) *Soziologie*. Berlin.

Simmel, G. (1917) *Grundfragen der Soziologie*. Berlin: Göschen.

Simmel, G. (1955) *Conflict and the Web of Group Affiliations*. Edited by L. Coser and translated by R. Bendix. Glencoe: Free Press.

Simmel, G. (1959) 'The Problem of Sociology', in G. Simmel et al. *Essays on Sociology, Philosophy and Aesthetics*. New York: Harper.

Simmel, G. (1968a) 'The Conflict in Modern Culture', in *The Conflict in Modern Culture and Other Essays*. Edited and translated by K.P. Etzkorn. New York: The Teachers' College Press.

Simmel, G. (1968b) 'On the Concept and Tragedy of Culture', in *The Conflict in Modern Culture and Other Essays*. New York: The Teachers' College Press.

Simmel, G. (1968c) 'Sociological Aesthetics', in *The Conflict of Modern Culture and Other Essays*. New York: The Teachers' College Press.

Simmel, G. (1977) *The Problems of the Philosophy of History*. Translated and edited by G. Oakes. New York: Free Press.

Simmel, G. (1980) *Essays on Interpretation and Social Science*. Translated and edited by G. Oakes. Manchester: Manchester University Press.

Simmel, G. (1983) *Philosophische Kultur*. Berlin: Wagenbach.

Simmel, G. (1984) *On Women, Sexuality and Love*. Translated and edited by Guy Oakes. New Haven: Yale University Press.

Simmel, G. (1986) *Schopenhauer and Nietzsche*. Translated by H. Loiskandl, D. Weinstein and M. Weinstein. Amherst: MIT Press.

Simmel, G. (1990) *The Philosophy of Money* (second edition). Translated by D. Frisby and T. Bottomore and introduced by D. Frisby. London: Routledge.

Simmel, G. et al. (1959) *Essays on Sociology, Philosophy and Aesthetics*. Edited by K.H. Wolff. New York: Harper.

Stauth, G. and B.S. Turner (1988) *Nietzsche's Dance*. Oxford: Blackwell.

Tenbruck, F. (1980) 'The Problem of Thematic Unity in the work of Max Weber', *British Journal of Sociology* 31.

Turner, J.H. (1991) *The Structure of Sociological Theory*. Belmont, CA: Wadsworth.

Weingartner, R.H. (1960) *Experience and Culture: The Philosophy of Georg Simmel*. Middletown, CT: Wesleyan University Press.

Weinstein, D. and M. Weinstein (1990a) 'Simmel and the Theory of Postmodern Society', in B.S. Turner (ed.), *Theories of Modernity and Postmodernity*. London: Sage.

Weinstein, D. and M. Weinstein (1990b) 'Deconstruction as Cultural History/The Cultural History of Deconstruction', *Canadian Journal of Political and Social Theory* 14(1–3).

Wolff, K.H. (ed.) (1950) *The Sociology of Georg Simmel*. New York: Free Press.

Wood, J. (1983) 'Georg Simmel', in M. Mann (ed.), *The Macmillan Student Encyclopedia of Sociology*. London: Macmillan.

Mike Featherstone teaches Sociology at Teesside Polytechnic, England.

Money in Modern Culture

Georg Simmel

If sociology wished to capture in a formula the contrast between the modern era and the Middle Ages, it could try the following. In the Middle Ages a person was a member bound to a community or an estate, to a feudal association or a guild. His personality was merged with real or local interest groups, and the latter in turn drew their character from the people who directly supported them. This uniformity was destroyed by modernity. On the one hand, it left the personality to itself and gave it an incomparable mental and physical freedom of movement. On the other hand, it conferred an unrivalled objectivity on the practical content of life. Through technology, in organizations of all kinds, in factories and in the professions, the inherent laws of things are becoming increasingly dominant and are being freed from any colouration by individual personalities, just as our image of nature is striving to eradicate its anthropomorphic traits and we impose an objective regularity on it. Thus modernity has made subject and object mutually independent, so that each can more purely and completely find its own development. How the two sides of this differentiation process are affected by the money economy is what I consider here.

Until the high Middle Ages in Germany, the relationship between a person and their property appears in two forms. In primeval times we encounter ownership of land as an authority to which the individual personality is entitled; it flows from the individual's personal affiliation to his market community. By the tenth century personal land ownership had disappeared, and all personal rights had become dependent on the ownership of real property.

In both forms, however, a tight local connection was maintained between person and property. For instance, in the fellowship of vassal farmers, where feudal tenure to a hide of land gave one full membership of the association, someone who owned a hide outside

Theory, Culture & Society (SAGE, London, Newbury Park and New Delhi), Vol. 8 (1991), 17–31

of the farmers' association *to which he personally belonged* was considered landless. Conversely, someone who owned a property within the socage community without belonging to it personally (free citizens, burghers, guilds and so on) was required to appoint a representative, who *personally* owed allegiance to the feudal lord and would take over the rights and duties of a member.

This interdependence of personality and material relationships, which is typical of the barter economy, is dissolved by the money economy. At every moment it interposes the perfectly objective and inherently qualityless presence of money and monetary value between the person and the particular object. It fosters a distance between personality and property by mediating between the two. Thus it has differentiated the formerly intimate association of the personal and the local elements to such a degree that today I can receive income in Berlin from American railroads, Norwegian mortgages and African gold mines. This form of long-distance ownership, which we take for granted today, has only become possible since money has moved between owner and possession, both as a connecting and a separating factor.

In this way, money produces both a previously unknown impersonality in all economic ownership and an equally enhanced independence and autonomy of the personality, and the relationship of personality to associations develops similarly to that with property. The medieval guild included the entire person; a weavers' guild was not an association of individuals that only pursued the mere interests of weaving. Instead, it was a *living community* in occupational, social, religious, political and many other respects. No matter how objective the interests around which the medieval association grouped, it still existed directly through its members and the latter were absorbed in it without rights of their own.

In contrast to this unity, the money economy has now produced innumerable associations which either only demand financial contributions from their members or proceed merely in terms of monetary interest. In this way, on the one hand, the pure objectivity of the purposes of the organization, their purely *technical* character, their lack of any personal colouration are made possible, while, on the other hand, the subject is freed from restrictive commitments, because it is no longer connected to the totality as an entire person, but principally by spending and receiving money. Since the interest of the individual participant in an association is expressible in money, directly or indirectly, money has slipped like an insulating layer between the objective totality of the association and the subjective totality of the personality, just as it has come between owner and property. This has allowed both a new possibility of development and a new independence from one another. The pinnacle of this development is represented by the joint-stock company, whose business is completely objective to, and uninfluenced by the individual shareholder, while the company has absolutely nothing to do with him personally except that he holds a sum of money in it.

By virtue of this impersonality and colourlessness — which is peculiar to money in contrast to all specific values, and which must continually increase if we follow this course of cultural development, money comes to compensate an ever-increasing number and variety of things, it has performed incalculable services. This brings into existence a community of action of those individuals and groups who stress their separation and reserve at all other points. Hence, an entirely new line is drawn through the elements of life susceptible to associations. I shall mention only two examples that seem to me to demonstrate nicely how money is able on the one hand to unify interests and on the other hand to maintain a separateness of interests.

In France after 1848, syndicates of workers' associations from particular trades were formed in such a way that each association delivered all its funds to the association and thus a joint-savings bank was formed. This was supposed to make retail purchasing possible, provide loans, etc. These syndicates, however, were certainly not intended to unite the participating associations into a single, large one; rather, each was supposed to retain its particular organization. This case is illustrative because at that time workers were seized by a veritable passion to found associations. If they expressly rejected the unification that seemed so natural, they must have had particularly strong grounds for their reluctance — yet at the same time they were able to effect the unity of their interests which nevertheless existed through the common possession of a fund of money.

Furthermore, the successes of the Gustavus Adolphus Society, the great society for the support of Protestant congregations, would have been impossible if the objective character of the monetary contributions had not blurred the denominational differences of the contributors. But because money enabled this to be a common creation of the Lutheran, Reformed and Unitarian churches, who could not have been moved to any other type of common organization, it served as an ideal adhesive and strengthened the feeling of community among all these sects.

Generally one can say that the trade union and all its enormous successes, a type of organization virtually unknown in the Middle Ages, which one could say unites individuals impersonally for a course of action, has only become possible by virtue of money. Money offers us the only opportunity to date for a unity which eliminates everything personal and specific, a form of unification that we take completely for granted today, but which represents one of the most enormous changes and advances of culture.

Thus when one laments the alienating and separating effect of monetary transactions, one should not forget the following. Through the necessity of exchanging it and receiving definitive concrete values for it, money creates an extremely strong bond among the members of an economic circle. Precisely because it cannot be consumed directly, it refers people to others, from whom one can obtain what is actually to be consumed. In that way, the modern person is dependent on infinitely more suppliers and supply sources than was the ancient Germanic freeman or the later serf; his existence depends at any moment on a hundred connections fostered by monetary interests, without which he could no more exist than could the limb of an organic creature cut off from the circulation of its vital fluids.

What brings about this intertwining and growing together of modern life more than anything else is our division of labour, which could not develop beyond the roughest beginnings under the system of bartering. For how was one to measure the values of various products against one another so long as there was no common standard of measurement for the most different things and qualities? How could exchange proceed smoothly and easily as long as there was no medium of exchange that could even up every difference, no medium into which one could convert every product and which one could convert into any product? And by making the division of production possible, money inevitably ties people together, for now everyone is working for the other, and only the work of all creates the comprehensive economic unity which supplements the one-sided production of the individual.[1] Thus it is ultimately money which establishes incomparably more connections among people than ever existed in the days of feudal associations or the arbitrary unifications most highly praised by the guild romantics.

Finally, money has produced a comprehensive common level of interests for all people such as could never have been produced in the days of the barter economy. Money provides a common basis of direct mutual understanding and an equality of directives which contributed an extraordinary amount to producing that dissimulation of the generally human which played such an important part in the cultural and social history of the preceding century. A similar phenomenon appeared in the history of the Roman Empire when the money economy had completely established itself.

But, just as money in general has brought into being an entirely new relation between freedom and dependence — this should be clear from what has already been said — similarly the pronounced closeness and inevitability of the integration that it brings about has the peculiar consequence of opening up a particularly wide scope to individuality and the feeling of personal independence. The person in those earlier economic epochs was mutually dependent on far fewer people, but those few were and remained individually determined, while today we are much more dependent on suppliers in general, but frequently and arbitrarily change the individuals with whom we interact; we are much more independent of any *particular* supplier. It is precisely these types of relationship which must produce a strong individualism, for what alienates people from one another and forces each one to rely only on himself is not isolation from others. Rather, it is the anonymity of others and the indifference to their individuality, a relationship to them without regard to who it is in any particular instance. In contrast to times when every external relationship to others simultaneously bore a personal character, in modernity the money economy makes possible a cleaner separation between the objective economic activity of a person and his individual colouration, his actual ego, which now completely retreats from those external relationships and in that way can concentrate more than ever on its inmost strata.

The streams of modern culture rush in two seemingly opposing directions: on the one hand, toward levelling, equalization, the production of more and more comprehensive social circles through the connection of the remotest things under equal conditions; on the other hand, towards the elaboration of the most individual matters, the independence of the person, the autonomy of its development. Both tendencies are supported by the money economy, which makes possible, first, a completely general interest and a means of connection and communication which is equally effective everywhere.

Second, it permits the most pronounced reserve, individualization and freedom for the personality.

The later point still requires evidence. The expressibility and redeemability of services by means of money has always been felt to be a means and support of personal freedom. Thus, classical Roman law provided that someone who was obliged to make a certain payment could refuse to fulfil it in kind and could settle it with money, even against the will of the recipient. That provided a guarantee that one could pay off all personal obligations in money, and in that respect, this provision has been deemed the *Magna Charta* of personal freedom in the arena of civil law.

The emancipation of serfs often proceeded in the same direction. The dependent artisans of a medieval manor, for instance, often attained freedom by a process where their services were first limited, then specified and finally transformed into a monetary tax. Thus it was considered a great advance toward freedom when the English counties were permitted, from the thirteenth century on, to substitute monetary payments for their obligations to provide soldiers and labourers. Similarly, one of the most important regulations with which Joseph II sought to introduce the emancipation of peasants was the provision that they were allowed, and in fact required, to redeem their socage labour and their payments in kind through monetary taxes. The substitution of a monetary tax for service immediately releases the person from the specific bondage that was imposed by that service. The other no longer has any claim to direct personal action, but only to the impersonal result of such action. By paying money the person no longer offers himself, but only something without any personal relationship to the individual.

But for that very reason, the substitution of a monetary payment for a service can also have a degrading character. The deprivation of the rights of the Athenian allies began when they substituted monetary payments for their previous contingents of ships and crews. This apparent liberation from their personal obligation, after all, contained the renunciation of any political activity of their own, of the importance which can only be claimed for the employment of a specific service, for the deployment of concrete forces. This is so often overlooked as the money economy expands: in the duties that are bought off with money there often lie less apparent rights and significances which are also abandoned.

This same double meaning attached to the payment of money is also connected with its receipt, with selling. On one hand, one senses the conversion of a possession into money as a liberation. With the assistance of money, we can now pour the value of the possession into any arbitrary form, while it was previously captured in that one particular form. With money in our pocket, we are free, whereas previously, the object made us dependent on the conditions of its conservation and fructification. But how often does this very freedom simultaneously mean a vapidity of life and a loosening of its substance! For that reason, the same legislation that prescribed the monetary settlement of peasant service also prohibited the compulsory enclosure of the peasants. It seemed of course, no injustice was being done to the latter if his master bought his rights to the land for a proper price (in order to add it to his estate's holdings). In the soil, however, there is much more for the peasant than the value of the property. For him it was the possibility of useful action, a centre of interests, a practical reality giving life direction which he lost as soon as he lost possession of the land and had only its value in money. The frequent enclosures of the farmers in the previous century did indeed give them a momentary freedom, but deprived them of the priceless thing which gives value to freedom: the steady object of personal activity.

That in turn is the questionable thing about a culture oriented to money, like that of late Athens, of late Rome, or of the modern world. Because more and more things are paid for with money and become attainable through it, and money accordingly stands out as the constant in the flow of activity, one overlooks all too often that even the objects of economic exchange still have aspects that cannot be expressed in monetary terms. It is all too easy to believe that one has their exact and complete equivalent in their monetary value. This is certainly a deep reason for the problematic character, the restlessness and the dissatisfaction of our times. The qualitative nature of objects lose their psychological emphasis through the money economy; the continuously required estimation according to monetary value eventually causes this to seem the only valid one; more and more, people speed past the specific value of things, which cannot be expressed in terms of money. The revenge for this is that very modern sensibility that the core and meaning of life slips through our fingers again and again, that definitive satisfactions become ever rarer, that all the effort and activity is not actually worthwhile. I do not wish to assert that our epoch is already entirely caught up in that state of mind, but where we are approaching it is certainly connected with the progressive obscuring of the qualitative values by a merely quantitative one, by an interest in a pure more-or-less, since after all it is only the qualitative values which ultimately satisfy our needs.

Indeed objects themselves are devalued of their higher significance through their equivalence with this means of exchange which can apply to anything at all. Money is 'common' because it is the equivalent for anything and everything. Only that which is unique is distinguished; whatever is equal for many is the same even for the lowest among them, and for that reason it pulls even the highest down to the level of the lowest. That is the tragedy of every levelling process: it leads directly to the position of the *lowest* element. For the higher can always descend to the lowest, but anything low seldom ascends to the highest level. Thus the innermost value of things suffers under the uniform convertibility of the most heterogeneous elements into money, and popular language is therefore justified in calling the very special and distinguished 'priceless'.

The 'blasé attitude' of our prosperous classes is only the psychological reflection of this fact. Because they now possess a means with which, despite its colourless uniformity, they can purchase the most varied and special things, and because therefore the question of what something is worth is increasingly displaced by the question of how much it is worth, the delicate sensibility for the specific and most individual charms of things must necessarily atrophy more and more. And that is just what a blasé attitude is: no longer reacting to the gradations and peculiarities of things with a corresponding nuance of sensibility, but rather valuing them within a uniform and thus dull colouration, no longer distinguished by variation.

Through this very character, however, which money increasingly assumes, the more things it compensates for — within a rising culture — it loses the significance it previously possessed. The monetary fine, for instance, has its sphere limited. Ancient Germanic law punished the severest crimes, including murder, with fines. From the seventh century, it was possible to substitute money for religious penance, while modern legal systems limit monetary penalties to relatively minor misdemeanours. This is not a sign against, but rather for, the increased importance of money; precisely because it now compensates for so many more things and has therefore become that much more characterless and colourless, it is said to be unsuitable to serve for compensation in very special and exceptional cases, in which the most inward and essential aspects of the personality are affected. It is not despite the fact that one can get everything with money, but precisely because of it, that it has ceased to settle the moral and religious requirements on which penance was based.

Characteristically, two major currents of historical development meet at this point. If murder could be atoned for in primitive society by money, then that meant on the one hand, that the individual and his value was not yet so recognized, that it was not yet felt to be so incomparable and irreplaceable as in later times when it stood out from the group more decisively and individually. On the other hand, it means that money had not yet become so indifferent, that it had not yet transcended any qualitative significance. The increasing differentiation of people and the equally increasing indifference of money converge to make the punishment of murder by monetary penalties impossible.

A second extremely important consequence of the prevailing monetary system runs in a similar direction to this grinding down and deterioration of money by the growth of its equivalents. This is the tendency to perceive money, a mere means to acquire other goods, as an independent good, whereas it has its entire meaning only as a transition, a link in a series that leads to a definitive purpose and enjoyment. If the series is broken off psychologically at this level, then our consciousness of the end stops at money. Because the majority of modern people must focus on the acquisition of money as their proximate goal for most of their lives, the notion arises that all happiness and all definitive satisfaction in life is firmly connected to the possession of a certain sum of money; it grows inwardly from a mere means and a presupposition to an ultimate purpose. But when this goal has been attained, then frequently deadly boredom and disappointment set in which are most conspicuous among business people who retreat into retired life after having saved up a certain sum. After the loss of the circumstances which caused the consciousness of value to concentrate on it, money reveals itself in its true character a mere means that becomes useless and unnecessary, as soon as life is concentrated on it alone — it is only the bridge to definitive values, and one cannot live on a bridge.

This colonization of ends by means is one of the major features and main problems of any higher culture. The latter has its essence in the fact that, by contrast to primitive circumstances, the intentions of people can no longer be achieved through simple, obvious, direct actions. Instead, they are gradually becoming so difficult, complicated and remote that one requires a multi-part construction of means and apparatus, a multi-level detour of preparatory steps for them. The first step can hardly ever lead to the goal in higher cultures, and not only is a means required, but this itself cannot often enough be achieved directly, but there is a multiplicity of means, one of which often supports the others, which finally flow into the definitive end. The greater danger is of getting stuck in the labyrinth of means and thereby forgetting the ultimate goal. Thus, the more intertwined, artificial and structured the technique of all areas of life becomes — that means after all the system of mere means and tools — it is felt increasingly as an intrinsically satisfying ultimate purpose, beyond which one can no longer enquire.

That is the origin of the stability of all external customs, which were originally only means to certain social ends, but continue to exist as intrinsic values, as self-supporting demands, while the ends have long been forgotten or become illusory. A feeling of tension, expectation and unresolved insistence runs through modernity, in particular as it seems, through its most recent stages — as if the main event, the definitive one, the actual meaning and the central point of life and things were yet to come. That is certainly the emotional outcome of that excess of means, of the compulsion of our complicated technique of life to build one means on top of another, until the actual end which they were supposed to serve recedes further and further towards the horizon of consciousness and ultimately sinks beneath it. But no element has a broader share in this process than money, never has an object which only has value as a means grown with such energy, such completeness and such success for the overall situation of life into a — really or apparently — satisfying goal of aspiration.

The importance that money has been given through the enormous growth of the range of objects that can be acquired by it radiates out into many individual character traits of modern life. Money has moved the complete satisfaction of an individual's wishes into a much greater and more tempting proximity. It gives the possibility of obtaining at a single stroke, as it were, whatever appears at all desirable. Between the human being and his wishes it inserts a mediating stage, a relieving mechanism and, because everything else becomes attainable with the acquiring of this one thing, it stimulates the illusion that all these other things are more easily obtained. But as one comes closer to happiness, the longing for it grows, for it is not that which is absolutely distant and denied us which inflames the greatest longing and passion, but rather that which is not owned, but seems to be becoming nearer and nearer.

The enormous desire for happiness of modern man, as expressed in Kant no less than in Schopenhauer, in social democracy no less than in the growing Americanism of the times, has obviously been nourished on this power and this result of money. The specifically modern 'covetousness' of classes and individuals, which one may condemn or welcome as a stimulus to the development of culture, was able to develop because there is now a slogan that concentrates everything desirable in itself, a central point one need only acquire, like the magic key in a fairy-tale, in order to attain all the joys of life.

Thus — and this is very important — money becomes that absolute goal which it is possible in principle to strive for at any moment, in contrast to the constant goals, not all of which may be wanted or can be aspired to all the time. This provides the modern person with a continuing spur to activity; he now has a goal which appears as the *pièce de résistance* as soon as other goals give it space; it is potentially always there. That is the reason for the restlessness, feverishness, the unrelenting character of modern life, which is provided by money with the unremovable wheel that makes the machine of life a *perpetuum mobile*. Schleiermacher emphasizes that Christianity was the first to make piety, the desire for God, into a permanent state of the psyche, whereas earlier times connected religious moods to particular times and places.

Thus the desire for money is the permanent disposition that the mind displays in an established money economy. Accordingly, the psychologist simply cannot ignore the frequent lament that money is the God of our times. Of course, he can only linger on it and discover significant relationships between the two ideas because it is the privilege of psychology not to commit blasphemy. The concept of God has its deeper essence in the fact that all the varieties and contrasts of the world reach unity in it, that it is the *coincidentia oppositorum*, in the beautiful phrase of Nicholas of Cusa, that peculiarly modern spirit of the waning Middle Ages. It is in this idea that all the strange and irreconciled aspects of being find unity and harmony, from which stem the peace, the security and the all-encompassing richness of feeling, which are part of the idea of God and of the idea that we possess Him.

The feelings stimulated by money have a psychological similarity to this in their own arena. By increasingly becoming the absolutely sufficient expression and equivalent of all values, it rises in a very abstract elevation over the whole broad variety of objects; it becomes the centre in which the most opposing, alien and distant things find what they have in common and touch each other. Thus money actually does grant us that elevation over the individual, that trust in its own omnipotence as in that of a supreme principle which can provide us these individual and lower elements at any moment, as if it could transform itself into these. This feeling of security and calm which the possession of money provides, this conviction of possessing the intersection of all values in the form of money, thus contains in a purely psychological sense, formally one could say, the equalization point which gives the deeper justification to that complaint about money as the God of our times.

Other, more remote character traits of modern mankind, directed differently, flow from the same source. The money economy brings along with it the necessity for continuous mathematical operations in everyday life. The life of many people is filled out with determining, weighing up, calculating and reducing of qualitative values to quantitative ones. This certainly contributes to the rational, calculating nature of modern times against the more impulsive, holistic, emotional character of earlier epochs. Thus much greater accuracy and sharper demarcations had to enter into the elements of life through monetary valuation, teaching people to determine and specify every value down to the penny. Where things are conceived of in their direct relationships to one another — thus not reduced to the common denominator of money — then much more rounding off and comparison of one unit to another occurs. The exactness, sharpness and precision in the economic relationships of life, which of course fade into its other elements, keep pace with the spread of the money economy, but not, of course, to the benefit of grand style in living.

The ever-growing use of smaller monetary units has the same effect, and heralds the spread of the money economy. Until 1759, the Bank of England did not issue notes under £20 sterling, but since then it has gone down to £5. And, more revealingly, until 1844 its notes circulated an average of fifty-one days before being broken into smaller change, while by contrast they circulated only thirty-seven days in 1871 — in twenty-seven years, then the need for small change increased by nearly 25%. The fact that people carry around small denominations of money in their pockets, with which they can immediately purchase all sorts of small articles, often on a whim, must encourage industries that thrive from this possibility. This and in general the divisibility of money into the tiniest sums certainly contributes to the frivolous style of the external, and particularly the aesthetic areas of modern life, as well as to the growing number of trivialities with which we furnish our life.

The punctuality and exactness — somewhat analogous to that of pocket watches — which the spreading of the monetary system has conferred on the external relationships of people, is by no means accompanied by an equivalent increased inner conscientiousness in the ethical sphere. Rather, through the quite objective and indifferent character with which it offers itself equally and unrelatedly to the highest and the lowest actions, money tempts us to a certain laxity and thoughtlessness of action, which would be inhibited in other cases by the particular structure of the exchange objects and the individual relationship of the agent to them. Thus persons who are otherwise honest may participate in deceitful 'promotions', and many people are likely to behave more unconscientiously and with more dubious ethics in money matters than elsewhere. The result that is ultimately achieved, money, bears few traces of its origins, while other possessions and situations, because they are more individual and have distinctive qualities, carry their origins within themselves, either objectively or psychologically; they are visible in those things and the things recall their origins. But once the act has flowed into the great ocean of money, by contrast, then it can no longer be recognized, and what flows out no longer bears any resemblance to that which flowed in.

Returning from these individual consequences of the circulation of money, I close with a general remark on its relationship to the deeper traits and motifs of our culture. If one would venture to summarize the character and greatness of modern life into a formula, then it could be this: that the contents of knowledge, of action and of the formation of ideals are being transformed from their solid, substantial and stable form into a state of development, movement and instability. Every look at the fates of those elements of life, which are occurring under our very eyes, unmistakably shows this line of formation: we are dispensing with the absolute truths that would be contrary to all development, and gladly sacrificing our knowing to continual reshaping, duplication and correction — for this is exactly what the continual emphasis on empiricism means.

The species of organisms are no longer considered eternal

thoughts of Creation, but transitional points of an Evolution striving towards infinity. The same tendency extends to the lowest inanimate and to the highest spiritual formations; modern natural science is teaching us to dissolve the rigidity of material into the restless turmoil of the tiniest particle. We now recognize that the uniform ideals of earlier times, once considered to be founded beyond any change and contradiction, are dependent on and adaptations to historical conditions. The fixed boundaries of social groups are dissolving more and more. The rigidity of caste and class ties and traditions is being increasingly broken — whether this be a benefit or a disadvantage — and the personality can circulate through a changing variety of situations, reflecting, as it were, the fluidity of things.

The rule of money takes its place in this great and uniform process of life, which the intellectual and social culture of modernity put in such decisive contrast to the Middle Ages as well as antiquity, supporting the process and supported by it. By finding their equivalent in a completely colourless means of exchange beyond any specific determinacy, by being able to be exchanged into such a means at any moment, things become worn down and smoothed, in a sense, their rough surfaces are reduced, and continual equalization processes occur between them. Their circulation, giving and taking occur at a quite different pace than in the days of the barter economy; more and more things that appeared to be beyond exchange are pulled down into its restless flow. I recall only, as one of the simplest examples, the fluctuating value of real property since the dominance of money. Since the advent of the money economy, the same transformation of stability to instability that characterizes the entire modern philosophy has also seized the economic cosmos, whose destinies, as they form a part of that movement, are also a symbol and reflection of its entirety.

Here we can only point out that a phenomenon like the money economy, no matter how much it appears to follow its own purely internal laws, nevertheless follows the same rhythm that regulates all contemporaneous movements in culture, even the most remote of them. Unlike historical materialism, which makes the entire cultural process dependent on economic conditions, the consideration of money can teach us that far-reaching effects on the entire psychic and cultural state of the period do indeed emanate from the formation of economic life. That formation itself, on the other hand, receives its character from the great uniform trends of historical life, whose ultimate sources and motives remain a divine secret.

But if these similarities and deep connections reveal the monetary system to us as a branch from the same root that produces all the other flowers of our culture, then one can take consolation from this against the complaints raised particularly by the preservers of spiritual and emotional values against the *auri sacra fames* and the devastation wrought by the financial system. For the more knowledge nourishes itself from that root, that much more clearly must the relationships of the money economy appear, both to the dark sides and to the subtlest and highest aspects of our culture. Thus, like all great historical forces, the money economy might resemble the mythical spear that is itself capable of healing the wounds it inflicts.

Translated by Mark Ritter and Sam Whimster.

Notes

This article was first given as an address to the Society of Austrian Economists, reported by the *Neue Freie Presse* of Vienna. It was first published as 'Das Geld in der modernen Kultur' in *Zeitschrift des Oberschlesischen Berg und Huttenmännnischen Vereins* 35: 319–24.

1. Monetary payment advances the division of labour, because as a rule only a one-sided service is paid for with money; this abstract, amorphous equivalent corresponds only to the objective individual product divorced from the personality. Money does not buy the entire person — except in the case of slavery — but only the atomized product of the division of labour. That is why the development of the latter must proceed hand in hand with the spread of the money economy. The deficiencies and contradictions in the modern condition of domestic servants are explained by this fact, for here an entire person is still being purchased with money.

Call for Papers

In summer 1991, the Georg Simmel Society in Bielefeld, Germany, will begin publication of a journal devoted to the documentation and co-ordination of international Simmel research. In view of the rapidly increasing number of academic publications, the journal will attempt to foster dialogue on all aspects of Simmel's writings and influence and will comprise two principal components: the biannual *Simmel Newsletter* (ISSN 0939-2327) will contain information on current research problems, announcements of forthcoming meetings and other news items, book and conference reports, as well as short articles; the annual *Simmel Abstracts*, to be included in the winter issue of the *Simmel Newsletter* and also available on disk, will provide information on recent books, dissertations and articles.

The *Simmel Newsletter* invites submission of articles (not exceeding 2000 words) and other items for publication (in German, English and French).

To be included in the *Simmel Abstracts*, authors should send detailed information on their work; forms for this are available on request. Please direct manuscripts, subscriptions and requests for information to:

Otthein Rammstedt and Gerhard Wagner
Simmel Newsletter
Fakultät für Soziologie
Universität Bielefeld
Postfach 8640
D-4800 Bielefeld 1
Germany.

Causality or Interaction? Simmel, Weber and Interpretive Sociology

Klaus Lichtblau

Behind the action is the person. (Max Weber, 1985: 496)

For the fabric of social life it is particularly true: no weaver knows what he's weaving. (Georg Simmel, 1905: 18)

Max Weber had made the attempt to throw out the idea — one could almost say — and to retain only the *subjectively intended meaning* (the parallel to Sombart's 'motif'), in order to construct the historical, social world in that way. Today one can probably state that this attempt — matchless in its monumentality — has failed *in this respect*. Objectivized contexts ('objects') cannot be dissolved completely in a nominalistic fashion. (Karl Mannheim, 1929: 239)

Causality is disappointing in a certain sense: as a principle of the proportionality of cause and effect it excludes significance. If the concessions become palpable under which science guarantees the conditions of life for us, but also cuts off questions, then mythology suggests itself. For the 'really moving question' is not necessarily also the one upon the solution of which our pure ability to exist depends. (Hans Blumenberg, 1971: 48)

I

In the course of the general reflection upon the historical origin of modern sociology as an academic discipline, the mutual relationship between the work of Georg Simmel and that of Max Weber has increasingly become the focus of international research in the recent past. This interest is due in part to the current resumption of the debate over the nature and characteristics of cultural modernity and its 'postmodern' irritations and excesses. At the same time it is also the expression of an irritation with the academic self-conception of modern sociology, which has never been able to master in a satisfactory way the *'hiatus irrationalis'* between conceptual-theoretical work and empirical-theoretical research. In addition, two different traditions of sociological research and thought seem to have had

Theory, Culture & Society (SAGE, London, Newbury Park and New Delhi), Vol. 8 (1991), 33–62

their beginnings in the works of Simmel and Weber — at least so far as the history of the response to them is concerned. The North American response by Albion W. Small and Robert E. Park on the one hand and Talcott Parsons on the other has tended more to amplify than to dampen this dissociation (Levine, 1971: xlviiiff.; Faught, 1985: 156ff.).

On the one hand, it seems as if Simmel's microscopic analyses of the everyday social interactions and modes of cultural experience in modern life confront Weber's sociological categories and his universal-historical investigation as if they were a different world. The two seem to drift even further apart through the contrast between Simmel's preference for an aesthetically rich literary expression and Weber's insistence on a 'clear' formation of concepts devoid of any stylistic attraction. On the other other hand, a number of substantive similarities in the works of the two great thinkers and founders of modern sociology had already been discussed at an early stage in the secondary literature, which ultimately made the questions as to their specific epistemological and methodological positions increasingly acute.

In particular, there appears to have been unanimity for many decades that Simmel's *Philosophy of Money* (Philosophie des Geldes) (1922) must be accorded an exceptional significance for Weber's theory of occidental rationalism and the corresponding studies in cultural history and the sociology of religion. This is an assessment, by the way, which found fertile soil in Weber's professed support for the tradition of scholarly cultural analysis as inaugurated by Simmel's *Philosophy of Money* (cf. Weber, 1920: 34; Frischeisen-Köhler, 1919/20: 18; Lukács, 1958: 175; Mannheim, 1980: 313; Salomon, 1945: 606; Tenbruck, 1959: 622ff.; Frisby, 1978: 22ff.; Faught, 1985; Pohlmann, 1987; Lichtblau, 1988: 33ff.). It is also a consensus that the commonalities in such analyses stem in part from a radical renunciation of the naive optimism on progress as expressed in the Enlightenment philosophy of the eighteenth century and in the industrial boom of the late nineteenth century in Germany (the *Gründerzeit*). In that sense they prepared the way for a *tragic consciousness* within German sociology (Lenk, 1964; Dahme, 1988; Liebersohn, 1988). There is an equivalent consensus in the history of dogma about moving the origin of *Western Marxism* and central motifs of the *Frankfurt School* back to the unconventional Simmel–Weber synthesis as marked out in the work of the young Georg Lukács (cf. Schnabel,

1974: 110ff.; Frisby, 1978: 22ff.; Beiersdorfer, 1986; Turner, 1986; Dannemann, 1987: 61ff., 83ff.; Scaff, 1987, 1989).

In that respect it is no coincidence that, particularly among theoreticians of cultural modernity who feel themselves obliged to this traditional context and the knowledge claims expressed in it, the work of Simmel and Weber is coming to occupy the centre of attention in a *comparative* perspective as part of the clarification of the fundamental conceptual premises for a sociologically significant cultural analysis of European modernity (cf. Scaff, 1987, 1989; Whimster, 1987: 268ff.; Frisby, 1988a, b; Lichtblau, 1988, 1989/90). Both Simmel's theory of the divergent development of 'subjective' and 'objective' culture, and Weber's analysis of the objectification and generalization of relations of domination that were originally genuinely personal have come into view as pre-formulations of Lukács's critique of the reification of consciousness in bourgeois society. Simmel's theory is likewise viewed as the possibility of an irrational questioning of the culture of modernity which is due to the 'life process' itself, or better, the emergence of new charismatic personalities and social revolutionary movements. This has finally turned even the question of the status of the respective individual freedom and of the concrete margins of action for the individual within this 'autonomization' of 'social forms' into an 'iron cage' of lifestyle and the routinization of action in the wake of the 'mechanisms of rationalization' (Davis, 1973: 322; Kalberg, 1978: 7ff.; Bevers, 1985: 140; Lichtblau, 1988: 87ff.).

This multiplicity of substantive relations between Simmel's and Weber's works is the actual reason why even their differing views of the nature and characteristics of sociology as an 'exact' and academically conducted specialized discipline have found an increased international audience and correspondingly more attention during the past few years. For some time, there have existed attempts to determine from a comparative perspective sociology's relationship with respect to the efforts at its institutionalization as a specialized academic discipline (Dahme and Rammstedt, 1984; Rammstedt, 1985; Weiss, 1988), and to explicate its handling of the problem of the semantic ambiguity of contexts of meaning and a corresponding aesthetic-literary form of representing them (Green, 1988; Levine, 1988). By now, there are also a considerable number of studies which claim to bring a bit more light into the tangled relationship between Simmel's conception of a *pure* or *formal sociology* and Weber's plan of an *interpretive sociology*.

Two differing evaluations can be observed, which dominate these methodological discussions and at the same time clarify the aporia of such a comparison of theories. The first case draws on Simmel's epistemological investigation on *The Problems of the Philosophy of History* (*Die Probleme der Geschichtsphilosophie*) from the year 1892, which appeared in 1905 in a heavily revised second edition. Here the conception of a *science of reality* (*Wirklichkeitswissenschaft*), i.e. the *theory of interpretation* and of *ideal-typical concept formation* that had already begun to be developed by Simmel, is considered the model and the heuristic frame of reference for Weber's own methodological works (Tenbruck, 1958: 604ff., 1959: 622ff; Levine, 1971: xlv, 1984: 326ff.; Schnabel, 1974: 104ff.; Bevers, 1985: 125ff.; Segre, 1987; Lichtblau, 1988: 20ff.). In the second approach, it is simultaneously pointed out that this epistemological investigation into the a priori presuppositions of history, which would become so important to Weber's work, does not in fact contain a methodological foundation of Simmel's own sociology. In that respect, his 'pure' or 'formal' sociology ought not be hastily equated to Weber's programme of an 'interpretive' sociology, since the two are based in part on completely different foundations and also pursue differing knowledge interests (Tenbruck, 1958: 604ff., 1959: 622ff.; Atoji, 1982: 5ff.; Bevers, 1985: 125ff.; Nedelmann, 1988).

The state of the debate in this area becomes totally confused if one additionally introduces the peculiar status of Simmel's *Philosophy of Money* into this tissue of relationships. That work was of no less importance than *The Problems of the Philosophy of History* for Weber's self-clarification and intellectual development at the time of his recovery, yet by Simmel's own admission it is neither a socioeconomic study in the specialized sense nor does it even contain an application of his 'sociology' (cf. Lichtblau, 1986). Furthermore, Weber's infrequent remarks on Simmel's sociological method in the narrow sense remain oddly enigmatic, and should probably be held responsible in part for the current confusion in relation to the significance of Simmel's work for Weber's plan of an 'interpretive' sociology. Indeed, it can be surmised that Weber's inadequate understanding relative to the particular characteristics of Simmel's different works and their corresponding methodological approaches can be traced back to an initial insecurity on Weber's part with respect to his *own* sociological self-understanding, which also left its mark on his contradictory judgements of Simmel's work.

Symptomatic of Weber's irritation and lack of understanding with respect to the cognitive status and the methodological peculiarity of Simmel's work is the fact that Weber did not distinguish at all between the various types of texts among Simmel's works and their disciplinary classifications. Instead, he refers to them in a quite undifferentiated way, and incidentally, very selectively in the context of his attempts to clarify the 'logical' problems of the 'human sciences' (*Geisteswissenschaften*) or 'historical cultural sciences' (*historische Kulturwissenschaften*). These 'logical' problems of historical cultural sciences are discussed in Simmel's works only in the various editions of his *Problems of the Philosophy of History*, as well as in his later works, *The Problem of Historical Time* (Das Problem der historischen Zeit) (1916), 'Historical Formation' (Die historische Formung) (1917/1918), and in *On the Nature of Historical Understanding* (Vom Wesen des historischen Verstehens) (1918b). There was no such discussion in *The Philosophy of Money* and Simmel's various sociological writings, whose specific cognitive status was not perceived by Weber at all.

By contrast to Weber himself, Simmel had developed at an early date, at the latest by the publication of *On Social Differentiation* (Über sociale Differenzierung) (1890), a clear and precise conception of sociology as a specifically new discipline which was certainly limited in its knowledge claims. Specifically, he conceived of it as 'pure' or 'formal' science, that is to say a specific *method of research*, which stands in a relation of form to content with respect to the other human and social sciences (*Geistes- und Sozialwissenschaften*), or 'cultural studies' (*Kulturwissenschaften*) (Simmel, 1890: 1–20; cf. Rammstedt, 1988). The only important enhancement of this programme of a *formal sociology* developed in the last decade of the preceding century is represented by the 'Digression on the Problem: How is Society Possible?' in the introductory chapter of his 'large' sociology from 1908. There, Simmel underscored the a priori character of the 'pure' forms of sociation over against the 'empirical' aspects of the 'contents' entering into these forms of sociation, i.e. the motives, needs, ends and inner 'experiences' of the specific individuals (cf. Simmel, 1968: 21–30).

On the other hand, Simmel's 1917 study of *The Fundamental Questions of Sociology* (Die Grundfragen der Soziologie) (1970), known as the 'little' *Sociology*, contains no further categorical expansion, much less a renovation, of his sociological approach as

fully and finally formulated in 1908. Rather, it offers only a refinement of this 'pure' or 'formal' sociology for pedagogical purposes
with respect to the *epistemology* of the social sciences on the one
hand, and *social philosophy* or 'philosophical sociology' on the
other (Simmel, 1970: 5-32; cf. Dahme, 1981: 248ff., 1984). At the
time Weber was increasingly turning to sociological research and
the problems of its methodological foundation, Simmel had in
essence already abandoned this terrain for newer areas of work
which seemed more personally important to him (cf. Troeltsch,
1922: 572ff.; Tenbruck, 1958: 593). This state of affairs documents
the fact that Weber was not a contemporary of Simmel's at all, but
in a sense already belonged to a new generation.

Unlike Simmel, Weber had not entered the scene with intentions
from the beginning to found a sociology operating as a specialized
discipline to form an alternative to the older and newer traditions
of a speculative and metaphysical 'social theory'. In the controver-
sies that had erupted in the 'methodological quarrel' between
Schmoller and Menger in economics, as well as in the historians'
quarrels over Karl Lamprecht's works on cultural history, regarding the relationship between a genuinely historical and a purely
systematic knowledge or between an 'individual psychological'
and a 'social psychological' method of knowledge, Weber's own
attempts to reach a new and independent solution to these
unresolved problems have the character of occasional pieces,
whose programmatic claims had not from the beginning intended
something like a sociology operating as an autonomous science.
Even the posthumously published 'Theory of Sociological Categories' in *Economy and Society* (1968) was, by Weber's own
self-understanding, purely a conceptual aid for his historical-
comparative investigations of universal history, and was only later
hypostatized by his later disciples into an end in itself (cf. Weber,
1972b: 1-180; Tenbruck, 1959; Hennis, 1987; Weiss, 1989: 7-19).
This may finally have been one of the reasons why Weber said so
little about Simmel's actual *sociological* writings and was more
interested in Simmel the 'logician' and 'cultural philosopher'.

In the following section, I will sharpen these 'ambivalent encoun-
ters' between Simmel and Weber in terms of the question of what
significance for Weber's attempts at clarification of the 'logical
problems' of the 'historical cultural sciences' in general can be
ascribed to Simmel's works in the *methodological sense*. To this
end, the various references of Weber to Simmel's work and

especially his critique of Simmel will be considered. Additionally, the inappropriateness of Weber's critique of Simmel will be discussed against the background of Simmel's own work, in order to clarify the question of the relationship Simmel's project of a 'pure' or 'formal' sociology has to Max Weber's 'interpretive' sociology.

II

Simmel never directly referred to Weber's work in publications that appeared during his life or posthumously. Besides his consistent practice of avoiding quotations, caused in part by his aesthetic 'attitude', the previously mentioned temporal gap between the sociological creative periods of the two authors may have also motivated this.

Weber, by contrast, refers directly and indirectly to Simmel in the various essays in his Wissenschaftslehre, in his writings on the sociology of religion, at the beginning of his *Basic Concepts of Sociology* (Soziologische Grundbegriffe) and in *Economy and Society*. Around 1908, he also began working out a critical reaction to Simmel's *Soziologie*, as announced in his essay on Knies, but, like so many of Weber's later projects, this remained a fragment, first published in 1972, in an English translation (Weber, 1972a). On the basis of Weber's own voluminous methodological discussions of the 'logical problems' of 'historical cultural sciences', and taking into account these different statements in Weber's writings directly related to Simmel's work, the following will strive to reconstruct the central critical points which Weber felt it necessary to assert against Simmel's sociological self-understanding and scientific method in general. It will be seen in the process that Weber attempted to comprehend Simmel's work with a standard that was not only wholly inappropriate to it, but also sheds some light on Weber's own theory and practice of 'interpreting'.

Let it be emphasized first that Weber attempted to define both Simmel's *Philosophy of Money* and his *Problems of the Philosophy of History* as well as his actual sociological writings with regard to their contributions to the project of an 'interpretive sociology' in the sense that Weber later pursued. Additionally, it is striking in this sense that Weber generally positively assessed Simmel's reconstruction of the epistemological problems of historiography and the theory of 'historical interpretation' he had sketched out from the *methodological* point of view. On the other hand he treated the *Philosophy of Money* as well as Simmel's *Soziologie* with critical distance or even rejection, because of their epistemological premises, which he considered problematic. He nevertheless felt ambivalent in this connection, because it was precisely the latter two 'main sociological works' of Simmel's to which he owed so many stimuli in the *substantive* sense. Let us therefore turn first to Weber's positive references to Simmel's writings, before submitting his critique of Simmel's 'sociological method' in the *The Philosophy of Money* and his actual *Soziologie* to a detailed discussion.

Quite early, Weber credited Simmel with the achievement of having worked out 'by far the most logically developed approaches to a theory of "interpretation" ', especially in the second edition of his *Problems of the Philosophy of History* (Weber, 1985: 92). In particular it is the rigid distinction between the nomological or nomothetic and ideographic or historical sciences (*Gesetzes- und Wirklichkeitswissenschaft*) which Weber draws from the works of Simmel, Windelband and Rickert, in order to underscore the distinctive character of the concept formation in the cultural sciences vis-à-vis the 'realistic' or 'naturalistic' self-misunderstandings of the historians and economists of his period (Weber, 1985; 4, 146, 237; Simmel, 1892: 41ff.; Simmel, 1905: 40ff.). Like Simmel and Rickert, Weber justifies the emphasis on the purely *hypothetical* character of the scientific 'interpretation' of historical and socio-economic processes with the argument that 'reality' as such constitutes an 'intensive infinity of *all* the empirically existing variety'. This necessarily forces the researcher into a rigid 'material selection', in order to distil a *conceived order* out of this 'heterogeneous continuum' of events, or to make it 'comprehensible' by relating it to an 'adequately' conceived and 'causally relevant' nexus of meaning (Weber, 1985: 75, 114). Similarly to Simmel, Weber emphasizes a *lower threshold of historical interpretation*, the criterion of which Simmel designates as the respective *degree of consequence* of a historical event, and Weber as its *causally relevant* aspect (Simmel, 1905: 131, 1957: 57; Weber, 1985: 233). Weber also refers positively to Simmel's emphasis on the *individual* character of 'mass phenomena', to the extent they can be reconstructed by the 'method of interpretation', as well as to Simmel's view of the necessity of specific *value relationships* that guide the researcher in the choice of material and the hypothetical construction of its meanings.

Along with Simmel, Weber advances the view that it is not only strongly characterized *historical personalities* and the motives of their actions that can be best interpreted, but also that a strongly marked *personality of the historian* himself is the best presupposition for the interpretation of individual courses of action by great historical individuals, as well as for grasping the meaning of apparently fortuitous events and mass phenomena (Simmel, 1905: 52ff.; Weber, 1985: 48, 101, 548). And just as much as Simmel, Weber views the manifestation of *social conflict* or struggle as an essential component of sociation processes, which finds expression on the methodological level in the recognition of a *pluralism* or '*absolute polytheism*'. Weber, however, sees the preconditions for a 'mortal struggle, as if between God and the Devil' in this pluralism of the various cultural 'value spheres' or 'possible points of view'. Simmel, on the other hand, relativizes that pluralism to the logical parallelism of possible value spheres or the more moderate form of a respective 'personal attitude', by which means the individual personality expresses its specific views towards the 'world' surrounding it (Weber, 1985: 463, 507; cf. Simmel, 1910: 23ff., 1918a: 30ff.). Finally, like Simmel, Weber considers the description of 'rational progress', or the various processes of rationalization which have shaped the formation of modern occidental culture, to be a major task of sociology and of a corresponding cultural theory (Weber, 1985: 525ff.; cf. Simmel, 1892: 40ff.; Weber, 1968: 147ff.).

Weber takes a critical if not hostile view of the thesis advanced by Simmel and Karl Lamprecht that this process of the increasing prevalence of the model of instrumentally rational action in the most varied areas of society, interpreted as *rational progress* and *social differentiation*, must necessarily be accompanied by an increasing differentiation of the subjective culture of inner 'experience'.[1] In this connection, with a glance at Karl Lamprecht's writing on cultural history, Weber criticizes the existence of an 'allegedly determinate and uniform succession of the various "impressionisms" in the social psyche'. He also asserts the objection to Simmel's 'impressionism' that the increasing significance of 'emotional nuances' need not necessarily contain at the same time an increasing differentiation in the forms of 'experience' itself. The 'race for sensations' and 'the intellectually interesting' which are characteristic of modern culture should, in Weber's view, be conceived rather as the 'product of diminishing power to master everyday life inwardly' and of a spreading 'aesthetic twilight mood' in the *fin de siècle* (Weber, 1985: 7f., 518f.; for a discussion of Simmel's 'impressionism' see Frisby, 1981; Böhringer, 1989). Weber does partially concur with regard to the view that there is a *progressive social differentiation and rationalization*, to the extent it is connected with the idea of an increase in *rational social organization*. Before naively transferring a pattern of differentiation borrowed from biology to sociocultural processes, however, he insists on a clarification of the question:

> how in the early stages of human social differentiation the realm of purely mechanical-*instinctive* differentiation should be assessed in relationship to that which is individually and sensually comprehensible and further to that which is consciously and rationally created. (Weber, 1985: 461, 473, 576f.)

This reservation, implicitly also directed against Simmel's theory of social differentiation, can also be sharpened into the methodological question of what is the relationship in Simmel's *Soziologie* between the *subjectively intended meaning* and that *objectively valid meaning* which 'interpretive sociology' attempts to reconstruct in the form of an empirical checking of the researcher's *adequacy of meaning* by the causal relevancy of his interpretations. Of course, Weber himself admits that Simmel's book on *The Problems of the Philosophy of History* deserves the merit of having 'clearly separated the objective "interpretation" of the *meaning* of a statement from the subjective "interpretation" of the motives of a (speaking or acting) person'. On the other hand, he later repeatedly accuses Simmel of causing the intended and the objectively *valid* meaning to 'blur deliberately', especially in *The Philosophy of Money* and *Soziologie*, whereas Weber would 'sharply distinguish them' (cf. Weber, 1985: 427, 541).

The apparent contradiction between Weber's first statement from the year 1905 and his later judgement from the years 1913–20 can be resolved in the following sense. Simmel was concerned in the quoted passage from *The Problems of the Philosophy of History* only with the distinction between the interpretation of a *sentence's meaning* independently of the context in which it was first uttered and the interpretation of the *intentions* of the speaking and acting persons. In the second case, however, Weber accuses Simmel of not having sufficiently distinguished within his 'sociological method', in the narrower sense, between the interpretation of the *motives* of the social actors and the *objective context of meaning* reconstructed by the researchers, in which a statement or an action appears both 'adequate to the meaning' and 'causally relevant' (cf. Levine, 1984: 328-34; Nedelmann, 1988: 13ff.).

This central objection that Weber raises against Simmel's 'method' can be supplemented and expanded by a series of further critical points, which Weber lodged against *The Philosophy of Money* and his *Soziologie* and which are directly connected to this main argument of Weber's. Weber additionally not only accuses Simmel of treating actual *problems of being* (*Seinsprobleme*) as *problems of meaning* (*Sinnprobleme*), that is, ultimately metaphysically, but also of drawing *illustrations* and *analogies* for 'interpreting' sociologically relevant facts from the most diverse spheres of meaning. To be sure, Weber also recognizes the *heuristic* value of uncovering 'parallelisms' between the most various 'causal series' and 'contexts of meaning' in the sense of the construction of 'comprehensible images' of events. Unlike Simmel, however, he views the 'comparison of "analogous" events' as only one of *several* means of 'attribution' and therefore merely a 'preliminary stage' of the actual work of an 'interpretive sociology' — that is, the formation of 'sharp concepts' and 'pure types' of 'causal relevance'. By contrast, he claims that for Simmel the 'analogous' side of a concrete phenomenon that is being cited is elevated to its 'actual nature' and therefore ultimately abstracted from its causal conditionality (Weber, 1972a: 160ff., 1985: 14, 26ff., 124, 232; on the positive evaluation of Simmel's 'brilliant images' in *The Philosophy of Money* see Weber, 1920: 34).

In reproaching Simmel's investigation of cultural philosophy and sociology for its causal irrelevance, Weber is attempting at the same time to strike at the heart of Simmel's 'sociological method'. Already in 1905, Weber had pointed to the problematics of the 'remarks on the concept of society and the duties of sociology scattered throughout his [Simmel's] various writings', and in that connection had quoted for the first time the corresponding critique of Simmel's positions by Othmar Spann (Weber, 1985: 93). In his fragmentary manuscript on 'Georg Simmel as Sociologist and Theoretician of the Money Economy' from 1908 (English trans. 1972a), Weber renews this appeal to Spann's critique of Simmel, seconding it 'in many essential points', although Spann had not been able to take account of Simmel's 'large' *Soziologie* of 1908, which Weber credited with 'a few notable, though not fundamental modifications with respect to Simmel's earlier stances that had been criticized by Spann'. Additionally, Weber launches an attack of his own on the central and fundamental concept in Simmel's 'method', which Spann had already scrutinized critically: the principle of *interaction* (*Wechselwirkung*) which Simmel conceived of as the 'global regulative principle' (cf. Simmel, 1890: 13ff.; Weber, 1972a: 162f.; Spann, 1905, 1907: 178ff.).

Weber, of course, recognizes that for Simmel sociology is a science concerned with the *interactions between individuals*. Nonetheless, this concept of 'interaction' appears deeply 'ambiguous' to him, since a 'relationship that is not somehow mutual . . . [is] scarcely constructible within physical reality in the most literal sense and as a *general* phenomenon'. Therefore, Weber reaches a conclusion he considers devastating for Simmel's sociology, that this idea is so abstract in its concept and broad in its contents 'that it would require the greatest artificiality to conceive of an influence of one person by another that would be purely "one-sided", i.e. not containing a certain element of "interaction"' (Weber, 1972a: 163).[2]

The thrust of Weber's argument becomes even clearer when we include the criticisms raised by Othmar Spann against Simmel's 'formal' sociology, objections to which Weber referred approvingly several times.[3] Spann had anticipated at a very early date a central problem of Simmel's 'speculative atomism', to which Simmel did not provide a satisfactory answer until 1908 — the question that remained to be cleared up: 'How is social science as a science of *complexes*, whose elements are already subject to universal research, possible at all?' Spann considered Simmel's 'solution of this preliminary epistemological question' by means of the 'global regulative principle' of *interaction* 'unsatisfactory in its implementation and contradictory and metaphysical in its construction' (Spann, 1905: 310; for a discussion of Simmel's 'speculative atomism' see also Böhringer, 1976). Spann criticizes Simmel's view that in principle there can be 'laws of events' only for the smallest part of the physical world. He argues that in the context of such epistemological premises it can no longer be plausibly shown in what form an 'independent law' could then be formulated for the 'complex as such' and the 'totality' of social phenomena. The 'sublimation of the concept of society' to a *mere name for the sum of all social interactions* is therefore said to be a necessary consequence of Simmel's 'formal' sociology, which makes *social science* 'impossible' as an *independent science*.

In opposition to that, Spann insists on the *uniform*, not purely *gradual* effect of social formations, which are likewise also accessible in principle to a *law-based causal analysis*. In that respect, he views even Simmel's concept of *interaction* as only the *special case of a double causal relationship*, in the sense of a 'mutual relationship of dependency between two quantities', whose 'exact causal-theoretical determination and justification' is a desideratum in Simmel's sociology. The same applies to the formulation of a 'material concept of society' because of Simmel's excessively abstract and unsubstantively formulated principle of interaction. Spann concludes his critique of the inadequacy of Simmel's epistemological foundation of the social sciences with the postulate that it remains to be shown how the individual interactions and complexes of phenomena can be constituted as *specifically social* at all, with respect to the premises advocated by Simmel (cf. Spann, 1905: 310–35, 1907: 189–220, 1923b: 25–46).

In what follows I demonstrate that these objections raised by Weber and Spann against Simmel's 'method' only represent his starting-points for an epistemological foundation of the modern social sciences in a completely inadequate way, and largely miss their mark. I will show that Simmel solved the criticisms raised against his methodological approach by means of a logically consistent *theory of interpretive understanding* (*Verstehen*), both in the second edition (Simmel, 1905, 1977) of his study of *The Problems of the Philosophy of History* as well as in his 'Digression on the Question: How is Society Possible?' from 1908 (Simmel, 1959, 1968). And he did this in a way that not only proves Weber's and Spann's criticism of him obsolete, but is also more capable than Weber's own approaches of satisfying the demands that we are compelled by the current state of knowledge to place on the foundation of 'interpretive sociology'. Finally, I will clarify the specific knowledge interests Simmel pursued with his carefully measured out and well reflected *trisection* of 'cultural sciences' (*Kulturwissenschaften*) into an *epistemology of the historical and social sciences* and the respective underlying *empirical scientific* correlatives on the one hand, and the *theory of cultural modernity* explicated in his *The Philosophy of Money* on the other.

III

In order to illustrate the difference between the basic epistemological positions of Simmel and Weber, it is worth taking a brief look at the history of the concepts of *causality* and *interaction* which they employ as 'global regulative principles'. It must first be stressed that Weber's insistence on the inescapable necessity of causal analyses in the area of the 'historical cultural sciences' no longer possessed any direct persuasive power as such at the beginning of the twentieth century. Following the revolutionizing of the *world view of natural science* around the turn of the century, the suitability of the causal category for the fundamental conceptual reconstruction of physical processes had been called into question. The crisis of the mechanical world view is owing in part to the insight from the physics of elementary particles as developed by Max Planck and Albert Einstein that the interactions between 'elementary quantities' or quanta on one hand, and 'matter' on the other, cannot be reconstructed along the pattern of cause and effect. Rather, all that can still be described are the constant relationships of changes in time in the sense of a fundamental *relativity*, that is, a 'dependence of phenomena on one another' (Ernst Mach). By completely cutting through the relationship between *causality* and *adherence to laws*, which was still constitutive for classical mechanics, Weber does react to the foundational crisis of the modern scientific world view. At the same time, however, he dissolves the concept of causality into a pure juridically inspired *problem of attribution* for the 'historical explanation' of phenomena which are always only *comprehensible individually* (on Weber's positive reference to Gustav Radbruch's concept of 'adequate causation' (1902) see Weber, 1985: 269ff.).

The understanding of causality in the mechanistic world view was already an extrication of the *causa efficiens* from a more encompassing understanding of being, such as was still self-evident for Greek antiquity and the European Middle Ages. The Aristotelian tradition that still prevailed in that era distinguished between four *different* types of 'causes', which were inwardly connected within underlying teleological world view: the *material*, the *form*, the *motive force* (*causa efficiens*) and the *end* (telos). According to this thought, the originator (or the *causa efficiens*), which is identical with the modern causal concept, was not the only presupposition for the 'being of that which has been created', but rather it was embedded into the context of the *structural totality* shaped by an overarching concept of purpose (cf. Gadamer, 1967: 196f.).

By reaching back to interaction (*Wechselwirkung*) as the basic category for his thought Simmel not only follows the relativistic world view of modern physics, but also consciously seeks to connect with an older tradition of thought. The latter always conceived of itself as an alternative to the modern predominance of the causal category, and not coincidentally, it rehabilitated the fourfold significance of the Aristotelian concept of 'cause' in that respect. In the etymological respect, the concept of 'change' (*'Wechsel'* — also meaning a draft, or promissory note) in the sense of the *exchange of goods* is one of the oldest German commercial terms. In Kant's philosophy, the concept of 'interaction' is explicitly equated with that of the *community*, and as an *analogy of experience* it is determined according to the principle of the *simultaneous being of substances in space* (cf. Kant, 1924: 302ff.). In the Romantic philosophy of nature, the concept of interaction is called upon for describing an *organism*, in which the whole *precedes* the parts, so that the 'endless interactions' of the parts cannot be interpreted as a causal relationship, since any effect is always already the cause of its own attainment.

Friedrich Schleiermacher finally attempted for the first time to make this idea of a fundamental *simultaneity* of the elements of an interaction fruitful in a genuinely social-philosophical form for his own philosophy in the context of his 'Theory of Social Behavior' (Theorie des geselligen Betragens) from 1799. As part of this theory, he defined society as an 'interaction winding through all its participants, but also completely determined and completed by them' (Schleiermacher, 1984: 169; for the history of the concept 'interaction' see Christian, 1978: 110ff.).

Simmel puts his own concept of 'interaction' into the theoretical context transmitted to him via Dilthey, by holding fast to the fundamental *boundlessness of all events*, by conceiving of these events *constantly* as *connected* by a variety of interactions, and by subjecting an analysis of these interactions to the *principle of simultaneity*. This preference for *synchronism* vis-à-vis *diachronism* distinguishes his approach fundamentally from a causal analysis in a Weberian sense, because the traditional concept of causality is necessarily dependent on the idea of a temporal succession in the sense of an afterwards (cf. Kant, 1924: 283ff.). The interaction, on the other hand implies a coexistence, which can be captured and described in the *mode of 'magnificent simultaneity'* (Friedrich Schlegel).

This determination of Simmel's fundamental principles has a variety of implications and consequences for his *method of interpreting*, which can only be treated summarily and in passing within the bounds of this investigation. First, according to Simmel, a description of historical events 'as they really happened' is fundamentally *not* possible for epistemological reasons. In that respect, *historical understanding*, like *any* kind of knowledge, is 'a transfer of that which directly exists into a new language' which 'follows only its own forms, categories and demands' (Simmel, 1905: 40ff.). Even the relationship between 'cause' and 'effect' is substituted in that way by the *logical form of a mutual relationship* or an 'interaction', in which 'the present has an effect on the past at the same time as the past on the present' (Simmel, 1919: 191; cf. Christian, 1978: 125). Historical understanding according to this view designates an intelligible level that is identical neither with the isolated acts of consciousness on the part of the historian nor with the 'motives' of 'historical individuals'.

Second, even in any ordinary example of reciprocal action or interaction a play of projection and rejection between the acting and the experiencing individuals occurs. We always see the *other* only in the mirror of our own generalizations and typifications, and we gain our *self image* conversely only through a 'generalized other' (cf. Simmel, 1968: 24ff.).

Third, this 'global regulative principle' in Simmel's 'method of interpretation' is furthermore deeply connected with his cultural philosophy, adopted from the aesthetic works of Baudelaire, that described *modernity* as an *eternal present*. In this respect then, Simmel's decision in favour of the category of interaction against that of causality owes something to the substantive results of his own analyses of modern and contemporary culture (cf. Frisby, 1981, 1985).

In rejecting all 'realistic' or 'naturalistic' reifications of 'ideal-typical' concept formations, Simmel was therefore no less rigorous than Max Weber. Unlike Weber, he additionally goes so far as to dissolve the 'external' successions within the empirical world of phenomena into a simultaneity or timelessness of 'inner contemplation'. Even so-called 'historical interpretation' is therefore only the expression of a logical process for Simmel, in which the difference between ego and non-ego, subject and object, as well as present and past is first *constituted*. By means of the example of his concept of *historical interpretation*, I will illustrate this commonality in the initial questioning between Simmel's attempt at an epistemological foundation of historical studies, on the one hand, and his quasi-transcendental constitutional theory of the forms of sociation, on the other. Then I will attempt to characterize the status of the *sociological* a prioris within Simmel's attempt to ground modern sociology, and the latter's logical relationship of that attempt to Weber's programme of an 'interpretive sociology'.

IV

Simmel starts from the fundamental *circularity* of human knowledge, according to which *external events* can only be symbolically interpreted by analogy to 'inner experience', and *inner events* conversely only by analogy to temporal-spatial, i.e. 'external' determinations. The two analogy formations do not enjoy a relationship of mutual 'cause' and 'effect', but occur *simultaneously* or produce one another *mutually*, and thus behave *correlatively* towards each other (Simmel, 1905: 20f., 1922: 534ff., 1968: 567f.; cf. Lichtblau, 1986: 64f.). This *mode of the simultaneous* characterizes in his view not only *current* actions and events, but also the *historical interpretation* of past events. The two types of understanding thus differ only *in degree* (cf. Simmel, 1957: 44, 64). Interpretation as such always contains a process of psychological *reforming, concentration and reshaping* of the 'acts of consciousness in others', yet it should not be understood as a pure 'projection'. Rather, it designates a 'completely idiosyncratic synthesis of the category of the general with the simply individual', which now takes the place of the *causality* of 'psycho-mechanical events' in describing those *reasons* which are based on the 'logical relationships of their contents' (Simmel, 1905: 30ff.). Of course this form of interpreting meaning also connects with the *motives* of the persons who are acting, but it subjects their analysis to the a priori *demands of thought*, through which the transmitted events are first formed into a *historical* context. The work of a historian, which Simmel did not compare to that of an artist by mere coincidence, concentrates the *singular* — hence also the 'subjective motives' insisted upon by Weber — into a *structure of meaning*, which:

> often was not present at all in the consciousness of its 'heroes', by unearthing meanings and values in its material that shape this past into an image worthy of presenting to us. (Simmel, 1905: 41, 45ff.)

With respect to what was *really experienced*, the categories of history thus represent a priori *categories of the second order*, as it were, the analysis of which constitutes the actual object of an epistemology of 'scholarly history' (Simmel, 1905: 50f.). In this sense, the difference between 'subjective' and 'objective meaning' asserted by Weber against Simmel is consciously 'sublated' in Simmel's theoretical analysis of the constitution of historical thinking within the framework of a *synthesis of the fantasy*. For, according to him, a reconstruction of the possibility of historical interpreting moves on a logical level situated *beyond* this dualism.

Nevertheless, Simmel does take up the problem of *historical individuality* and the fundamental issue of the *possibility of understanding other minds* as part of his a priori grounding of historical studies. The latter in particular were extensively discussed in his later works *The Problem of Historical Time* (Vom Problem der historischen Zeit) and *On the Nature of Historical Understanding* (Vom Wesen des historischen Verstehens) (for translations see Simmel, 1980). There, Simmel repeats his view that the *process of understanding* as such constitutes *something completely timeless*, and cannot therefore be described in the form of a causal relationship. For him, 'historical' is the epitome of an event that is unambiguously determined in its *date*, and thus is accorded the 'character of individualization', which results solely from its position within the context of meaning reconstructed by the historian. Simmel, however, denies the character of the temporal to that context, because any time-span conceived in that way is subject to the law of causality. The historical concept of *duration*, on the other hand, expresses a *unity of understanding* whose individual elements determine each other *correlatively*, i.e. in a hermeneutically conceived mode of *mutual* 'interaction' (cf. Simmel, 1957: 44ff., 71ff.).

What is fundamental for Simmel's theory of historical understanding, then, is not the difference between *cause* and *effect*, or between *subjective* and *objective* meaning, but that between 'I' and 'You' in the sense of the constitutive 'relationship of one spirit to another'. This relationship already *finds* a 'fragmentary outline' of itself in the practice of the lifeworld, and is to be analysed by epistemology solely with respect to its a priori premises. The categories of *You* and *understanding* prove identical in this process; in them, the *condition humaine* is 'expressed once as a substance, as it were and once as a function — an elemental phenomenon of the human mind . . . it is the transcendental foundation for the fact that the human being is a *zoon politikon*'. Those categories are therefore 'about as decisive for the construction of the practical and historical world as are the categories of *substance* and *causality* for the physical world' (Simmel, 1957: 67f.).

In the introductory chapter of his large *Soziologie* (1968) from 1908, Simmel attempted to make this *transcendental* nature of understanding and the implicit fundamental conceptual difference between 'I' and 'You' fruitful for an a priori foundation of the social sciences. In this way he hoped to be able to provide a definitive answer to the question Othmar Spann had still raised against his 'formal method', of how *society* can be possible at all as an *objective form of subjective souls* (cf. Simmel, 1968: 21ff.). Animated by a corresponding attempt by Max Adler (1904), Simmel now made an effort to show that an a priori design occurs in the most varied forms of social interaction which always places the contents of these interactions, that is, 'drives', 'motives', subjective 'experiences', and 'purposes', into a context of sociation. These concrete 'contents' come under consideration in Simmel's sociological approach only in the sense that they have already entered into this quasi-transcendental *shaping*; that is to say, they have been *synthesized* or *sociated* to an extent by a corresponding *social* a priori. A fundamental conceptual difference between the 'subjectively intended' and the 'objectively valid meaning' has thus in fact become *irrelevant* not only for Simmel's metatheory of history, but also for his sociological analyses of the various forms of social 'interaction' — and Max Weber rightly emphasized this. The only *difference*, or better, the 'original difference' that therefore still plays a part in Simmel's a priori formal foundation of sociology, is the difference between 'I' and 'You' built into the act of interpretation itself, which as a *primeval phenomenon* lies *beyond* the conflict between 'subjective' and 'objective.'[4]

As compared to Weber's approach in this respect, Simmel's analysis of the *sociological* a prioris contains a completely *autonomous* theory of interpretation which was taken up quite productively not only by his student Martin Buber, but also by the 'Chicago School of sociology', and became fruitful for a *dialogic social philosophy* or an *interpretive sociology*. In the variant of an interpretive sociology that Max Weber represents, by contrast, he no longer discusses the act of 'interpreting' as reconstructed by Simmel and his successors. Instead, he presumes the possibility of interpretation as if 'selfevident', in order to functionalize it for his real cognitive interest — that of 'causal explanation'.[5]

Simmel, by contrast, would like to show two things with his analysis of the a priori preconditions of interpretation and the original difference implied in it. First, according to him, all the possible reference points of a sociological causal analysis, that is, both the 'social actors' and the 'social constructs', are to be conceived of as the results of *simultaneously* occurring *interactions*, which alone constitute them as *relative* interaction units at all. Simmel had developed and presented this train of thought already back in 1890 as part of his attempt to overcome 'speculative atomism' with the epistemological means of that very same 'atomism'. On the other hand, the 'original phenomenon' of *interpretation* itself is explicated as the *specific form of an interaction*, by means of which the 'subjects' of interpretation and the possible 'points of attribution' of a causal analysis are first hermeneutically constituted, as it were.

Simmel expresses this line of thought most succinctly in his discussion of the 'first sociological a priori'. There he alludes to the thought he had already asserted in his epistemology of history, that we can always interpret 'external' events *symbolically* only according to 'inner' *analogies* and vice versa, and that both of these analogy formations are performed in the *mode of the simultaneous*, that is to say, in the form of a *hermeneutic circle* or of an *interaction*. In this connection, Simmel says that we can never grasp another person in his full *individuality* or *uniqueness*, but instead always create a more or less *general image* of him, or *typify* him, since a *real knowledge* of him would presume an equality of subject and object, or of ego and non-ego that never exists in reality. Conversely — and in this view Simmel follows not only the poet but also the neurologist — we ourselves are only:

> *fragments* not just of the general human being, but also of ourselves. . . . This fragmentary quality, however, completes the view of the other into something that we ourselves never are purely and completely. He cannot see only the fragments lying next to one another that really exist, but just as we supplement the blind spot in our field of vision, so that one is not even aware of it, similarly we make of this fragmentary data the completeness of his individuality. . . . This fundamental procedure, although it is seldom carried out to perfection in reality now takes effect within the already existing society as the a priori of the further interactions that unfold between individuals. . . . Certain suppositions emerge from the common basis of life, through which people catch sight of each other, as if through a veil. (Simmel, 1968: 281f.)

But it is precisely this veil, however, which Simmel invokes with its indirect allusion to Plato's famous metaphor for the eyes, which is at the same time what makes 'society' in the sense described by

Simmel possible at all. For the pure immediacy and simultaneity of understanding oneself and others represents a logical limiting case, which may of course be possible as a mystical 'experience' or in the gazes of lovers as a language of the eyes, but which is completely irrelevant to those everyday interactions that constitute the central forms of sociation.[6] In this connection, Simmel also frequently uses the metaphor of *detours* in order to indicate that we can neither conceive and know ourselves nor understand the other in his immediacy through pure self-referentiality, because that is *both near to and far from us*. These detours and 'deviations' from the immediacy of self-relationship and of an understanding of others are also what constitute the actual object of Simmel's formal sociology as well as of his cultural theory as sketched out in *The Philosophy of Money*. In this context, he occupied himself particularly with those 'detours' which the individual must put up with in pursuing his subjective purposes and valuations, in order to attain his actual 'final goals'. The extent of such detours indicates the degree of *social differentiation* in each case, the increase of which Simmel generally evaluated as *cultural progress*. He compared these increasing 'distances' to taxes which the individual had to pay to 'society' in order to pursue his own motives and purposes (cf. Simmel, 1890: 42ff, 1922: 480ff.).[7] Precisely these 'detours', 'distances' and *forms* which shape individual action acquire a specific *socializing or sociating function* that can be described according to Simmel as a completely new and *genuinely autonomous nexus of meaning*, without any 'causal attribution' to subjective 'motives' being required for the *understanding* of these 'immeasurable contexts'. The real place where, according to Simmel, individuality in a qualitative sense can still unfold in the culture of modernity is less the sphere of the 'social' than that of artistic, erotic and religious 'experience', in which the 'modern soul' is able to preserve and build up its particularity (cf. Simmel, 1922: 529ff.; Lichtblau, 1988: 54ff., 89ff.).

V

In concluding, we still must discuss Weber's charge that in Simmel's works 'problems of being' are often treated as 'problems of meaning', and that the latter thereby give expression not only to a *metaphysical* but also to an *aesthetic need*. Now Simmel himself repeatedly pointed out that every 'exact' specialized science possesses both an *upper* and a *lower limit*. Beyond these there lies, on the one hand, the *epistemology* of a specialized science based on a priori assumptions and, on the other, a corresponding *metaphysics*. In the case of history an attempt is made to satisfy this 'metaphysical need' with the *philosophy of history*, while the same is done in the case of 'pure' or 'formal' sociology with 'philosophical sociology' or *social philosophy* (cf. Simmel, 1892: 71ff., 1905: 112ff., 1922: v–ix, 1968: 20f., 1970: 29ff.).

Within such a metaphysics *beyond* exact science, Simmel actually does attempt to provide an answer to the question of the meaning of life and the inner contents of the underlying 'ultimate' *values*. According to Simmel, the basis for the legitimacy of such an enquiry is that the 'empirical' (*wirklichkeitswissenschaftlich*) approach necessarily loses sight of the *totality of life*, because it breaks concrete events and the sum of their interactions down into a number of *fragments*. Unlike Marx and the 'universalist' stance of Othmar Spann, Simmel has long since abandoned the hope that this lost totality of life could be reconstructed by means of a specialized science. His own sociological analyses are thus consciously 'conceived as examples in their methods and, in their content, only as fragments of what I must consider the science of society' (Simmel, 1968: 14).

He attempts a philosophical clarification of the *value* of sociation for the *further development of individuals*, and he has a metaphysical need for the *unity of an overall view*, which would condense the abbreviation of phenomena in a purely *symbolic* manner. The attempt is owed to that deep 'dissatisfaction with the fragmentary character of detailed knowledge' which later logically *led him away from* sociology in favour of a more intensive concern with the fundamental problems of metaphysics, aesthetics and the philosophy of religion and life. To reproach him for this is not only improper but also inadequate, because Simmel always indicated precisely where his respective works are logically situated *within* and *beyond* the mode of knowing characteristic of a specialized discipline.

Here Simmel's *Philosophy of Money* assumes an outstanding importance for his cultural-philosophical and metaphysical interpretation of the *fragments of modernity*. He had characterized that work's logical position clearly enough *within* and *beyond* the range of validity of a *scientifically* organized economics. Reproaching him in this context for not differentiating clearly enough between 'determinations of fact' and 'valuations' is like carrying coals to

Newcastle. For Simmel had always said unambiguously that he was concerned in his *Philosophy of Money* with tracing the *primeval phenomena of value* as such. Therefore he was also engaged in a clarification of the premises which determine the *nature of money* and *meaning of its existence* on the one hand, and at the same time with a presentation of its effects on the 'inner world', i.e. on the *vital consciousness* (Lebensgefühl) *of individuals*, on the *concatenation of their fates* and on the *development of general culture* (cf. Simmel, 1922: viff., Frisby, 1978; Lichtblau, 1986, 1988: 37ff.). Thus, Simmel consciously conceived of his 'philosophy of money' simultaneously as an *aesthetic theory*, and incidentally also determined his concept of *social formation* by analogy to the aesthetic concept of form (cf. Davis, 1973; Hübner-Funk, 1976, 1984; Ritter, 1976; Böhringer, 1984; Boella, 1986; Frisby, 1989).

Similarly to a 'self-contained' *work of art*, the *objectivity of values* crystallized and symbolized in money appeared to him as a social construct which has *consumed the motions of its becoming within itself* and has become 'indifferent' to them when understood according to those *purely immanent determinations* (cf. Simmel, 1957: 73). And like the consideration of art, the 'philosophy of money' also proceeds from an apparently purely peripheral individual example, in order to 'do justice to it through its expansion and extension to the totality and the most general case'. In the sense that 'its entire practical meaning lies not in itself but only in its conversion into other values', money thus becomes pure *indifference*, the most general expression and the *symbol* of a culture in which things and people have lost their autonomy and now determine their relative value *mutually* (Simmel, 1922: viii, 98ff., 584f.).

Max Weber attempted to judge Simmel's work according to a standard which is simply inappropriate to the uniqueness of this oeuvre. It is a different question, however, whether Weber himself stringently adhered in his *own* research work to the methodological postulates summarized in his 'theory of science'. Doubts as to the 'freedom from value judgments' of his historical analyses arise, for instance, when Weber constructs a *heroic age* of modern capitalism in order to emphasize the *decadent* and *derivative* character of the contemporary culture surrounding him (cf. Weber, 1920: 20f., 55f., 203f., 1985: 139). Doubts also come up when he describes the overall course of the occidental rationalization process over against the 'organically prescribed circulation of life' as an *ever more devastating senselessness* (Weber, 1920: 570f.). Justified doubts are likewise in order as to whether Weber actually maintained the difference he postulated between *ideal* and *real types* strictly in his material sociology, or whether he is not describing something like a *realization of values* here, that is, a crystallization of the *subjective* 'value relationships' into *objective* 'contexts of meaning' or *objective constructs* (cf. Mannheim, 1929: 239ff.; Habermas, 1981: I, 263; Levine, 1984: 333ff.; Bevers, 1985: 132ff.).

Finally, one must also be dubious with respect to his postulate that neither symbol-rich *illustrations* nor *analogy formations* nor *quasi-aesthetic categories* may be employed in 'historical cultural sciences'. For Weber repeatedly employed a meaning-laden literary topos in order, for instance to characterize a central methodological problem of his study of Protestantism: the metaphor of *elective affinities*. With his novel of the same title Goethe intended to create a *chemical allegory* which he based on the constellation of Ottilie, Eduard, Charlotte and the Captain. The neologism 'elective affinities' therefore denotes in this context a *constraint of natural law*, so to speak, or a *magical attractive power of love* which threatens to destroy the moral and legal foundations of the bourgeois institution of marriage.

Weber criticized Simmel not only for basing his works on a 'sociologically amorphous' concept of *interaction*, but also for making use of the 'problematic', 'aesthetically charged' methods of *analogy formation* and *symbolic interpretation* of the 'correlations' between 'inner' and 'outer', or 'psychic' and 'social' facts in the *Philosophy of Money* and his sociological writings. Now, in order to characterize an *aporia not soluble causally* ('magnificent simultaneity'), Weber himself repeatedly makes use of a literary topos that has been decoded in Germanist studies as a *mythical mode of thought* ever since Walter Benjamin's ground-breaking study of Goethe's *Elective Affinities* (cf. Benjamin, 1980: 123ff.; Buschendorf, 1986). Is it perhaps a coincidence that this 'mythical shadow play', which Weber was able to make metaphorically fruitful for research into the cultural history of ascetic capitalism and the genesis of the modern professional ethos, is additionally oriented toward the *model case of a collapsing marriage*? By the way, Talcott Parsons elegantly 'solved' or better, evaded this symptomatically overdetermined problem by translating *Wahlverwandschaften* as 'correlations' rather than the more accurate 'elective affinities', thus favouring an expression more closely connected to Simmel's than Weber's terminology (cf. Weber, 1976: 90). Is this not perhaps *also* a symptomatic shift within his *own* 'discourse of the other'?

Translated by Mark Ritter.

Notes

1. Simmel first systematically developed his theory of social differentiation in the work of the same name from 1890, and later based both his *Philosophy of Money* as well as the 'large' *Soziologie* (1968) of 1908 on it (see Lichtblau, 1984).

2. For the sake of clarity, I have taken the liberty of quoting from a scarcely legible reproduction (due to multiple copying) of the German-language original manuscript. This has been circulating 'unofficially' in the scholarly world for years, and was kindly provided to me by a colleague. The original, currently held in the Max Weber Depository at the Bavarian State Library in Munich under the call number 'Ana 446', will soon be published in the *Max-Weber-Gesamtausgabe*.

3. The problematic nature of this positive reference to Spann's critique of Simmel lies of course, in the fact that Weber's own 'methodological individualism' was later likewise harshly criticized by Spann's 'universalism' (cf. Spann, 1923a, 1925: 149–67; on Weber's later dissociation from Spann's 'universalistic method' cf. Weber, 1985: 557f.).

4. Here I consciously emphasize the fundamental conceptual 'elective affinity' between Simmel's approach and the difference-theoretical deconstruction of classical metaphysics by Gilles Deleuze (1968) and with Jacques Derrida's meditations on 'différance' (1968, 1974: 44ff.). Here one is concerned with the same model based on a constitutional logic of an origin of all differences from an *original difference* which as such can no longer be derived from anything else. Such a model also plays an important part in Heidegger's thought and has recently been injected into sociological discussions by Niklas Luhmann. On the corresponding 'elective affinities' between Luhmann's autopoietic systems theory and French structuralism as inspired by Ferdinand de Saussure's foundation of modern linguistics, see Lichtblau, 1980: 249ff.

5. Therefore, the idea that Simmel's 'sociological method' in the sense described above, and not Weber's 'methodological individualism' was the most suitable starting-point for the development of a genuinely 'interpretive sociology' was the unanimous opinion that connected the participants in a discussion of Werner Sombart's paper on 'Interpretation' (Das Verstehen) at the Sixth Congress of German Sociologists in Zürich, bearing in mind the other differences expressed there (cf. Sombart, 1929). Considering this, one of the most interesting questions in the framework of a sociological analysis of the recent history of sociology is the problem of why after 1945 it was Weber's work and not that of Simmel which was hypostatized as the real origin of the tradition of an interpretive sociology.

6. On the significance of a specific language of the eyes in this sense, cf. the lucid analysis in Simmel's 'Sociology of the Senses' [Soziologie der Sinne] (1968: 484ff.).

7. On the significance of the expression 'pathos of distance' which occurs in Simmel's works and its 'elective affinity' to Nietzsche's critique of culture, cf. Lichtblau, 1984.

References

Adler, M. (1904) 'Kausalität und Teleologie im Streite um die Wissenschaft', pp. 193–433 in M. Adler and R. Hilferding (eds), *Marx-Studien. Blätter zur Theorie und Politik des wissenschaftlichen Sozialismus*, Vol. I. Vienna: Ignaz Brand.

Atoji, Y. (1982) 'Georg Simmel and Max Weber', *Sociologia* 7(1): 1–49.

Beiersdorfer, K. (1986) *Max Weber und Georg Lukács. Über die Beziehung von Verstehender Soziologie und westlichem Marxismus.* Frankfurt: Campus.

Benjamin, W. (1980) 'Goethes Wahlverwandtschaften', pp. 123–201 in W. Benjamin, *Gesammelte Schriften. Werkausgabe*, Vol. I, Frankfurt: Suhrkamp.

Bevers, A.M. (1985) *Dynamik der Formen bei Georg Simmel. Eine Studie über die methodische und theoretische Einheit eines Gesamtwerkes.* Berlin: Duncker & Humblot.

Blumenberg, H. (1971) 'Wirklichkeitsbegriff und Wirkungspotential des Mythos', pp. 11–66 in M. Fuhrmann (ed.), *Terror und Spiel. Probleme der Mythenrezeption.* Munich: Fink.

Boella, L. (1986) 'Visibilité et surface. Le possible et l'inconnu dans le concept de forme de Georg Simmel', *Social Science Information* 25: 925–43.

Böhringer, H. (1976) 'Spuren von spekulativem Atomismus in Simmels formaler Soziologie', pp. 105–17 in H. Böhringer and K. Gründer (eds), *Ästhetik und Soziologie um die Jahrhundertwende: Georg Simmel.* Frankfurt: Klostermann.

Böhringer, H. (1984) 'Die "Philosophie des Geldes" als ästhetische Theorie. Stichworte zur Aktualität Georg Simmels für die moderne bildende Kunst', pp. 178–82 in H.-J. Dahme and O. Rammstedt (eds), *Georg Simmel und die Moderne.* Frankfurt: Suhrkamp.

Böhringer, Hannes (1989) 'Simmels Impressionismus', pp. 151–5 in W. Schmidt-Biggemann (ed.), *Disiecta membra. Studien. Karlfried Gründer zum 60. Geburtstag.* Basel: Schwabe.

Buschendorf, B. (1986) *Goethes mythische Denkform. Zur Ikonographie der 'Wahlverwandtschaften'.* Frankfurt: Suhrkamp.

Christian, P. (1978) *Einheit und Zwiespalt. Zum hegelianisierenden Denken in der Philosophie und Soziologie Georg Simmels.* Berlin: Duncker & Humblot.

Dahme, H.-J. (1981) *Soziologie als exakte Wissenschaft. Georg Simmels Ansatz und seine Bedeutung in der gegenwärtigen Soziologie.* Stuttgart: Enke.

Dahme, H.-J. (1984) 'Das Abgrenzungsproblem von Philosophie und Wissenschaft bei Georg Simmel', pp. 202–30 in H.-J. Dahme and O. Rammstedt (eds), *Georg Simmel und die Moderne.* Frankfurt: Suhrkamp.

Dahme, H.-J. (1988) 'Der Verlust des Fortschrittsglaubens und die Verwissenschaftlichung der Soziologie. Ein Vergleich von Georg Simmel, Ferdinand Tönnies und Max Weber', pp. 222–74 in O. Rammstedt (ed.), *Simmel und die frühen Soziologen.* Frankfurt: Suhrkamp.

Dahme, H.-J. and O. Rammstedt (1984) 'Die zeitlose Modernität der soziologischen Klassiker. Überlegungen zur Theoriekonstruktion von Emile Durkheim, Ferdinand Tönnies, Max Weber und besonders Georg Simmel', pp. 449–78 in H.-J. Dahme and O. Rammstedt (eds), *Georg Simmel und die Moderne.* Frankfurt: Suhrkamp.

Dannemann, R. (1987) *Das Prinzip Verdinglichung. Studie zur Philosophie Georg Lukács'*. Frankfurt: Sendler.

Davis, M.S. (1973) 'Georg Simmel and the Aesthetics of Social Reality', *Social Forces* 51: 320–9.

Deleuze, G. (1968) *Différence et répétition*. Paris: Presses Universitaires de France.

Derrida, J. (1968) 'La "Différance"', *Bulletin de la Société française de Philosophie* 62(3): 73–120.

Derrida, J. (1974) *Grammatologie*. Frankfurt: Suhrkamp.

Faught, J. (1985) 'Neglected Affinities. Max Weber and Georg Simmel', *British Journal of Sociology* 36: 155–74.

Frisby, D. (1978) 'Introduction to the Translation', pp. 1–49 in Georg Simmel, *The Philosophy of Money*. Translated by Tom Bottomore and David Frisby. London: Routledge & Kegan Paul.

Frisby, D. (1981) *Sociological Impressionism. A Reassessment of Georg Simmel's Social Theory*. London: Heinemann.

Frisby, D. (1985) *Fragments of Modernity: Theories of Modernity in the Work of Simmel, Kracauer and Benjamin*. Cambridge: Polity Press.

Frisby, D. (1988a) 'Die Ambiguität der Moderne: Max Weber und Georg Simmel', pp. 580–94 in W.J. Mommsen and W. Schwentker (eds), *Max Weber und seine Zeitgenossen*. Göttingen: Vandenhoeck & Ruprecht.

Frisby, D. (1988b) 'Soziologie und Moderne: Ferdinand Tönnies, Georg Simmel und Max Weber', pp. 196–221 in O. Rammstedt (ed.), *Simmel und die frühen Soziologen*. Frankfurt: Suhrkamp.

Frisby, D. (1989) 'The Aesthetics of Modern Life: Simmel's Interpretation'. Paper Presented to the Culture Section at the American Sociological Association Annual Meeting, San Francisco. (Revised version in this volume).

Frischeisen-Köhler, M. (1919/20) 'Georg Simmel', *Kant-Studien* 24: 1–51.

Gadamer, H.-G. (1967) 'Kausalität in der Geschichte?', pp. 192–200 in H.-G. Gadamer, *Kleine Schriften I*. Tübingen: Mohr.

Green, B.S. (1988) *Literary Methods and Sociological Theory: Case Studies of Simmel and Weber*. Chicago: University of Chicago Press.

Habermas, J. (1981) *Theorie des kommunikativen Handelns*. Frankfurt: Suhrkamp.

Hennis, W. (1987) *Max Webers Fragestellung. Studien zur Biographie seines Werks*. Tübingen: Mohr.

Hübner-Funk, S. (1976) 'Ästhetizismus und Soziologie bei Georg Simmel', pp. 44–70 in H. Böhringer and K. Gründer (eds), *Ästhetik und Soziologie um die Jahrhundertwende: Georg Simmel*. Frankfurt: Klostermann.

Hübner-Funk, S. (1984) 'Die ästhetische Konstituierung gesellschaftlicher Erkenntnis am Beispiel der "Philosophie des Geldes"', pp. 187–201 in H.-J. Dahme and O. Rammstedt (eds), *Georg Simmel und die Moderne*. Frankfurt: Suhrkamp.

Kalberg, S. (1978) 'Max Weber and Georg Simmel. On Modern Culture and Individual Freedom'. Unpublished manuscript, Trier.

Kant, I. (1924) *Kritik der reinen Vernunft*. Edited by V.R. Schmidt. Leipzig: Reclam.

Lenk, K. (1964) 'Das tragische Bewusstsein in der deutschen Soziologie', *Kölner Zeitschrift für Soziologie und Sozialpschologie* 16: 257–87.

Levine, D.N. (1971) 'Introduction', pp. ix–lxv in D.N. Levine (ed.), *On Individuality and Social Forms. Selected Writings*. Chicago: University of Chicago Press.

Levine, D.N. (1984) 'Ambivalente Begegnungen: "Negationen" Simmels durch Durkheim, Weber, Lukács, Park und Parsons', pp. 318-87 in H.-J. Dahme and O. Rammstedt (eds), *Georg Simmel und die Moderne*. Frankfurt: Suhrkamp.

Levine, D.N. (1988) 'Das Problem der Vieldeutigkeit in der Begründung der Soziologie bei Emile Durkheim, Max Weber und Georg Simmel', pp. 181-95 in O. Rammstedt (ed.), *Simmel und die frühen Soziologen*. Frankfurt: Suhrkamp.

Lichtblau, K. (1980) 'Die Politik der Diskurse. Studien zur Politik- und Sozialphilosophie'. PhD dissertation, University of Bielefeld.

Lichtblau, K. (1984) 'Das "Pathos der Distanz". Präliminarien zur Nietzsche — Rezeption bei Georg Simmel', pp. 231-81 in H.-J. Dahme and O. Rammstedt (eds), *Georg Simmel und die Moderne*. Frankfurt: Suhrkamp.

Lichtblau, K. (1986) 'Die Seele und das Geld. Kulturtheoretische Implikationen in Georg Simmels "Philosophie des Geldes"', pp. 57-74 in F. Neidhardt, M.R. Lepsius and J. Weiss (eds), *Kultur und Gesellschaft*. (*Kölner Zeitschrift für Soziologie und Sozialpsychologie*, 27.) Opladen: Westdeutscher Verlag.

Lichtblau, K. (1988) *Gesellschaftliche Rationalität und individuelle Freiheit. Georg Simmel und Max Weber im Vergleich*. Hagen: Fernuniversität.

Lichtblau, K. (1989/90) 'Eros and Culture. Gender Theory in Simmel, Tönnies and Weber', *Telos* 82: 89-110.

Liebersohn, H. (1988) *Fate and Utopia in German Sociology, 1870-1923*. Cambridge, MA: MIT Press.

Lukács, G. (1958) 'Georg Simmel', pp. 171-6 in K. Gassen and M. Landmann (eds), *Buch des Dankes an Georg Simmel*. Berlin: Duncker & Humblot.

Mannheim, K. (1929) 'Diskussionsbeitrag zu dem Vortrag von Werner Sombart über "Das Verstehen"', pp. 238-43 in: *Verhandlungen des Sechsten Deutschen Soziologentages vom 17. bis 19. September 1928 in Zürich*. Tübingen: Mohr.

Mannheim, K. (1980) *Strukturen des Denkens*. Frankfurt: Suhrkamp.

Nedelmann, B. (1988) '"Psychologismus" oder Soziologie der Emotionen? Max Webers Kritik an der Soziologie Georg Simmels', pp. 11-35 in O. Rammstedt (ed.), *Simmel und die frühen Soziologen*. Frankfurt: Suhrkamp.

Pohlmann, F. (1987) *Individualität, Geld und Rationalitat. Georg Simmel zwischen Karl Marx und Max Weber*. Stuttgart: Enke.

Radbruch, G. (1902) *Die Lehre von der adäquaten Verursachung*. Berlin: Guttentag.

Rammstedt, O. (1985) 'Zweifel am Fortschritt und Hoffen aufs Individuum. Zur Konstitution der modernen Soziologie im ausgehenden 19. Jahrhundert', *Soziale Welt* 36: 483-502.

Rammstedt, O. (1988) 'Die Attitüden der Klassiker als unsere soziologischen Selbstverständlichkeiten. Durkheim, Simmel, Weber und die Konstitution der modernen Soziologie', pp. 275-307 in O. Rammstedt (ed.), *Simmel und die frühen Soziologen*. Frankfurt: Suhrkamp.

Rammstedt, O. (1989) Georg Simmels 'Soziologie von 1908'. Manuscript for a talk at the Symposium 'Georg Simmel e le Origini della Sociologia moderna', Trento 19-21. October.

Ritter, H. (1976) 'Diskussionsbeitrag zu Sibylle Hübner-Funk, Ästhetizismus und Soziologie bei Georg Simmel', pp. 61-9 in H. Böhringer and K. Gründer (eds), *Ästhetik und Soziologie um die Jahrhundertwende: Georg Simmel*. Frankfurt: Klostermann.

Salomon, A. (1945) 'German Sociology', pp. 586-614 in G. Gurvitch and W.E. Moore (eds), *Twentieth Century Sociology*. New York: The Philosophical Library.

Scaff, L.A. (1987) 'Weber, Simmel und die Kultursoziologie', *Kölner Zeitschrift für Soziologie und Sozialpsychologie* 39: 255–77.

Scaff, L.A. (1989) *Fleeing the Iron Cage. Culture, Politics, and Modernity in the Thought of Max Weber.* Berkeley: University of California Press.

Schleiermacher, F.D.E. (1984) 'Versuch einer Theorie des geselligen Betragens', pp. 163–84 in F.D.E. Schleiermacher (ed.), *Kritische Gesamtausgabe. I. Abteilung, Schriften und Entwürfe*, Vol. I and *Schriften aus der Berliner Zeit 1796–1799*, Vol. 2. Berlin, New York: de Gruyter.

Schnabel, P.E. (1974) *Die soziologische Gesamtkonzeption Georg Simmels.* Stuttgart: G. Fischer.

Segre, S. (1987) *Weber contro Simmel. L'epistemologia di Simmel alla prova della 'sociologia comprendenete'.* Genova: ECIG.

Simmel, G. (1890) *Über sociale Differenzierung. Soziologische und psychologische Untersuchungen.* Leipzig: Duncker & Humblot.

Simmel, G. (1892) *Die Probleme der Geschichtsphilosophie. Eine erkenntnis-theoretische Studie.* Leipzig: Duncker & Humblot.

Simmel, G. (1905) *Die Probleme der Geschichtsphilosophie* (second revised edition). Leipzig: Duncker & Humblot.

Simmel, G. (1910) *Hauptprobleme der Philosophie.* Leipzig: Göschen.

Simmel, G. (1916) *Das Problem der historischen Zeit.* Berlin: Reuther & Reichard.

Simmel, G. (1917/18) 'Die historische Formung', *Logos*: 113–52.

Simmel, G. (1918a) *Lebensanschauung. Vier Metaphysische Kapitel.* Leipzig: Duncker & Humblot.

Simmel, G. (1918b) *Vom Wesen des historischen Verstehens.* Berlin: Mittler.

Simmel, G. (1919) *Philosophische Kultur. Gesammelte Essays.* Leipzig: Kröner.

Simmel, G. (1922) *Philosophie des Geldes.* Leipzig: Duncker & Humblot.

Simmel, G. (1957) *Brücke und Tür. Essays des Philosophen zur Geschichte, Religion, Kunst und Gesellschaft.* Stuttgart: Köhler.

Simmel, G. (1959) 'Digression on the Question: How is Society Possible?', in K. Wolff (ed.), *Essays on Sociology, Philosophy and Aesthetics by Georg Simmel et al.* New York: Harper.

Simmel, G. (1968) *Soziologie. Untersuchungen über die Formen der Vergesellschaftung.* Berlin: Duncker & Humblot.

Simmel, G. (1970) *Die Grundfragen der Soziologie.* Berlin: de Gruyter.

Simmel, G. (1977) *The Problems of the Philosophy of History.* Translated and edited by Guy Oakes. New York: Free Press, (translation of Simmel, 1905).

Simmel, G. (1980) *Essays on Interpretation in Social Science.* Translated and edited by Guy Oakes. Manchester: Manchester University Press (Translations of Simmel, 1916, 1917/18, 1918a).

Sombart, W. (1929) 'Das Verstehen', pp. 227–47 in W. Sombart (ed.), *Verhandlungen des Sechsten Deutschen Soziologentages vom 17. bis 19. September 1928 in Zürich.* Tübingen: Mohr.

Spann, O. (1905) 'Untersuchungen über den Gesellschaftsbegriff zur Einleitung in die Soziologie. Erster Teil: Zur Kritik des Gesellschaftsbegriffes der modernen Soziologie. Dritter Artikel: die realistische Lösung', *Zeitschrift für die gesamte Staatswissenschaft* 61: 301–44.

Spann, O. (1907) *Wirtschaft und Gesellschaft. Eine dogmenkritische Untersuchung.* Dresden: Böhmert.

Spann, O. (1923a) 'Bemerkungen zu Max Webers Soziologie', *Zeitschrift für Volkswirtschaft und Sozialpolitik* 3: 761-70.

Spann, O. (1923b) *Gesellschaftslehre.* Leipzig: Quelle & Meyer.

Spann, O. (1925) *Tote und lebendige Wissenschaft. Abhandlungen zur Auseinandersetzung mit Individualismus und Marxismus.* Jena: Gustav Fischer.

Tenbruck, F.H. (1958) 'Georg Simmel (1888-1918)', *Kölner Zeitschrift für Soziologie und Sozialpsychologie* 10: 587-614.

Tenbruck, F.H. (1959) 'Die Genesis der Methodologie Max Webers', *Kölner Zeitschrift für Soziologie und Sozialpsychologie* 11: 573-630.

Troeltsch, E. (1922) *Der Historismus und seine Probleme.* Tübingen: Mohr.

Turner, B.S. (1986) 'Simmel, Rationalization and the Sociology of Money', *The Sociological Review* 34: 93-114.

Weber, M. (1920) *Gesammelte Aufsätze zur Religionssoziologie*, Vol. I Tübingen: Mohr.

Weber, M. (1968) *Economy and Society*, 3 Vols. New York: Bedminster Press.

Weber, M. (1972a) 'Georg Simmel As Sociologist'. Introduced by D.N. Levine, *Social Research* 39: 155-63.

Weber, M. (1972b) *Wirtschaft und Gesellschaft. Grundriss der verstehenden Soziologie.* Tübingen: Mohr.

Weber, M. (1976) *The Protestant Ethic and the Spirit of Capitalism.* Translated by Talcott Parsons and introduced by Anthony Giddens. London: Allen & Unwin.

Weber, M. (1985) *Gesammelte Aufsätze zur Wissenschaftslehre.* Tübingen: Mohr.

Weiss, J. (1988) 'Georg Simmel, Max Weber und die "Soziologie"', pp. 36-63 in O. Rammstedt (ed.), *Simmel und die frühen Soziologen.* Frankfurt: Suhrkamp.

Weiss, J. (ed.) (1989) *Max Weber heute. Erträge und Probleme der Forschung.* Frankfurt: Suhrkamp.

Whimster, S. (1987) 'The Secular Ethic and the Culture of Modernism', pp. 259-90 in S. Lash and S. Whimster (eds), *Max Weber, Rationality and Modernity.* London: Allen & Unwin.

Klaus Lichtblau teaches Sociology at the University of Kassel, Germany.

The Problem of Style

Georg Simmel

It has long been said that the practical existence of humanity is absorbed in the struggle between individuality and generality, that at almost every point of our existence the obedience to a law valid for everyone, whether of an inner or an outer nature, comes into conflict with the purely internal determination of our existence, with the individuality of the person who obeys only his own vital sense. But it might seem paradoxical that in these collisions of the political, economic and moral fields only a much more general form of contrast expresses itself, which is no less able to bring the nature of artistic style to its fundamental expression.

I begin with a very simple experience from the psychology of art. The deeper and more unique the impression of a work of art is on us, the less the question of style tends to play a role in this impression. On viewing any of the countless, rather ungratifying statues of the Seventeenth century, we are above all aware of their baroque character; with the neo-classical portraits from around 1800 we think mainly of the style of their times; nothing about numerous quite indifferent pictures from the present excites our attention, except perhaps that they display the naturalistic style. Facing a statue by Michelangelo, however, a religious painting by Rembrandt, or a portrait by Velasquez, the question of style becomes completely irrelevant; the work of art takes us utterly prisoner in the unified wholeness with which it confronts us, and whether it additionally belongs to some temporal style or other is a question which will not occur, at least not to the merely aesthetically interested observer. When a foreignness of sensibility does not permit us to grasp the real individuality in the work of art, so that we can only penetrate to its more general and typical features — as is often the case for instance with oriental art — only then does our consciousness of style remain active and especially effective even with regard to great works. For the decisive thing is

Theory, Culture & Society (SAGE, London, Newbury Park and New Delhi), Vol. 8 (1991), 63–71

this: style is always that type of artistic arrangement which, to the extent it carries or helps to carry the impression of a work of art, negates its quite individual nature and value, its uniqueness of meaning. By virtue of style, the particularity of the individual work is subjugated to a general law of form that also applies to other works; it is, so to speak, relieved of its absolute autonomy. Because it shares its nature or a part of its design with others it thus points to a common root that lies beyond the individual work — in contrast to the works that grow purely out of themselves, that is, from the mysterious, absolute unity of the artistic personality and its uniqueness. And just as the stylization of a work contains the note of a generality, a law of perception and feeling that applies beyond the specific artistic individuality, the same can be said with respect to the *subject* of the work of art. A stylized rose is supposed to represent the general character of a rose, the style of a rose, not the individual reality of a specific rose. Different artists attempt to achieve this through quite different constructions, just as for different philosophers that which appears as common to all realities is quite different, even opposite. For an Indian artist, a Gothic artist, or one from the Empire period, such stylization will therefore lead to quite heterogeneous phenomena. But the meaning of each is nonetheless not to make the rose perceptible, but rather its law of formation, the root of its form, which is universally active as the unifying force in all the multiplicity of its forms.

Here, however, an objection seems unavoidable. We do speak after all, of Botticelli's or Michelangelo's style, of Goethe's or Beethoven's. The right to do so is the following: that these great figures have created a mode of expression flowing from their very individual genius, which we now sense as the general character in all their individual works. Then such a style of an individual master may be adopted by others so that it becomes the shared property of many artistic personalities. In these others it expresses its destiny as a style, of being something over or beside the expression of personality, so that we quite rightly say, 'These have Michelangelo's style', just as we have a possession that has not grown from us ourselves, but been acquired externally and only subsequently incorporated into the sphere of our ego.

Michelangelo, by contrast, is this style himself, it is identical to Michelangelo's own being, and by virtue of that it is also that general character which is expressed in and colours all artistic utterances of Michelangelo, but only because it is the root-force of these works and these works only. Therefore, it can only be distinguished logically, so to speak, and not objectively from what is unique to the individual work as such. In this case, saying that style is the man himself is well justified, even more clearly in the sense that the man is the style. In the cases of a style coming from outside, on the other hand, shared with others and the period, that maxim has at best the meaning that it shows where the limits of the originality of the individual lie.

From this general theme — that style is a principle of generality which either mixes with the principle of individuality, displaces it or represents it — all the individual features of style as a psychic and artistic reality are developed. It displays in particular the fundamental distinction between applied arts and fine art. The essence of the work of applied art is that it exists many times; its diffusion is the quantitative expression of its usefulness, for it always serves a need that is shared by many people. The essence of the work of fine art, on the other hand, is uniqueness. A work of art and its copy are something totally different from a model and its realization, something different from the copies of a fabric or piece of jewellery manufactured according to a pattern. The fact that innumerable fabrics and pieces of jewellery, chairs and book bindings, candelabras and drinking glasses are manufactured without distinction from a single model, is the symbol that each of these things has its law outside itself. Each such object is only the chance example of something general, in short, its sense of form is style and not the singularity with which a psyche is expressed according to its uniqueness in precisely this one object.[1] This is by no means a denigration of applied art, no more than the principle of generality and the principle of individuality possess a ranking among themselves. Instead, they are the poles of the human creative ability, neither of which could be dispensed with, and each of which determines every point of life, inward and outward, active and enjoying, only in cooperation with the other, although in an infinite variety of mixtures. And we will become acquainted with the vital needs which can only be satisfied by the stylized, not the artistic individual object.

Just as previously the concept of artistic individual design was disputed by the fact that even great artists have a style — namely, their own, which is a law, and therefore a style, of their own — the corresponding objection comes up here. We also observe, especially today, how the objects of applied art are individually designed, by definite personalities with the unmistakable cachet of such; we often see only one copy of an individual object, perhaps manufactured for only one user. But there is a peculiar situation, which can be pointed out here, that keeps this from being a counter-example. To say of some things that they are unique, and of others that they are one individual thing out of many, often has only a symbolic meaning, and certainly that is the case here. With that we refer to a certain quality which is characteristic of the thing and gives its existence the meaning of singularity or repetitiveness, without some contingent exterior fate always having to realize this quantitative expression of its nature. We have all had the experience that a sentence we hear disgusts us with its banality, without being able to maintain that we have often heard it, or even ever heard it at all. It is just inwardly, qualitatively old hat, even if no one else has ever actually used it; the sentence is banal because it deserves to be banal.

And conversely we have the irrefutable impression that certain works and certain people are unique — even if chance combinations of existence actually produce another or many other exactly identical personalities or objects. That doesn't affect any of these, because they have the right, one could say, to be unique, or rather, this numerical designation is only the expression of a qualitative nobility of nature, whose basic nature is incomparability. And such is the situation with the singularities of applied art: because their essence is style, because the general artistic substance of which their particular shape is formed always remains tangible in them, it is their *meaning* to be reproduced, they are internally constituted for multiplicity, even though expense, caprice or jealous exclusivity only permit them by chance to become reality once.

Matters are different with those artistically formed objects of use which actually refuse this style-meaning through their design and wish to have or do indeed have the effect of individual works of art. I should like to lodge the strongest protest possible against this tendency of the applied arts. Those objects are destined to be incorporated into life, to serve an externally given end. In this they contrast completely with the work of art, which is imperiously closed within itself. Each work is a world unto itself, it is its own end, symbolizing by its very frame that it refuses any participation as a servant in the movements of a practical life outside itself. A chair exists so that one can sit on it, a glass in order that one can fill it with wine and take it in one's hand; if due to their design these two give the impression of that self-satisfied artistic nature which follows only its own laws and expresses the autonomy of its psyche totally within itself, then the most repulsive conflict arises. Sitting on a work of art, working with a work of art, using a work of art for the needs of practice — that is cannibalism, it is the degradation of the master to the status of slave, and this is not a master who occupies that status by the contingent favour of fate, but inwardly, in accordance with the law of his nature. The theoreticians, whom one hears pronouncing in the same breath that the piece of applied art should be a work of art and that its highest principle is practicality, do not seem to sense this contradiction: that the practical is a means — which therefore has its end outside itself — while the work of art is never a means, but a work closed in itself, one that unlike the 'practical' never borrows its law from anything that is not itself. The principle that if possible every object of use should be a work of art like Michelangelo's *Moses* or *Jan Six* by Rembrandt is perhaps the most common misunderstanding of modern individualism. It would give to things that exist for other people and purposes the form of those whose meaning resides in the pride of being-for-themselves; to the things that are used and used up, moved and handed around it would give the form of those which outlast the bustle of practical life unmoved, like a blessed island; finally to those things that appeal because of their utilitarian end to the general in us, to that which we share with others, it would give the form of those objects which are unique because an individual soul has embodied its uniqueness in them, so that they gravitate towards the point of uniqueness in us, where each man is alone with himself.

And here finally lies the reason why all this conditionality of the applied arts does not signify a denigration. Instead of the character of individuality, applied art is supposed to have the character of style, of broad generality — which of course does not mean absolutely broad, open to every philistine and all tastes — and thus it represents in the aesthetic sphere a different principle of life than actual art, but not an inferior one. We must not be deluded into thinking that the subjective achievement of its creator can display the same refinement and nobility, the same depth and imagination as that of the painter or the sculptor. The fact that style also appeals to the observer at levels beyond the purely individual, to the broad emotional categories subject to the general laws of life, is the source of the calming effect, the feeling of security and serenity with which the strictly stylized object provides us. From the stimulation points of individuality to which the work of art so often appeals, life descends with respect to the stylized object into the more pacified levels, where one no longer feels alone. There — or so at least these unconscious events can be interpreted — the supra-individual law of the objective structure before us finds its counterpart in the feeling that we too are reacting with the supra-individual part of ourselves, which is subject to universal laws. Thus we are saved from absolute responsibility, from balancing on the narrowness of mere individuality.

This is the reason why the things that surround us as the basis or background of daily life should be stylized. For in his own rooms, a person is the main thing, the point, so to speak, which must rest on broader, less individual, subordinate layers and distinguish himself from them, in order to bring about an organic and harmonious overall feeling. The work of art hanging in its frame on the wall, resting on its pedestal, or lying in a portfolio, shows by this external demarcation alone that it does not intervene in direct life, like tables and glasses, lamps and rugs, that it cannot serve people as a 'necessary extra'. The principle of calm, which the domestic surrounding of a person must support, has lead with miraculous instinctive practicality to the stylization of this environment: of all the objects we use, it is probably furniture which most consistently carries the cachet of some 'style'. This becomes most evident in the dining-room, which even for physiological reasons is supposed to favour relaxation, the descent from the surging excitements of the day into a broader comfort shared with others. Without being aware of this reason, the aesthetic tendency has always encouraged that the dining-room be especially stylized, and the 'style movement', beginning in Germany in the 1870s, concentrated initially on the dining-room.

Just as the principle of style as well as that of the uniqueness of form have everywhere tended to display some sort of a mixture and reconciliation with their respective opposite, a higher power also rectifies the exemption of home furnishings from individual artistic design with the demand for their stylization. Oddly enough this demand for style only exists — for modern man at least — for the individual objects of his surroundings, but not for the surroundings as a whole. The residence, as furnished by the individual in accordance with his taste and needs, can by all means have the personal, unmistakable tone that flows from the special nature of this individual, which would nonetheless be unbearable if every single object in it betrayed the same individuality. This might seem paradoxical at first glance. But assuming that it is true, it would first of all explain why living in rooms that are kept strictly in a certain historical style has a peculiarly unpleasant, strange and cold quality for us, while those that are composed of pieces in different but no less strict styles according to individual taste, which must of course be firm and consistent, seem most liveable and warm to us.

An environment consisting entirely of objects in *one* historical style coalesces into a closed unity which excludes the individual who lives there, so to speak; he finds no gap where his personal life, free from any past style, could enter into it or join it. This becomes quite different, oddly, as soon as the individual constructs his environment of variously stylized objects; by his doing the objects receive a new centre, which is not located in any of them alone, but which they all manifest through the particular way they are united. This centre is a subjective unity, an experience by a personal psyche and an assimilation to it which becomes tangible in the objects. This is the irreplaceable attraction which leads us to furnish our rooms with objects from past times, and especially those which bear the calm happiness of a style, i.e. a supra-individual law of form, to create a new whole, whose synthesis and overall form are of a thoroughly individual nature and suited to one and only one specially attuned personality.

What drives modern man so strongly to style is the unburdening and concealment of the personal, which is the essence of style. Subjectivism and individuality have intensified to breaking-point, and in the stylized designs, from those of behaviour to those of home furnishing there is a mitigation and a toning down of this acute personality to a generality and its law. It is as if the ego could really no longer carry itself, or at least no longer wished to show itself and thus put on a more general, a more typical, in short, a stylized costume. There is a very delicate shame in the fact that a supra-individual form and law are placed between the subjective personality and its objective environment. Stylized expression, form of life, taste — all these are limitations and ways of creating a distance, in which the exaggerated subjectivism of the times finds a counterweight and concealment. The tendency of modern man to surround himself with antiquities — that is, things in which the style, the character of their times, the general mood that hovers around them is essential — this tendency is certainly not a contingent snobbery. Instead it goes back to that deeper need to give the individually excessive life an addition of calm breadth and typical lawfulness. Earlier times, which only had one style which was therefore taken for granted were situated quite differently in these difficult questions of life. Where only one style is conceivable, every individual expression grows organically from it; it has no need to search first for its roots; the general and the personal go together without conflict in a work. The unity and lack of problems we envy in Greek antiquity and many periods of the Middle Ages are based on such an unproblematic general foundation for life, that is to say, on the style, which arranged its relationship to the individual production much more simply and freer of contradictions, than is possible for us, who have a variety of styles at our disposal in all areas, so that individual work, behaviour and taste have a loose optional relation to the broad foundation, the general law, which they do require after all. That is the reason why the products of earlier ties often seem to have so much more style than those of our own age. For we say an object is devoid of style if it appears to have sprung from a momentary, isolated, temporary sentiment, without being based on a more general feeling, a non-contingent norm. This necessary fundamental aspect can very well be what I term the individual style. In great and creative people, the individual work flows from such an all-encompassing depth of being that it is able to find there the firmness and the foundation, the transcendence of here and now, which comes to the work of the lesser artist from an external style. Here the individual is the case of an individual law; anyone who is not that strong must adhere to a general law; if he fails to, his work fails to have style — which, as is now easily understood, can only happen in periods with multiple style possibilities.

Finally, style is the aesthetic attempt to solve the great problem of life: an individual work or behaviour, which is closed, a whole, can simultaneously belong to something higher, a unifying encompassing context. The distinction between the individual style of the very great and the general style of the lesser expresses that broad practical norm: 'and if you cannot become a unity yourself, then join a unity as a serving partner'. It expresses this in the language of art, which grants even the most modest achievement at least a ray of the splendour and unity that shine in the practical world only on the very great.

Translated by Mark Ritter.

Notes

This article was published as 'Das Problem des Stiles' in *Dekorative Kunst* 16 (1908).

1. Therefore, *material* also has such a great importance for style. The human form, for instance, demands quite a different type of expression if it is presented in porcelain or in bronze, in wood or in marble. For the material is in fact the *general* substance, which offers itself equally to an arbitrary number of different forms, and thus determines these as their general prerequisite.

Human Studies

A Journal for Philosophy and the Social Sciences

Editor:

George Psathas, *Dept. of Sociology, Boston University, USA*

Human Studies is devoted primarily to advancing the dialogue between philosophy and the human sciences. In particular, such issues as the logic of inquiry, methodology, epistemology and foundational issues in the human sciences exemplified by original empirical, theoretical and philosophical investigations are addressed. Phenomenological perspectives, broadly defined, are a primary, though not an exclusive focus.

Human Studies is attractive to scholars in a variety of fields, since it provides a forum for those who address these issues in attempting to bridge the gap between philosophy and the human sciences. The contributions published have been drawn from sociology, psychology, anthropology, history, geography, linguistics, semiotics, ethnomethodology, political science and, of course, philosophy.

Human Studies is partially supported by the Department of Sociology, Boston University, Boston, Massachusetts.

Journal
Highlight

KLUWER
ACADEMIC
PUBLISHERS

Subscription Information   **ISSN** 0163–8548
1991, Volume 14 (4 issues)
Subscription rate: Dfl.234.00/US$133.00
incl. postage and handling
*Private rate: Dfl.110.00/US$62.50
incl. postage and handling*

P.O. Box 322, 3300 AH Dordrecht, The Netherlands
P.O. Box 358, Accord Station, Hingham, MA 02018-0358, U.S.A.

The Aesthetics of Modern Life: Simmel's Interpretation

David Frisby

. . . the culture of things as a culture of human beings . . . (G. Simmel, 1989b)

All sense interest connects with the perceptible, with what is real or whose reality we wish; all moral interest with that which *should* really exist, however unlikely it will be realised. *Aesthetic judgement, however, connects with the mere image of things, with their appearance and form, regardless of whether they are supported by an apprehendable reality.* (G. Simmel, 1918)

I

After the completion of *The Philosophy of Money* in 1900, Simmel wished to write a comprehensive philosophy of art or aesthetics — something which never came to fruition. Nonetheless, Simmel's contribution to the understanding and interpretation of the aesthetic dimension of life and of the social world permeates much of his writing (and not merely his explicit essays on aesthetics or monographs and essays on artists such as Rembrandt [1916], Rodin, Michelangelo, Böcklin and others). In his teaching too, Simmel lectured on aesthetics and culture almost every year from 1902 to 1915 (1903 is the only exception). A full analysis of his treatment of the aesthetic dimension would also have to deal with his often critical relationship to major modern aesthetic movements: such as naturalism, impressionism, symbolism, art nouveau and expressionism.[1]

More significantly for our theme, however, it can be argued that Simmel's emphasis upon the *forms* of interaction (*Wechselwirkung*) or sociation (*Vergesellschaftung*) in his programme for sociology — first tentatively announced in 1890 (Simmel, 1890a) — indicates an interest in revealing an aesthetic dimension of all social interaction that we do not immediately perceive in our everyday life, composed as it is of a multiplicity of diverse and intersecting interactional

Theory, Culture & Society (SAGE, London, Newbury Park and New Delhi), Vol. 8 (1991), 73–93

frames. In other words, and without diminishing Simmel's major contribution to establishing sociology as an independent social science disipline, the sociologist can reveal and analyse aesthetic constellations and configurations that both exist in and are originally hidden in 'the flat surface of everyday life'.

What are the facets of the aesthetic dimension of social life which interest Simmel? In the fifteenth lecture devoted to Kant's aesthetics in his book on *Kant* (Simmel, 1904; 1918, fourth edition — all references are to this edition) Simmel announces that we enjoy what is beautiful because it is valuable: this enjoyment, however, 'depends not on the existence but on the qualities or *forms* of the thing which we must judge to be valuable' (Simmel, 1918: 188). Indeed, following Kant, 'only the form of things bears its beauty' (Simmel, 1918: 189). Aesthetic judgement applies to things themselves 'and not their significance for ends and values' (Simmel, 1918: 190). The work of art constitutes a unity out of diversity 'and its fundament therefore lies in the interaction of its parts'; it '*is form*' for this is what relates the elements to one another. Art is the representation of that which one characterizes as the formation of things.

This crucial dimension of form, in turn, reveals other facets of aesthetic judgement. The latter 'connects with *the mere image of things, with their appearance and form*, regardless of whether or not they are borne by a graspable reality' (Simmel, 1918: 197). Whereas the reality of existence 'exhausts itself in concrete individual elements', the aesthetic dimension is felt in 'the lightness and freedom of *play*', for the latter implies that 'one exercises functions . . . purely formally' without regard to 'the reality-contents of life' (Simmel, 1918: 194). Hence, beauty does not lie in the objective existence of things but rather is a *subjective* reaction which the latter arouses in us. It follows, too, that the justification for aesthetic judgement 'does not lie in definite concepts . . . but in that quite general *internally harmonious* feeling' (Simmel, 1918: 197) which we experience. In turn, this feeling of satisfaction with respect to the work of art arises out of the latter's success in creating a totality out of the fragmentary: it is 'the feeling that the fortuitous elements of the phenomenon are dominated by a *single* meaning, that the mere facticity of the individual elements is permeated by the significance of a totality, that *the fragmentary and disintegrating dimension of existence*, at least in this single point, *has gained a living unity*' (Simmel, 1918: 194).

The dialectic of the fragment and the totality is paralleled by that of the individual and the universal. Simmel suggests that 'what has recently attracted modern people so strongly to aesthetic values is *this unique play between the objective and the subjective stand-point*, between the individuality of taste and the feeling that it is indeed rooted in a supra-individual, universal' (Simmel, 1918: 198). It may be that this aesthetic enjoyment is possible because it excites constellations 'that remain beneath the threshold of consciousness'. Simmel posits that 'the feeling with respect to art of being released from every detail and one-sidedness of existence perhaps emerges out of the fact that a boundlessness of the individual element, as emanating from a central point and on which the work of art rests, is brought to life in us, and indeed *not with the confusion of fortuitous associations but rather, in each case, in typical and meaningful forms of relations, attractions and connections of conceptions*' (Simmel, 1918: 199). When Simmel speaks here of the sense of release from existence he is again recalling the connection between the aesthetic of the play form and that of reality: 'Precisely the lightness of playing with which in their indifference to all reality, aesthetic elements, have their effect, makes possible this coming into being of spheres of the soul as a whole which would be restricted if the inner processes were burdened with the serious emphases of reality' (Simmel, 1918: 199; cf. also Simmel, 1901). This somewhat abstract formulation acquires a concrete instance in Simmel's discussion of sociability (*Geselligkeit*) as the play form of society (*Gesellschaft*), as a form of sociation unburdened by any specific content.

However, returning to Simmel's representation of Kant's aesthetics, we already have the following dimensions of the aesthetic. We respond *subjectively* to the *form* of things, 'to the mere *image of things*', to 'their *appearance* and form' with an '*internally harmonious* feeling'. The aesthetic dimension creates a *totality* out of the *fragmentary*; it *plays* with form and thereby abstracts from content; what is *individual* is transformed into the *universal*. The relationship between fragment and totality, between the particular and the universal is more precisely formulated in Simmel's earlier essay 'Sociological Aesthetics' (Simmel, 1896a: 204–16) in which he asserts that the aesthetic interpretation 'lies in the fact that the typical is to be found in what is unique, the law-like in what is fortuitous, the essence and significance of things in the superficial and transitory. It seems as if no phenomenon is able to escape from this reduction to that which is significant and eternal in it.' This is true of 'the meanest things', 'the ugliest thing', 'the most indifferent thing'. Hence it follows that 'every point conceals the possibility of being released into absolute aesthetic significance. To the adequately trained eye, the *total* beauty, the *total* meaning of the world as a whole radiates from every single point' (Simmel, 1896a: 205).

But if this were the case in an absolute sense, Simmel continues, then the individual element or fragment would lose its significance as a distinctive individuality. The equal valuation of things cannot be sustained aesthetically, for all valuation requires making distinctions and creating a distance from each individual phenomenon. At this point, Simmel introduces two further dimensions of the aesthetic that are crucial to understanding his interpretation of the modern period. Aesthetic judgement requires the tension of *nearness* and *distance*, and ultimately its most modern expressions are based on distance. The second dimension to which Simmel here refers follows from the first: 'the first aesthetic step . . . leads beyond the mere acceptance of the meaninglessness of things to *symmetry*, until later refinement and enhancement once more connects the irregular, the *asymmetrical* with the most heightened aesthetic judgement'. As a modern instance of distance Simmel cites the reaction to naturalism, a 'reaction in painting that was supplied by the Scottish School [the 'Glasgow Boys'] and in literature which led from Zolaism to Symbolism' (Simmel, 1896a: 215). With the asymmetrical we return again to the fragment, to the aesthetic appeal of that which 'almost exclusively bears an individualistic character', to 'the rhapsodic fortuitousness' of the individual element (in contrast, as Simmel argues, to the socialistic tendency to search for symmetry, harmony and to view the ideal society itself as a totality, a symmetrical work of art): 'hence . . . the nowadays so lively experienced enjoyment of the fragment, of the mere impression, the aphorism, the symbol, the undeveloped artistic style' (Simmel, 1896a: 214). All these are appreciated as a result of their *distance* from their object.

The 'pathos of distance', which reappears in *The Philosophy of Money* (1989b) as a central theme and which has its origin in the work of Nietzsche, is already important in this earlier essay on sociological aesthetics (cf. Lichtblau, 1984). Indeed, Simmel already suggests that 'the inner significance of artistic styles reveals itself to be a consequence of *the diverse distance which they create between ourselves and things'* (Simmel, 1896a: 213). The subjective response to distance from the object — including the aesthetic object — is a differentiated one. For those with refined tastes, 'the whole secret attraction of distance from things lies *in the artistic formation of the object'*; for those less sensitive, the creation of the attraction of distance requires *'a greater distance of the object itself*: stylized Italian landscapes, historical dramas; the more uncultivated and childlike is the aesthetic sensibility, the more fantastic, the further from reality must the object be' in order to achieve its effect. Both cases, however, testify to the fact that 'present day artistic sensibility basically strongly emphasises the attraction of distance as opposed to the attraction of proximity' (Simmel, 1896a: 214).

Such a 'tendency to create a distance' in modern culture, in fact 'the tendency to *enlarge* the distance between human beings and their objects' which manifests itself in the aesthetic sphere, is symbolized in other spheres: 'the destruction of the family', arising out of the rejection of its presumed excessive closeness, extends to the rejection of contact with other intimate circles; 'the ease of transport to the furthest distant points strengthens this "anxiety with regard to contact" '; 'the "historical spirit", the wealth of inner relationships to spatially and temporally more distant interests makes us all the more sensitive to the shocks and the disorder that confront us from the immediate proximity and contact with human beings and things'. A 'major cause' of this anxiety with regard to contact is 'the ever deeper penetration of the money economy' (Simmel, 1896a: 215–16).

Like Simmel's own argument, we have begun to move from the elucidation of the aesthetic dimension to a more specific treatment of the aesthetics of modern life. In particular, it is appropriate here to examine in some detail the far-reaching consequences of the mature money economy for the aesthetic domain and for the aesthetics of everyday life.

II

We can commence this analysis by remaining for a moment with Simmel's essay on sociological aesthetics. Although admitting that the destruction of earlier economic relations is not complete, Simmel outlines the effect of the increasing influence of the mature money economy upon social relations as follows: 'Money intervenes between one human being and another, between human beings and commodities as a mediating instance, as a common denominator, to which each value must be reduced in order to be able to be translated further into other values. With the development of the money economy, the objects of economic transactions no longer confront us immediately.' Rather, we are confronted by 'this inter-mediate value', so much so that our intentionality comes to rest upon this intermediate stage,

> as if upon the centre of interest and the fulcrum of rest, whilst all concrete things pass by in restless flight, burdened by the contradiction that in fact they alone can secure all definite satisfactions but nonetheless acquire their degree of value and interest only after their devaluation into this characterless, qualityless standard. In this way, with the enlargement of its role, money places us at an ever more basic distance from objects; the immediacy of impressions, the sense of value, interest in things is weakened, our contact with them is broken and we experience them, as it were, only by means of a mediation that does not permit their complete, autonomous, immediate existence to gain full expression. (Simmel, 1896a: 216)

The increasing predominance of the mediating value announces the domination of the exchange value of things over their use value.[2] The domination of exchange value is the domination of *quantitative* valuation and therefore ostensibly signifies the impos-sibility of aesthetic valuation. The levelling tendency of monetary and commodity exchange is problematical in this context insofar as the equalization of exchange value removes the possibility of qualitative valuation but, at the same time, to refer to one dimen-sion of the aesthetic, still possesses the aesthetic dimension of symmetry. Indeed, this is not the only aesthetic dimension present in the mature money economy, in the sphere of circulation and exchange of commodities. Money transactions, for instance, appear to create that distance which is a necessary prerequisite for aesthetic judgement. When, in his article on 'The Seventh Ring' (Simmel, 1922a: 74–8) — in fact, a review of Stefan George's poetry — Simmel declares that 'art gives unity to otherwise unrelated and unresolved elements that exist side by side' (Simmel, 1922a: 78)[3] has he not shown earlier in *The Philosophy of Money* that the mediating value (money) performs precisely this task in its capacity as the universal equivalent of 'unrelated and unresolved' use values? Does not the 'beautiful illusion' (*schöne Schein*) (Hegel) that is art and the aesthetic realm have its counterpart in the seemingly autonomous realm of the circulation and exchange of commodities (made possible by the mediation of money)? In the course of his reflections on the picture frame, Simmel maintains that 'the essence of the work of art . . . is to be a totality for itself, to require no relationship to an external entity, to weave each of its threads back once more into its focal point. Insofar as the work of art is that which otherwise only *the world as a whole* or the soul can be: a *unity* out of individual elements — it encloses itself as *a world for itself* against all that exists external to it' (Simmel, 1922b: 46). In *The Philosophy of Money*, Simmel seeks to demonstrate that 'the world as a whole' in the mature economy 'appears' as 'a world for itself', as 'the culture of things', as 'the objective culture' (*die Sachkultur*) which not merely stands against subjective culture, against human subjects themselves but creates the possibility of 'the culture of things *as* the culture of human beings' (Simmel, 1990). In order to substantiate these and other claims, which at least posit an 'elective affinity' between the aesthetic domain and the domain of the circulation and exchange of commodities we must turn to Simmel's analysis in *The Philosophy of Money* and those insights associated with this work.

As Simmel declares in the preface to *The Philosophy of Money*, it is not intended as a work on the economics or the history of money. As well as being a major contribution to a sociology of money, its 'philosophy' of money contains at least fifty references to the aesthetic domain, most of which cannot be dealt with here. But before looking at the seemingly more direct discussion of the aesthetic domain, we should recall Simmel's association of beauty with *subjective* reactions and, along with Kant, the attendant need for valuation. For Simmel the construction of his subjectivist theory of value proved most difficult. Drawing on contemporary marginal utility theorists such as Menger and von Wieser, Simmel constructs a theory of value that is grounded in subjective desire and enjoyment. The transition from value as substance in barter economies to value as function in money economies creates an unresolved tension between the subjectivist (and psychological) presuppositions of marginal utility theory (some of which were later criticized by Weber in another context) and the objectivist presuppositions of money exchange (i.e. between subjective needs and enjoyment and the objective, autonomous measurement and exchange of one object with another) (Simmel, 1990). This significant shift in the mode of valuation and its consequences is already dealt with in Simmel's first comprehensive outline of some of the major themes in *The Philosophy of Money* in his essay 'Money in Modern Culture'

(Simmel, 1896b: 319–24). There, Simmel maintains that money as the mediating instance between commodities intervenes between the individual and commodity as an 'in itself qualityless instance'. Indeed, its domination signifies a shift from qualitative to quantitative valuation (and implicitly carrying with itself an attendant devaluation and levelling of value). The absolute mediator of values, objects and persons 'thus emerges as the secure fulcrum in the flight of phenomena' (Simmel, 1896b: 321). As the equivalent for everything, it displaces that which is exceptional — 'only what is individual is exceptional' — and replaces it with a common denominator. Furthermore, as the absolute expression of all value, it is also the ultimate means 'in this labyrinth of means' created by the universalization of exchange transactions. Ends are replaced by means and by techniques (another key to distinguishing the work of art and the product of the applied arts). Money's domination in the teleology of ends and means accounts for 'the unrest, the feverishness, the unceasing nature of modern life whose unstoppable wheel is given in money, and which makes the machine of life into a *perpetuum mobile*'. At the same time as it penetrates everyday life, 'it elevates itself in the totally abstract heights above the whole broad diversity of objects, it becomes the centre in which the most opposed, alienated, distant things find their common element and resting point'. This unification of the most contradictory elements is a dynamic process. The 'transition from stability to lability' is an accelerating process that manifests itself in the speed and rhythm of exchange transactions. At the elementary level, 'the divisibility of money into the smallest sums certainly contributes to the small style in the external and especially the aesthetic arrangement of modern life, to the growing number of little things with which we adorn our life' (Simmel, 1896b: 323). For Simmel, such seemingly fortuitous phenomena are related to the most profound currents of modern life.

The detailed analysis of the effects of the mature money economy, which this earlier outline prefigures but which is given greater depth in *The Philosophy of Money*, prompts the question as to the possible existence and survival of the aesthetic domain in the reified and alienated world which it creates. Although Simmel declares exchange to be 'a sociological phenomenon *sui generis*' that in some respects constitutes pure interaction, its reified form is the mature money economy. Money is 'the reification of the pure relationship between things as expressed in their economic motion', it 'stands between the individual objects . . . in a realm organized according to its own norms' (Simmel, 1990: 176). Such exchange relations acquire a spectral objectivity, they become 'the embodiment of a pure function' — they play with values just as the aesthetic judgement 'exercises functions . . . purely formally'. It seems, however, as if the more reification extends to social and cultural relations, the more the aesthetic dimension is stultified. But does not the world of the circulation and exchange of commodities and of money exchange relations create the same illusions as the aesthetic realm? Does not this sphere acquire an autonomy in which its individual elements achieve a reconciliation? Is there not a parallel between the aesthetic judgement associated with the image, appearance and form of things and the world of the circulation and exchange of commodities (with its creation of harmony through a pure function that is indifferent to the reality of all use values)?

We might question whether the sphere of circulation and exchange of commodities (facilitated by the universal commodity, the universal equivalent that is money) creates a 'beautiful' illusion, but, in securing the domination of exchange value, it certainly creates an illusory world of inverted value. Simmel argues that 'all concrete things drive on in restless flight' towards their monetary evaluation and, implicitly, their devaluation. As Scheible (1980: 158) puts it, 'the exchange principle, rendered universal, brings about a genuine reversal of the poles of the static and the dynamic. That which is apparently stable, use value, declines totally into the economic dynamic, whilst the dynamic principle, exchange, because of the universitality in which it prevails, becomes the ultimate "stabilizing pole".' In Marx's terms, 'circulation appears as a *simply infinite* process', 'as that which is immediately present on the surface of bourgeois society' but it exists in this manner 'only so far as it is constantly mediated . . . As immediate being it is therefore pure semblance. It is the phenomenon of a process taking place behind it' (Marx, 1973: 254–5). Although Simmel is seldom concerned explicitly with the production of commodities (i.e. with what lies behind this process), his examination of the phenomenal forms in which the circulation process of money exchange appear to us is consonant with this interpretation. In this respect, his theory of alienation not merely anticipates the then unknown analysis of alienation in Marx's (1975) 'Paris Manuscripts' but, in some respects at least, Simmel's phenomenological analysis of the sphere of circulation and exchange goes beyond Marx's hints at such an analysis of it in the then equally unknown *Grundrisse* (1973) which is only tangentially concerned with 'the daily traffic of bourgeois life'.

Where Simmel does dramatically extend the analysis of the everyday world of circulation (in the metropolis) and exchange (in the money economy) is in revealing its aesthetic dimension. This is announced at least in the title of the last chapter of *The Philosophy of Money* — 'The Style of Life', implicitly of modern life but explicitly not the 'beauty' of modern life. Is his aesthetics of modern life concerned not merely with the crisis in the work of art, in the possibility of the beautiful, but also with the illusion of the aesthetic realm in the sphere of the circulation and exchange of commodities?

If such an interpretation is justified, then it is all the more remarkable that Simmel does not draw upon the distinction which Kant makes between the beautiful and the sublime (*das Erhabene*).[4] In *The Critique of Judgement*, Kant draws the following pertinent distinctions between the two: 'The beautiful . . . is a question of the form of the object, and thus consists in limitation, whereas the sublime is to be found in an object even devoid of form, so far as it immediately involves, or else its presence provokes, a representation of *limitlessness*, yet with a super-added thought of its totality. Accordingly the beautiful seems to be regarded as a presentation of an indeterminate concept of understanding, the sublime as a presentation of an indeterminate concept of reason. Hence the delight is in the former case coupled with the representation of *Quality*, but in this case with that of *Quantity*' (Kant, 1982: 90–1). And whereas the beautiful is associated with a sense of 'the furtherance of life', the sublime might be equally attracted and repelled by it, creating 'a negative pleasure'. The beautiful may be contained in sensuous form, the sublime 'concerns ideas of reason'. The latter is associated with quantity and with a dynamic.

Only one-half of this distinction between the beautiful and the sublime is explicitly and consciously thematized by Simmel, namely the beautiful in relation to the work of art. But it is surely legitimate, and possibly illuminating, to see his treatment of the sphere of exchange and circulation facilitated by the mature money economy as the other half of this juxtaposition. Such a sphere provides 'a representation of limitlessness', a notion of totality, a presentation of the concept of reason, a quantitative and dynamic sphere. In the wider context of the aesthetics of modern life, it is surely the case that the work of art and the possibilities for the beautiful are increasingly limited in a context in which the transition to the functional values of money exchange not merely relativize all values but produce an indifference to value as such (manifested in Simmel's analysis of the domination of the blasé attitude in the mature money economy). The aesthetic viewpoint, on the other hand, is capable of transcending the indifference of things, but the problem here is that insofar as the universalization of money exchange reinforces the culture of things, the culture of human subjects (and the creation of the work of art) becomes increasingly threatened. This constitutes a central theme of his dialectic of subjective and objective culture, in fact the growing gap between the two. There exists within the context of the mature money economy an antagonism between an aesthetic tendency and money interests which is that of form versus quantitative valuation. For Simmel, this makes all the more important the investigation of the possibilities for the aesthetic, for 'the feeling of liberation, which is part of the aesthetic mood, the release from the dull pressure of things, the expansion of the joyful and free self into things, the reality of which usually oppresses it' (Simmel, 1990: 328). Unfortunately, the experience of modernity that is located in the mature money economy and the metropolis is not conducive to such feelings. Nonetheless, as Böhringer has persuasively argued, *The Philosophy of Money* can be read as an aesthetic theory, even as an analogy for modern art (Böhringer, 1984).

III

Is it possible that the distinction between the beautiful and the sublime has its parallel in the distinction between the work of art and the applied arts, between form and style? Certainly, for Simmel, there exists a major difference between the work of art and the product of the applied arts, the stylized product (Simmel, 1950: 338–44). The unique work of art arouses in us an excitement that is related to its reconciliation of the growing gap between subjective and objective culture, between subject and object. The work of art embodies the talent, the uniqueness of the artist, the product of applied art signifies the domination of technique. In the former case, it is creative subjectivity that is paramount, in the latter the results of an evermore sophisticated objective culture. The product of the applied arts stands closer to the claims of utility, its 'form' is embodied in a generalized 'style'. Is it the fate of the products of the applied arts, including the mechanical reproduction of the work of art, to be the manifestation of a false reconciliation of subject and object? Even though Simmel argues that 'the perfection of the mechanical reproduction of phenomena' would not 'make the visual arts superfluous' (Simmel, 1990: 53) he elsewhere recognizes that the then still popular panoramas artificially produced the effect of the third dimension which he associated with the work of art. In the metropolis, of course, it is the applied arts in all their varied forms, including the multiplicity of ornamentation, with which we are confronted. As we shall see, however, the distinction between the work of art and the product of the applied arts address only part of the problem. The work of art reduced to an object of consumption, of passive appreciation, is itself so seriously compromised that it cannot stand uncritically juxtaposed to the already compromised stylized product of the applied arts.

The distinction between the work of art and the product of the applied arts is certainly a significant one for Simmel. It is true that the distinction is not a universal one, but rather one that is associated with the development of a market for cultural objects, with a money economy and especially with the development of capitalism. However, at the turn of the century there was a heated debate on the significance of the applied arts that was, in part, associated with machine production. It also comes to the fore in discussion of art nouveau. For another sociological account of the distinction see Sombart's essay on the applied arts (Sombart, 1907). In *The Philosophy of Money* it is already apparent in the distinction between beauty and utility: 'In those cases that offer *realistic* pleasure, our appreciation of the object is not specifically aesthetic, but practical; it becomes aesthetic only as a result of *increasing distance, abstraction and sublimation*' (Simmel, 1990: 74). In the same context, Simmel announces that

> the whole development of objects from utility value to aesthetic value is a process of objectification. . . . *So long as objects are merely useful they are inter-changeable* and everything can be replaced by anything else that performs the same service. But *when they are beautiful they have a unique individual existence* and the value of one cannot be replaced by another even though it may be just as beautiful in its own way . . . The more remote for the species is the utility of the object that first created an interest and a value and is now forgotten, the purer is the aesthetic satisfaction derived from the mere form and appearance of the object. (Simmel, 1990: 74–5)

The distinction between the work of art and the product of the applied arts here relies upon the categorial distinctions we alluded to earlier in Simmel's general aesthetic.

When we turn to Simmel's reflections upon adornment or ornamentation, we find this same distinction is given greater precision. In his 'Psychology of Adornment' (Simmel, 1908a: 1685–9) — and here adornment (*der Schmuck*) can be extended to the ornament (thereby giving it a broader realm of application that extends to architecture, one of the largely neglected spheres of Simmel's aesthetics of everyday life, but one which is as apparent in the public sphere just as much as adornment, jewellery, etc. is apparent in the private sphere; cf. Müller, 1987) — the distinction is made as follows: 'The work of art is something *for itself*, the product of applied art is something *for us* . . . [whose] significance is the enlargement into general accessibility and practical recognition' (Simmel, 1950: 341). The product of the applied arts 'because of its use value [*Gebrauchszweck*] applies to a plurality of human beings' and has a style that appeals to a plurality of people. We must return to the issue of style later, as does Simmel in his essay 'The Problem of Style' (Simmel, 1908b: 307–16).

For the moment, let us go back to the fate of the work of art itself in a society increasingly dominated by the money economy and the consumption of commodities. The work of art, in this context, also becomes the object of *passive consumption*. This can be illustrated by an examination of three of Simmel's lesser known essays concerned with art as a passive object of consumption and the housing of the work of art. The fate of the work of art itself in modernity is associated with the fate of other things in this objectified and reified everyday world. In the earliest of the three essays, 'On Art Exhibitions' (Simmel, 1890b: 474–80), Simmel views the art exhibition as a symbolic microcosm of 'the rich coloration of metropolitan life on the street and in the salon'. The all too close juxtaposition of the most diverse works of art (typical of the display techniques of nineteenth-century art galleries that are still to be found today) arouses in the observer a wealth of impressions and images. At the same time, the contradictory serialized display of works of art arouses two typically modern reactions: 'the blasé attitude and superficiality'. The arbitrary sequentiality of diverse pictures acts as a burden to the nerves of the observer and produces merely a superficial overview of the whole. Simmel suggests that in this respect the response of the observer in the building devoted to the display of modern works of art is merely a parallel or a further manifestation of the same response that we experience in the metropolis with its excessive impressions that can no longer be mastered. Just as elsewhere in 'The Philosophy of Landscape' (Simmel, 1957a) Simmel virtually declares that the metropolitan 'cityscape' (Benjamin) cannot be a landscape, so in the museum devoted to the display of works of art (that are themselves framed) the totality is itself incapable of being 'framed'.

In an even more critical essay, published anonymously, 'Berlin Art Letter' (Simmel, 1896c: 186-7) Simmel attacks the contents and mode of presentation of works of art in the Berlin National Gallery. In contrast to his earlier critique in which he saw the response to the exhibition of works of art as having a parallel in our response to the everyday metropolitan experience of modernity, Simmel here emphasizes the absence of an adequate expression of modernity:

> The fact that there exists something akin to a modern art, that a style strives to express the representation of a new affinity between meaningful appearance and the meaningless significance of things, that a state gallery for modern art must above all lay out such changes . . . in a wealth of attempts as it were in the form of an archive — of all this one has no inkling; rather there is amassed one trash after another of 'recognized' masters, those miserable stale pictures that at their inception were antiquated. (Simmel 1896c: 186)

'In these antiquated circumstances', Simmel continues, one must struggle for a living modern art. In this context, Simmel argues against an exhibition of the work of a now forgotten artist — Gustav Graef — as an instance of such *unmodern* art. Against the likes of his stylized art, Simmel insists that, 'Beauty is for him . . . something different from *us moderns*; he does not extract it from the genuine significance of phenomena, it does not reveal itself to him as the depths of life that lives each essence for itself, without comparison with all others, it does not accompany for him, as it does for us, as a *character indelibilis* of the autonomous movement of things' (Simmel, 1896c: 186). And here we should highlight two aspects of Simmel's critique. Firstly, that Simmel is arguing against the typical stylization of images, the recourse to empty clichés. Second, we should note his extremely modern call for art to represent 'the autonomous movement of things' as being an appropriate task of modernity. Here are faint echoes of the displaced object, the decentred subject so beloved of postmodern theorists.

And, to remain for a moment with this critique, we should recall Simmel's attack upon the kitsch products of modern popular taste. Here the context is the then popular collection of Japanese wood-cuts. Simmel suggests that 'Berlin at last has started to imitate Paris with the taste in Japanese art. But unfortunately we have already arrived too late, for the market is almost exclusively filled with the modern Japanese products which emerged under European influence and which thus represent such *a bastardised style of the most impure kind'* (Simmel, 1896c: 187).

As a third example of applied works in the broadest sense as passive objects of consumption — and for a rare commentary upon contemporary architecture — we may take Simmel's essay 'The Berlin Trade Exhibition' (Simmel, 1896d) whose analysis in part anticipates Walter Benjamin's later analysis of the 'universe of commodities' (Benjamin, 1973). In this exhibition (which contemporaries viewed as a symbol of Berlin's elevation from a major city to a world metropolis) a profusion of commodities (and works of art and products of applied arts) were exhibited in the social context of *amusement*:

> The close proximity within which the most heterogeneous industrial products are confined produced a paralysis in the capacity for perception, a true hypnosis . . . but in its fragmentation of weak impressions there remains in the memory the notion that one should be amused here. (Simmel, 1896d)

Simmel also emphasizes the *passivity* of such consumption. As compensation for the one-sided restrictions of the labour process's extreme division of labour, people look for 'the increasing crowding together of heterogeneous impressions . . . the increasingly hasty and colourful change in emotions. The differentiation of the active spheres of life evidently complement one another through the comprehensive diversity of their passive and receptive spheres' (Simmel, 1896d).

A specifically aesthetic dimension of such exhibitions Simmel finds in their architecture with 'the conscious negation of the monumental style' giving them 'the character of a creation for transitoriness' (like the life of the commodities exhibited). Above all, an 'aesthetic super-additum' exists in the arrangement of such exhibitions 'just as the ordinary advertisement has advanced to the art poster' (the poster as an aesthetic representation of the representation of use value as exchange value). Indeed, the exhibition increases 'what one can term *the shop-window quality of things*. Commodity production . . . must lead to a situation of *giving things an enticing external appearance* over and above their usefulness . . . one must attempt to *excite the interest of the buyer* by means of the external attraction of the object'. Simmel terms this process *'aesthetic productivity'* (Simmel, 1896d).

Later, in *The Philosophy of Money* and in a somewhat different context, Simmel reflects upon the production of 'an enticing aesthetic appearance' as the production of a plurality of styles. Here he declares that 'the entire visible environment of our cultural life has disintegrated into a plurality of styles' (Simmel, 1990: 463). Style is seen here as a disguise, indeed as 'a veil that imposes a barrier and a distance in relation to the recipient of the expression of these feelings' (Simmel, 1990: 473). Style is capable of expressing any number and variety of contents in related forms. More generally, 'the aesthetic interest of recent times has tended towards an increase in the distance produced by *transposing objects into art*' (Simmel, 1990: 474). Written in 1900, this is probably a reference to art nouveau's conception of the total work of art (*Gesamtkunstwerk*) whose aim was to transform not merely the exterior and interior of a building into an artistic whole but also the whole of its contents. This is confirmed in the essay 'The Picture Frame' in the context of Simmel's attack on 'the conviction that furniture is a work of art', on the grounds that 'the work of art is something for itself, furniture is something for us' (Simmel, 1922b: 50). Again there is a distinction derived from Kant's aesthetics at work here — in however muted a form — namely the distinction between two types of 'objective finality': either internal (the perfection of the object, in this case the work of art) or external (the utility of the object, in this case the product of the applied arts). What is explicitly absent from Simmel's discussion but present in this period is the heated debate on the relationship between art and industry, between craft production and mass production (hinted at in Simmel's discussion of custom production) and the long-standing debate surrounding the useful arts (e.g. the relation between architecture and engineering).

The great work of art which reconciles subject and object, which resolves the contradictions of modern experience ('the modern *transmutabilita*' of restless, fleeting movement and fragmentation and 'the impression of the supra-monetary, the timeless impression') is seldom found in everyday modern experience. Where 'salvation from the trouble and whirl of life, the peace and conciliation beyond its movements and contradictions . . . [is] the permanent goal of art' (Simmel, 1923: 197), then it is certainly realized only in exceptional works such as — for Simmel — Rodin's sculpture. Of course, there are, for Simmel, many instances in works of art of a false reconciliation, culminating in a 'satisfaction with the sunlit surface of things' (Simmel, 1896c: 186).

IV

Nonetheless, Simmel is one of the first social theorists to examine the inner consequences for individual experience (*Erlebnis*) of the domination of the cultural things in everyday experience as the culture of human beings. His investigation of the two sites of modernity — the mature money economy and the metropolis — as the showplaces of modernity is also a study of the fragmentary objectifications and the fragments of experience that are to be found in the surface of the everyday world. This surface, as it is immediately experienced, is one of constant dissolution of forms. Where it becomes a permanent feature of everyday experience, its attendant fragmentation and disintegration threatens a crucial component of aesthetic experience. At one level, Simmel seeks to retrieve the aesthetic by revealing the wealth and diversity of forms, however fragmentary and fleeting they may be. In part, this is achieved through 'the deepening of the surface of life', 'the digging out of every intellectual stratum beneath its appearance' (Simmel, 1923: 11). Where practical necessities and the division of labour seldom permit us to see life in its totality, we must have recourse to another mode of viewing its objectifications. Since life is in permanent flux 'each moment is the whole' (Simmel, 1916: 2).

The domination of the objective culture, of a reified world of things, even, in Benjamin's words, the recognition of 'the force of the extinct world of things' (Benjamin, 1980: 620) makes the search for its aesthetic dimension all the more difficult. It has been argued here that Simmel does reveal the illusory aesthetic of the sphere of circulation and exchange, the sphere in which we normally experience the everyday world of capitalism. However, in his later writings Simmel seems to question the possibility of excavating the culture of things: 'the pessimism with which the majority of more profound thinkers seem to view the contemporary state of culture has its foundation in the ever-wider yawning abyss between the culture of things and that of human beings' (Simmel, 1957b: 95).

But if we reject the tragic vision of the separation of subjective and objective culture as a permanent 'fate' and start out from Simmel's earlier examination of the culture of things, of the phenomenal life of the commodity and the inner consequences of consumption, and of the aesthetic features of 'this' world and the world of everyday interaction, then we could investigate the transformations of aesthetic experience that are taking place without falling back upon the resignatory stance of cultural pessimism. If Simmel shows that the study of everyday modern life is a difficult task, then it is not an impossible one (Frisby, 1986).

Its starting-point — and this is true also for an investigation of the aesthetics of modern life — can be 'the daily traffic of bourgeois life' (Marx), 'the flatness of daily life' (Simmel). Kracauer suggests that Simmel shows us 'how mundane everyday understanding consigns all flowing connections between phenomena to oblivion, severs the web of appearances and endorses its now isolated parts — each of them autonomous — in a single conception' (Kracauer, 1977: 220). Simmel himself alludes to attempts at an aesthetic flight from 'the flatness of daily life' in his investigation of the adventure and travel, and even possibly to a qualified resistance to it in fashion. Their examination would take us into Simmel's contribution to the study of modern leisure (Frisby, 1989, 1991a). But, at all events, Simmel was surely one of the first social theorists to make us aware of the aesthetics of modern life, even in a manner that is relevant to the study of a putative postmodern culture. A 'prehistory' of postmodernity could do worse than reexamine the constellation and context of Simmel's 'modern' aesthetic concerns.

At all events, Simmel's analysis of modernity is significant in that it does highlight the aesthetic dimensions of our modern experience. In particular, if we accept the previous argument as to the affinity between the aesthetic realm and that of the circulation and exchange of commodities, then we can at least plausibly assert that the analogous aesthetic experience in this latter sphere is that of the sublime.

Notes

This article is a revised version of a paper given to the Culture Section of the American Sociological Association Annual Meeting in San Francisco, August 1989. I am grateful to the anonymous reviewers for their comments.

1. Such a comprehensive examination has hardly commenced. On impressionism see my *Sociological Impressionism* (1981; second edn 1991b). On *The Philosophy of Money* (1990) as a major instance of aesthetic theory see Hannes Böhringer (1984) and Sybille Hübner-Funk (1984). More generally, on Simmel's philosophy of art see Atoji (1986).

2. Simmel's use of the concept of value is complex and requires a detailed examination. Simmel at times participates in the neo-Kantian discourse of value spheres and, at others, in the then not totally dissociated discourse of Nietzsche on value. Not surprisingly, it was his theory of value in the first chapter of *The Philosophy of Money* which caused him the greatest difficulties and it is there that revisions were made when he came to write the second edition that appeared in 1907. In terms of economic theory, we can see Simmel oscillating between a subjective and objective theory of value, seeking out a critical position that is, as it were, neither that of Carl Menger nor of Karl Marx. In addition, the opening section of *The Philosophy of Money* (1990: 73–5) takes up aesthetic valuation too. The different nuances in the application of the concept of value are compounded by the ambiguous relationship between value and worth. This is most obvious in Chapter 5 of *The Philosophy of Money* on the money equivalent of personal values, where it would be more appropriate to use the concept of human worth.

3. Simmel's argument here on art's unification of diversity and disparity and elsewhere on art's capacity to resolve contradictory tensions is a central *leitmotif* of other areas of existence. Aside from the obvious applications in *The Philosophy of Money*, a great deal of his discussion of religion revolves around a sometimes explicit analogy between God and society (a comparison with Durkheim would be instructive here) and the unification of diversity. See *Die Religion* (Simmel, 1912). The central conception of sociation as the social process of interaction (*Wechselwirkung*) also implies that the reciprocal effects of two elements creates a third entity, the interaction itself.

4. In addition to Kant's *Critique of Judgement* (1982), his *Observations on the Feeling of the Beautiful and Sublime* (1960) should also be consulted on the concept of the sublime. For a recent secondary discussion in Kant's philosophy see Crowther (1989). A stimulating collection of essays on the sublime is edited by Pries (1989).

References

Atoji, Yoshio (1986) 'Georg Simmel's Philosophy of Art', pp. 147–64 in *Georg Simmel's Sociological Horizons*. Tokyo: Ochanomizu-shobo.

Benjamin, Walter (1973) *Charles Baudelaire*. Translated by Harry Zohn. London: New Left Books.

Benjamin, Walter (1980) *Gesammelte Schriften II*. Frankfurt: Suhrkamp.

Böhringer, Hannes (1984) 'Die "Philosophie des Geldes" als ästhetische Theorie', pp. 178–82 in H.J. Dahme and O. Rammstedt (eds), *Georg Simmel und die Moderne*. Frankfurt: Suhrkamp.

Crowther, Paul (1989) *The Kantian Sublime*. Oxford: Clarendon Press.

Frisby, David (1986) *Fragments of Modernity*. Oxford: Polity; Cambridge, MA: MIT Press.

Frisby, David (1989) 'Simmel and Leisure', in C. Rojek (ed.), *Leisure for Leisure*. Basingstoke: Macmillan.

Frisby, David (1991a) *Simmel and Since*. London: Routledge.

Frisby, David (1991b) *Sociological Impressionism*, second edn. London: Routledge.

Hübner-Funk, Sybille (1984) 'Die äesthetische Konstituierung gesellschaftlicher Erkenntnis am Beispiel der "Philosophie des Geldes"', pp. 193-201 in H.J. Dahme and O. Rammstedt (eds), *Georg Simmel und die Moderne*. Frankfurt: Suhrkamp.

Kant, Immanuel (1960) *Observations on the Feeling of the Beautiful and Sublime*. Translated by John T. Goldthwait. Berkeley/Los Angeles: University of California Press.

Kant, Immanuel (1982) *The Critique of Judgement*. Translated by J.C. Meredith. Oxford: Oxford University Press.

Kracauer, Siegfried (1977) 'Georg Simmel' in *Das Ornament der Masse*. Frankfurt: Suhrkamp.

Lichtblau, Klaus (1984) 'Das "Pathos der Distanz". Präliminarien zur Nietzsche — Rezeption bei Georg Simmel', pp. 231-81 in H.J. Dahme and O. Rammstedt (eds), *Georg Simmel und die Moderne*. Frankfurt: Suhrkamp.

Marx, Karl (1973) *Grundrisse*. Translated by M. Nicholaus. Harmondsworth: Penguin.

Marx, Karl (1975) *Early Writings*. Harmondsworth: Penguin.

Müller, Michael (1987) *Schöner Schein*. Frankfurt: Athenäeum.

Pries, Christine (ed.) (1989) *Das Erhabene*. Weinheim: VCH Verlag.

Scheible, Hartmut (1980) 'Georg Simmel und die "Tragödie der Kultur"', *Neue Rundschau* 91(2/3): 133-64.

Simmel, Georg (1890a) *Über sociale Differenzierung*. Leipzig: Duncker & Humblot (see also 1989a).

Simmel, Georg (1890b) 'Ueber Kunstausstellungen', *Unsere Zeit* 26(2): 474-80.

Simmel, Georg (1896a) 'Soziologische Aesthetik', *Die Zukunft* 17: 204-16 (see also 1968).

Simmel, Georg (1896b) 'Das Geld in der modernen Kultur', *Zeitschrift des Oberschlesischen Berg und Hüttenmännischen Vereins* 35: 319-24 (see also 1989b). English translation 'Money in Modern Culture' in this issue.

Simmel, Georg (1896c) 'Berliner Kunstbrief', *Die Zeit* 8: 186-7.

Simmel, Georg (1896d) 'Berliner Gewerbe-Ausstellung', *Die Zeit* 8. English translation 'The Berlin Trade Exhibition' in this issue.

Simmel, Georg (1901) 'Ästhetik der Schwere', *Berliner Tageblatt*, 10 June.

Simmel, Georg (1908a) 'Psychologie des Schmuckes', *Morgen* 2: 1685-9 (see also 1950).

Simmel, Georg (1908b) 'Das Problem des Stiles', *Dekorative Kunst* 16: 307-16. English translation 'The Problem of Style' in this issue.

Simmel, Georg (1912) *Die Religion*. Frankfurt am Main: Rütten u. Loening.

Simmel, Georg (1916) *Rembrandt*. Munich: Kurt Wolff Verlag.

Simmel, Georg (1918) *Kant. Sechzehn Vorlesungen*. Munich and Leipzig: Duncker & Humblot. First published in 1904.

Simmel, Georg (1922a) 'Der siebente Ring', pp. 74-8 in *Zur Philosophie der Kunst*. Potsdam: Gustav Kiepenheuer.

Simmel, Georg (1922b) 'Der Bildrahmen', pp. 46-54 in *Zur Philosophie der Kunst*. Potsdam: Gustav Kiepenheuer.

Simmel, Georg (1923) 'Rodin', pp. 179-97 in *Philosophische Kultur*. Potsdam: Gustav Kiepenheuer.

Simmel, Georg (1950) 'Adornment', pp. 338-44 in K.H. Wolff (ed.), *The Sociology of Georg Simmel*. New York: Free Press.

Simmel, Georg (1957a) 'Philosophie der Landschaft', pp. 141–52 in *Brücke und Tür*. Stuttgart: K.F. Koehler.

Simmel, Georg (1957b) 'Vom Wesen der Kultur', pp. 86–94 in *Brücke und Tür*. Stuttgart: Koehler.

Simmel, Georg (1968) 'Sociological Aesthetics', in *The Conflict in Modern Culture and Other Essays*. Translated by Peter K. Etzkorn. New York: Teachers' College Press.

Simmel, Georg (1989a) *Aufsätze. Über sociale Differenzierung. Die Probleme der Geschichtsphilosophie (1892)* (Gesamtausgabe 2). Edited by H.J. Dahme. Frankfurt: Suhrkamp.

Simmel, Georg (1989b) *Philosophie des Geldes* (Gesamtausgabe 6). Edited by D.P. Frisby and K.C. Köhnke. Frankfurt: Suhrkamp.

Simmel, Georg (1990) *The Philosophy of Money*. Translated by T. Bottomore and D. Frisby. London: Routledge.

Sombart, Werner (1907) 'Probleme des Kunstgewerbes in der Gegenwart', *Neue Rundschau* 18(1): 513–36.

David Frisby teaches Sociology at the University of Glasgow, Scotland. His latest books are *Simmel and Since* and *Sociological Impressionism*, second edn, both published by Routledge.

eine Generation der andern das Schönheitsideal und den Glauben daran übergeben und jede hat es auf ihre Weise gepflegt und sich immer fester daran gewurzelt, bis schließlich ein ungeheurer Durst nach Schönheit, die Erbschaft so langer Entwicklung, der Seele angeboren wird, das Geschenk der Gattung, das sie jedem in die Wiege legt — als stünden die Danaer zu Pathen. Denn darum ist ja das Leben so dunkel und schaal, so arm und verzerrt, weil über ihm das Ideal der Schönheit steht, strahlend und fleckenlos, ein Meer von Glanz überall hingießend, wo Seele ist und wo die Dinge nicht sind. Wie sollen sie denn hell und leuchtend bleiben, gemessen an dem Licht unsrer Schönheitsträume? Ach, die Schönheit kennt kein Erbarmen, sie ist die unbarmherzige Waage, auf der unser Leben Tag für Tag gewogen und zu leicht befunden wird. Mit den halben Wahrheiten haben wir uns abgefunden, resignirt, daß alles Wissen Stückwerk ist und daß die letzte Wahrheit der Dinge sich nur in einem göttlichen Auge spiegeln kann — ja, mit dem stillen Trost, daß eben dies Nicht-Wissen der große Segen der Menschheit ist und daß nichts so sehr die Weisheit der Vorsehung beweist, als unsre Nicht-Weisheit. In der unvollkommnen Moral sind wir erst recht eingewohnt und denken garnicht im Ernste daran, auszuziehen — nicht nur, weil die halbe Moral so oft gleich dem ganzen Glück ist, sondern an dem nie rastenden Kampf des Besten in uns mit dem Schlechtesten in uns ein unendlich viel höherer Werth und Bedeutsamkeit des Lebens haftet, als an der kühlen, von aller Versuchung gelösten Unverführbarkeit des Heiligen. Soviel wie diese aber läßt das Ideal der Schönheit sich nicht abhandeln. Es trägt in sich das geheime Versprechen voller Erreichbarkeit und zieht damit einen Wechsel auf die Wirklichkeit, den diese doch niemals honorirt, nicht strömt es, wie jene andern, den milden Trost aus, daß das menschliche Wesen seine letzte Erfüllung und Ganzheit nicht ertragen würde, eine Semele in Zeus' Armen — nein, wir könnten sie ganz und restlos genießen, unsre Sinne sind weit genug, unser Sinn tief genug. So fordert Schönheit sich ganz von den Dingen und damit zerstört sie die stille Genüßamkeit halber Befriedigungen. Sie macht noch auch wirklich, als ob immer nur ein Geringes fehlte, damit die Dinge schön seien, ein Hauch und Schimmer nur noch, ein erlösendes Wort, ein letztes Sich-Aufraffen und Aufgipfeln, als stünde

die Schönheit ganz dicht hinter den Dingen, und sie und wir brauchten nur zuzugreifen — und so schärft sich die Qual des Entbehrens durch die täuschende Nähe und Lockung des Glücks.

Ein Teufel muß die Schönheit erfunden haben, damit sie uns das Leben verleide. O sanftes, trautes, lebenverschönerndes Ideal der Häßlichkeit! Mit wie inniger Befriedigung würde unser Auge die Welt empfangen, mit wie ungestörten Harmonieen würde sie unser Ohr erfüllen, wenn wir sie an der Sehnsucht nach vollendeter Häßlichkeit, statt an der nach vollendeter Schönheit messen wollten! Da gäbe es zwischen Ideal und Wirklichkeit keine Dissonanz mehr, an der wir uns die Ohren wund zu hören hätten, da läsen wir zwischen den Zeilen der Welt keine unerfüllten Forderungen mehr, da sähen wir die natürliche Entwicklung der Menschen und der Dinge sich ruhig und stetig ihrem Ideale nähern, sicher, daß das heut noch nicht Erreichte morgen gelungen sein wird. Ein stiller, gesättigter Friede wird über die Welt kommen, wenn sie nicht mehr nach dem irren Traume der Schönheit, sondern nach der klaren Unbedingtheit des Häßlichen die Erscheinungen schätzen, nicht mehr in widerhaarigem Trotz von ihnen verlangen wird, was sie doch nicht gewähren, sondern sich zu ihrem unzweideutigen Sinne bekehren wird. Dann erst, wenn wir uns nicht mehr durch die freche Forderung der Schönheit die Dinge verleiden, sondern unsre Ideale gefügig so erbauen, daß die Wirklichkeit darin Platz hat, wenn unsre inneren Wallfahrten dem Allerheiligsten des Häßlichen, dem Allerhäßlichsten des Heiligen gelten werden — dann wird die Welt uns wirklich gehören und wir werden des Schauspiels genießen, daß nicht mehr die Wirklichkeit hinter dem Ideale, sondern manchmal sogar das Ideal hinter der Wirklichkeit zurückbleibt — —

Erst wenn das Ideal der Häßlichkeit uns zur Norm und Maaß aller Dinge geworden ist, die Plattheit statt der Tiefe, die Dürre statt der Fülle, der Mißklang statt des Wohlklangs — erst dann wird die unversöhnliche Tragik der Schönheitsforderung Platz gemacht haben der organischen Anpassung der Seelen an ihre Welt und es wird Freude auf Erden sein und den Menschen ein Wohlgefallen —

Tief ergriffen von der Weihe des neuen Evangeliums und in drängender Begierde, dessen erster Blutzeuge zu werden, erhob sich unser Freund und trat vor den Spiegel.

G. S.

C. Schmidt-Helmbrechts (München).

The Alpine Journey

Georg Simmel

A process which has been in the making for decades in the
Swiss transport system has recently been completed. It is something
more than an economic analogy to call it the wholesale opening-up
and enjoyment of nature. Destinations that were previously only
accessible by remote walks can now be reached by railways, which
are appearing at an ever-increasing rate. Railways have been built
where the gradients are too steep for roads to be constructed, as in
the Muerren or Wanger Alps. The railway-line up the Eiger appears
to have been finalized, and the same number of climbers who have
scaled this difficult peak can now be brought up in a single day
by rail. The Faustian wish, 'I stand before you, nature, a solitary
individual' is evermore rarely realized and so increasingly rarely
declared. Alpine journeys had a pedagogic value in that they were
a pleasure that could only be had by a self-reliance that was
both external and internal to oneself. Now there is the lure of
the ease of an open road, and the concentration and convergence
of the masses — colourful but therefore as a whole colourless —
suggesting to us an average sensibility. Like all social averages this
depresses those disposed to the higher and finer values without
elevating those at the base to the same degree.

All in all I accept that the advantages of this socialistic wholesale
opening up of the Alps outweigh the reliance on the efforts of the
individual. Countless people who previously were barred because
of their lack of strength and means are now able to enjoy nature.
I disagree with that foolish romanticism which saw difficult routes,
prehistoric food and hard beds as an irremovable part of the stimulus of the good old days of alpine travel; despite this it is still possible for those who wish, to find solitude and quiet in the Alps. But
the increased accessibility of alpine travel does cause us to question the benefit our civilization draws from it; since alpine travel

Theory, Culture & Society (SAGE, London, Newbury Park and New Delhi), Vol. 8
(1991), 95–98

has already to be seen as an important element of the psychic life (*Seelenleben*) of our upper strata and as such as a matter of social psychology (*Volkerpsychologie*).

It is said that it is part of one's education (*Bildung*) to see the Alps, but not education alone for its twin sister is 'affluence' (*Wohlhabenheit*). The power of capitalism extends itself to ideas as well; it is capable of annexing such a distinguished concept as education as its own private property. Furthermore, profound and spiritual (*geistige*) human beings believe they are cultivating their inner depths and spirituality when they visit the Alps. Alongside the physical act of climbing and the temporary pleasure it creates is a certain moral element and spiritual satisfaction which appear to be located outside egoistic pleasure. By distancing their own spiritual and educational values from other sensual pleasures, it seems to me that these people employ one of those easy self-deceptions whereby their own culture, which would find egoism shocking, retains a subjectivity despite its lofty sentiments and seeks shamelessly to cloak its own pleasures with objective justifications. I think that the educative value of alpine travel is very small. It gives the feeling of tremendous excitement and charge in its incomparable merging of forbidding strength and radiant beauty, and at the time the contemplation of those things fills us with an unrivalled intensity of feeling, prompting undisclosed inner feelings as if the high peaks could uncover the depths of our soul. Strangely this excitement and euphoria, which drive the emotions to a level more intense than normal, subside remarkably quickly. The uplift which a view of the high Alps gives is followed very quickly by the return to the mood of the mundane. In particular compared to travel in Italy this is very pronounced. The difference between the strength and depth of that momentary rapture and the lasting value on the formation and mood of the soul, encourages comparison between the Alps and music. In this way I also believe that music is given an exaggerated educational value. It also takes us into fantastic regions of the life of the senses, whose riches are so to speak tied to those areas; we take little or nothing from them to adorn other areas of our inner life. All of the verve and heightening that music brings out in us and which we claim as our own, fades away with the notes and leaves the state of one's soul exactly at the point where it was before. Like a talent for music, the effect of music belongs to something beyond the other faculties for learning (*Bildungssphaeren*). The magnificence of music should be as accessible as that of the Alps;

I think that the idea that the value of both to education in its deepest sense, in its effect upon the integrity of the soul, is in need of revision.

The clearest expression of this error is the confusion of the egoistic enjoyment of alpine sports with educational and moral values. In alpine clubs there is the idea that the surmounting of life-endangering difficulties is morally commendable, a triumph of the spirit over the resistance of the material, and a consequence of moral strength: of courage, will power and the summoning of all abilities for an ideal goal. One forgets that the forces deployed are a means to goals which have no moral claim and indeed are often unethical; as a means for momentary enjoyment, which comes from the exertion of all one's energies, from playing with danger and the emotion of the panoramic view. Indeed, I would place this enjoyment as the highest that life can offer. The less settled, less certain and less free from contradiction modern existence is the more passionately we desire the heights that stand beyond the good and evil whose presence we are unable to look over and beyond. I do not know anything in visible nature that bears the character of the materially transcendent as a snowscape that expresses 'the summits' in its colour and form. Whoever has once enjoyed this will yearn for the release in something that is simply other than the 'I' — the 'I' with its melancholy disquiet, full of the life of the plains, choking the exercise of the will. This is so more with respect to the mountains than the sea, which, with its foam waiting to drain away only to come flooding back in, with the purposeless *circulus vitiosus* of its movement, reminds us only too painfully of our own inner life. Admittedly many are attracted by this. Since not only the addition to the 'I' through its opposite releases us, but also the sea as symbol and picture, shorn of all incidentals, mirrors our destiny and unhappiness, rather like a secret homeopathy, and discloses a reconciliation and a healing elevation over life. Nevertheless, this is only a soothing, a forgetting and a reverie and, as such, merely a passive enjoyment. From the loneliness of the icy wilderness, however, bursts out the sensation of a desire for action, that feeling of joy and being beyond life that can be derived from perhaps no other external situation, even though this is admittedly only the temporary delusion of aesthetic stimulation.

But this pleasure remains completely egoistic and, therefore, the risking of life as mere enjoyment is unethical; indeed even more unethical since for the hire of a guide for fifty or hundred francs one risks another's life through possible accident. An alpinist would be indignant if one wanted to compare him or her to a gambler. And yet both wish to place their existence at risk as a purely subjective excitation and gratification. Frequently the gambler does not look for material profit but the excitement of risk and the gripping combination of the cold-bloodedness and passion of one's own skill and the incalculability of fate. The alpinist plays for a stake which from an ethical viewpoint should be wagered for only the highest objective values and not for the sake of selfish and immediate gratification. Only a romantic excitation can delude itself that every voluntary risking of life is part of tradition when social and religious commitments could supposedly only be gained at the price of life, thereby conferring on their goals the veneer of ethical dignity.

Translated by Sam Whimster.

Note

This article is a translation of 'Alpenreisen', *Der Zeit* (Wien) 4, 13 July 1895.

Simmel as Educator: On Individuality and Modern Culture

Donald N. Levine

In his preface to *The Philosophy of Money*, Simmel espouses a genre of speculative work — in later years he would name it 'philosophical sociology' — which offers general interpretations of history and society that empirical disciplines simply cannot provide, either because these disciplines are partial and incomplete or because they cannot encompass the required valuative emphases and integrative perspectives. This genre seems necessary because it deals with questions 'that we have so far been unable either to answer or to dismiss' (Simmel, 1978: 53).

Although valuable diagnoses of this sort have been produced by colleagues in our own time — such as Daniel Bell, Norbert Elias, Jürgen Habermas, Morris Janowitz and Talcott Parsons — the classics of social theory remain a goldmine of such speculative conceptions. More particularly, every one of the classic authors offers models and metaphors with which to grasp the nature of that historically unprecedented social and cultural context which we typically gloss as 'modernity'.

Of the many ways to represent the classic texts on modernity, the interpretive schema I apply here sees them as advocates of a new kind of educational programme. Their advocacy tends to proceed by means of a three-term argument. First, *they analyse key features of the new order which seem to promote human welfare*; second, *they criticize certain features of the new order which seem to affect humanity adversely*; and third, *they propose some form of education which will serve to counteract these adverse features*.

Thus, in the *Essay on the History of Civil Society* (1966), Adam Ferguson, whom some have called the 'first sociologist', defined modern civilization by its improvement of arts and sciences, its attainment of efficient administration and its perfection of

Theory, Culture & Society (SAGE, London, Newbury Park and New Delhi), Vol. 8 (1991), 99–117

commercial practices. On the other hand, Ferguson also found this civilization marked by a regime of selfishness and luxury, over-estimation of material wealth and neglect of political participation and the public good. Ferguson offered his own work as an educational tract designed to cultivate the liberal spirit and stimulate devotion to public affairs, thereby to counteract the corrupting tendencies of the modern commercial order.

Adam Smith likewise took the defining feature of modern societies to be their organization for commerce, and he hailed the division of labour as the key factor in raising the average standard of living of their members. On the other hand, Smith criticized the division of labour in industry for the way it cripples the mental faculties of labourers, making them 'as stupid and ignorant as it is possible for a human creature to become' (1965: 734). He indicted the division of labour for rendering people unfit for rational conversation and unsuited for making sensible judgements regarding private and public interests. Consequently, Smith advocated a system of public education which would counteract the mind-numbing and narrowing effects of the division of labour with broadening and enriching experiences.

For Auguste Comte, the hallmarks of modernity included both the overthrow of prescientific belief systems and the diversification of social functions. While these developments vastly expand the cooperative domain of modern societies as well as their productive capacities, they lead to conditions of intellectual anarchy which threaten the viability of modern societies as consensual systems. In response, Comte advocated the development of a common curriculum based on the positive sciences for the new elites of modern societies, as well as a simplified set of scientifically grounded beliefs to be disseminated to all their members.

Karl Marx located the great advances of the modern order in the astonishing productivity and internationalization made possible by the capitalist organization of production, and its correlative defects in the alienation of workers from the productive process. Despite passages which disparage efforts to change human consciousness through education, Marx at times signalled a need for new forms of consciousness as a means of overcoming the exploitative and alienating features of this system.

Herbert Spencer located the progressive aspect of modern societies in the extent to which they embodied functionally differentiated structures. The vulnerability of such an order lay in the tendency of functionaries to acquire vested interests in their specializations, and in the tendency of unenlightened activists to effect harmful interventions in complicated social realities. Although Spencer's general educational theory aimed at far more than the redress of such problems, he advocated the study of sociology as a resource to enhance the adaptive flexibility of modern citizens and to enable them to understand the complexities of natural processes so that they would avoid retrograde actions and pathological interventions.

Emile Durkheim rebutted Comte by arguing that modernity entailed such extensive specialization it was no longer plausible to base social solidarity on an extensive system of shared beliefs. Durkheim welcomed the modern order as a matrix of diversity, individualization, innovation and societal interdependence. At the same time, he viewed its erosion of traditional norms and social obligations as a source of disorientation and pathological personal strivings. To counteract these pathologies, Durkheim advocated a system of education whose goal was to cultivate both intellectual autonomy and moral regulation.

For Max Weber, by contrast, the modern order entailed unprecedented levels of social coordination and regulation. The rationalization of business, law and public administration vastly enhanced human instrumental capacities and the achievement of equality under the law; however, these processes of rationalization threatened to turn human actors into robots. To counter this, Weber advocated a strenuous process of 'education for judgment', a process which prodded people to think critically for themselves and to escape the 'unreflective determination of social decisions by value habits and emotions built into public language' and conventional practice (see Green, 1988: Ch. 7).

For John Dewey and George Herbert Mead, finally, one could say that they viewed the modern order as entailing unprecedented capabilities for rational discourse and public communication. On the other hand, they criticized contemporary society for not having developed the kinds of public consciousness needed for pluralistic urban communities. In response, they advocated new kinds of educational programmes to cultivate habits of social cooperation and elevate discourse about public problems.

I

Applying this interpretive schema to Simmel's widely scattered comments on the modern order may enable us to appreciate some features of his thought which may be particularly pertinent at present and which have hitherto been neglected. I contend that Simmel's two-sided diagnosis of modernity remains illuminating, and that the educational programme he projects can be a source of fruitful debate about the future of (post)modern humanity.

In developing this argument I have occasion to challenge two common interpretations of Simmel: the thesis of Simmel's alleged indifferentism and the thesis of Simmel's alleged pessimism. I challenge the view, espoused by commentators like Georg Lukács and David Frisby, that Simmel lacked a centre of firm commitments and wholly retreated from social reality (Levine, 1985: 134) — and argue instead that Simmel's writings reveal a consistent commitment to the value of human individuality and personal integrity. I also challenge the view frequently espoused by those who find Simmel an articulate critic, rather than indifferent to the human condition in modern culture, but who represent him as an unrelieved pessimist — commentators like Bryan Green, who acknowledges Simmel's 'commitment to the cultivation . . . of unique individuality', but hold that when he came to considering its conditions, he could find only 'a fateful tragedy, an inevitable overwhelming of subjective cultivation by cultural forms and techniques' (Green, 1988: 93). Instead, I argue that Simmel both analyses conditions which favour individuality in modern society and suggests ways in which to cultivate it.

In representing Simmel's conception of modernity[1] one must take care to consider at least four different lines of his work: his extension of Spencerian differentiation theory, as embodied in his first monograph, *On Social Differentiation* (1890); his writings on culture, reflecting the influence of Moritz Lazarus, writings which include his doctoral work on music and a number of later essays on the philosophy of culture; his highly original explorations on money, assembled in the two editions of *The Philosophy of Money* (1900, 1907); and his equally original explorations on urban life which appear in the 1903 essay, 'The Metropolis and Mental Life' (Simmel, 1978/89).

In reviewing Simmel's writings on modernity one is struck by the lack of regard for issues which loom large in the work of most other classic authors. Simmel paid little or no attention to such familiar themes as political centralization, social stratification, bureaucratization, social solidarity, equality, justice, the rationalization of law and secularization. On the other hand, these writings exhibit a

notable coherence owing to their focus on one major interpretive theme: the scattered texts where Simmel plants his diagnoses of modernity all pose the question of what effects the
conditions of modern life have for the fulfilment of individual
personality.

This theme appeared already in the very first sociological
essay which Simmel published, the 'Bemerkungen zu socialethischen
Problemen' (1888), where he argues that the expansion of the
sphere in which people associate promotes the development of their
individuality — an argument which gets elaborated in chapter 3
of *On Social Differentiation* and further developed in chapter 10
of *Soziologie* (1908). The remaining substantive chapters of *On
Social Differentiation* depict different patterns of evolutionary
development from 'more primitive epochs' to the modern era which
represent other modes of increased individuation. These include
the transition from a form in which jural responsibility is invested
in groups to one in which liability is assigned to individual persons (Ch. 2); from a condition in which shared beliefs embody
the lowest common denominator of mental activity to one which
permits individualized intellectual attainment (Ch. 4); and from
a relatively compulsory pattern of group affiliations based on the
accidents of birth and propinquity to one in which persons associate voluntarily on the basis of shared interests, thereby creating
more individuated constellations of group affiliation (Ch. 5; revised
to form Ch. 6 of *Soziologie*).

In *The Philosophy of Money*, Simmel extends these lines of
argument in several ways. First, he supplements his analysis of
group structural properties as sources of individuation by considering the ways in which the use of money as a general medium
of exchange similarly *advances the processes of personal emancipation*. Thus, just as the enlargement of spheres of social contact
liberates individuals by removing them from the conventional constraints of local communities, so money promotes freedom in the
sense of liberation from external constraints: indirectly by enlarg-
ing the effective sphere of exchange relations through an expanded
market, and directly, by facilitating transactions in which the obligations by which persons are bound to one another can be limited
to a very precise and specific exchange. Second, he considers the
repercussions within the personality of this withdrawal of external restraints. Negatively, that signifies the 'independence from and
exclusion of all extraneous factors, and development exclusively

according to the laws of one's own being which we call freedom' (Simmel, 1978: 302). Positively, it signifies the differentiation of a person's impulses, interests and capacities such that these 'various individual energies develop and run their course exclusively in accord with their own purposes and norms' (Simmel, 1989: 418, 1978: 313, translation modified).

In addition, Simmel considers the way in which *money promotes individuation by granting new powers to the individual*. Just as the shift from associations based on kinship and local territorial bonds to voluntary interest associations provides new resources for pursuing one's goals and realizing the unhampered development of one's unique personality, so money provides the freedom to carry out one's intentions. Again, it does this both indirectly, by facilitating the formation of innumerable voluntary associations organized around particular objective interests, and directly in a number of ways. Money enhances the freedom to act in that, of all objects, money offers the least resistance to an agent. It is the most possessable of all things, hence completely submissive to the will of an ego. It can be acquired in countless ways. The amount of it that one can possess can be increased indefinitely, and its uses are without number.

In yet another, more abstract line of argument about the process of individuation, Simmel associates the modern order with an unprecedented degree of emancipation of human subjectivity from the demands of objects and objectivity. By providing an effective means of differentiating between the subjective centre and the objective achievements of a person, money figures as the great agent of this process. For example, an individual's performance may be paid for with money while her or his person remains outside the transaction. Or else individual persons can be supported (by monetary contributions from many others) while their specific performances remain free from financial considerations and constraints. Further in this vein Simmel argues that the separation of workers from their means of production (for which a 'money economy paved the way'), while viewed by some as the focal point of social misery, may rather be viewed 'as a salvation' insofar as it provides conditions for the liberation of the worker as a human subject from the objectified technical apparatus of productivity (1978: 337). Summarizing many of these lines of argument, Simmel concludes that money 'frees us both when we give it away and when we take it' and as a consequence 'the continuous processes of liberation occupy an extraordinarily broad section of modern life' (1989: 555, 1978: 403–4).

In view of the foregoing, I find it puzzling to find interpretations of Simmel's theory of modernity which ignore what Simmel regards as enormous emancipatory developments in the modern order, developments which for him signal a great advance for humanity by virtue of encouraging an unprecedented degree of individuation.[2] (What is more, I believe that Simmel's main lines of argument on this point are valid and significant, and that they are consistent with a good deal else that has been written about modernity by Durkheim and by a number of later sociologists.) Even so, while the emancipation of individuality figures as a major hallmark of modernity for Simmel, *an even more basic feature of the modern order is its capacity to differentiate and to promote opposed characteristics*. This is particularly true for those structural features of modernity which Simmel singles out for intensive analysis: the use of money as a generalized medium of exchange, and the psychic effects of metropolitan living. As Simmel puts it with regard to the former, money 'cultivates all the opposites of historical-psychological possibilities' (1978: 409). And so, if it is true that money transforms human life by opening up unparalleled kinds of freedom, it is also true that for Simmel a number of negative tendencies accompany that transformation. He addresses certain *negative consequences of this new freedom* and some *new forms of unfreedom*.

II

The negative consequences of freedom include the possibility of a lowered standard of living, especially for emancipated peasants, as well as the economic insecurities attendant on the fluctuations of a free market economy. Above all, Simmel emphasizes the sense of deracination which often accompanies the emancipation of persons from objects to which they have been bound, but which have given their lives stability and meaning. He describes the emptiness and instability experienced by peasants who have been liberated by cash payments, and the boredom and inner restlessness of the tradesman who has sold his entire business for cash. In sum, 'since under very rapid money transactions possessions are no longer classified according to the category of a specific life-content, that inner bond, amalgamation and devotion in no way develops which, though it restricts the personality, none the less gives support and content to it. This explains why our age, which, on the whole, certainly possesses more freedom than any previous one, is unable to enjoy it properly' (1978: 403).

Simmel goes on to elaborate this theme of the detachment of human subjects from traditional moorings in his later writings on modern culture, especially 'The Conflict in Modern Culture' (1968c). In that essay he argues that the perennial struggle between contemporary forms filled with life and old, lifeless forms appears to have given way in the modern era to an opposition of vital energies to the very principle of form itself. This antagonism is self-destructive, however. Life wishes here to obtain something impossible: although subjects may seek to transcend all forms and to express the energy of life in its naked immediacy, life can only proceed by producing and utilizing forms. As a result of this intensification of the perennial conflict between form and life process, 'we gaze into an abyss of unformed life beneath our feet' (1971: 393). The phenomenology of this condition is luxuriantly described in the closing sections of *The Philosophy of Money*, where Simmel depicts the lability and fecklessness of modern cultural tastes.

In other writings, Simmel alludes to the fragmentation of personal experience under modern conditions. The multiplication of intersecting social circles gives each person an increasingly unique constellation of social connections but also multiplies the competing demands for their attention. The separate and incommensurable spheres of culture make conflicting claims — 'we are constantly circulating over a number of different planes, each of which presents the world-totality according to a different formula; but from each our life takes only a fragment along at any given time' (1918: 37) — and this fragmentation gets amplified by the diversification of specialized spheres in modern culture.

Beyond noting the negative effects of the modern economy in the personal disorientation produced by excessive freedom, *The Philosophy of Money* identifies other difficulties which appear in the form of new kinds of oppression. For example, restricting personal obligations to something that may be fulfilled by a monetary payment can produce a kind of disenfranchisement in instances where the obliged person had acquired some sort of influence or special rights by virtue of that relationship (1978: 395). Moreover, the modern objectification of the process of production brings about new forms of enslavement, both the enslavement of workers to an impersonal production process and the enslavement of consumers to products which come to seem indispensable, yet 'could and even ought to be dispensed with as far as the essence of life is concerned' (1978: 483).

Simmel goes on to analyse other consequences of an advanced money economy which threaten the individual person. He describes ways in which persons are debased by virtue of the translation of personal qualities and values into monetary terms. He also discusses the consequences of the extension of the 'teleological series' — the addition of numerous techniques in modern life which add so many new means into the cultural repertoire that chains of means-ends relationship get inordinately lengthened. As a result, individuals tend to lose sight of the ultimate ends of their strivings, and become fixated on goals which are nothing but instrumental means.

Above all, Simmel identifies a new order of oppressiveness with the autonomization of objective culture in the modern period. Thanks to the division of labour and the modern money economy, objectified cultural forms get created at a rate which exceeds the capacity of human subjects to absorb them. The unceasing production of new techniques and diverse cultural objects creates the 'typically problematic situation of modern man, his sense of being surrounded by an innumerable number of cultural elements which are neither meaningless to him nor, in the final analysis, meaningful. In their mass they depress him, since he is not capable of assimilating them all, nor can he simply reject them, since after all they do belong potentially within the sphere of his cultural development' (1968b: 44).

Just as money cultivates opposed historical-psychological possibilities, so the modern metropolis provides a place where 'conflicting life-embracing currents find themselves with equal legitimacy' (1971: 339). Simmel's essay on this subject constitutes an enquiry into the specifically modern aspects of contemporary life which bear on the struggle of individuals to maintain their autonomy and individuality in the face of overwhelming supra-individual forces of social organization, technology and cultural tradition. His analysis focuses on three pairs of opposed tendencies.

First, Simmel discusses the forces which *threaten and promote the modern ideal of individual autonomy* in the metropolis. The individual's freedom of action is seriously curtailed by the pressures for adhering to precise social arrangements, punctuality and impersonal kinds of transactions which are demanded by the rationalistic ethos of the big city and its money economy. These same factors, however, promote a psychic defence of reserve and aversion behind which individuals gain a new kind of freedom of response. This façade forms the protective covering for 'a type and degree of personal freedom to which there is no analogy in other circumstances' (1971: 332). The freedom in question is that gained by the enlargement of the sphere of social association and the corresponding diminution of those smothering social controls exerted over dwellers in small towns and villages.

Secondly, the essay discusses the forces which *threaten and promote the modern ideal of individuality*, the freedom to develop a unique self. Cities promote this individuality by supporting an extreme degree of specialization. At the same time, the division of labour threatens individuality, not only by exacting a one-sided kind of performance which permits the personality as a whole to deteriorate, but also, through its relentless productivity, by engulfing the individual in a world of cultural objects. These reduce him to a 'mere cog' in 'the vast overwhelming organization of things and forces which gradually take out of his hands everything connected with progress, spirituality and value' (1971: 337). In response to this oppressive situation, however, the conditions of modern urban life make possible a new source of individuality, that which arises in protest against the mass of depersonalized cultural accomplishment and expresses itself in the form of accentuated idiosyncratic traits and eccentric personalities, and the popularization of culture heroes who preach doctrines of extreme individuality. Were he writing today, Simmel would doubtless make reference to such phenomena as rock stars and individualized T-shirts.

Finally, there is the opposition between those two ideals of individualism themselves — between the ideal of autonomy, which Simmel associates with the eighteenth-century liberalist struggle against traditional constraints, and the ideal of individuality, which Simmel associates with the nineteenth-century romantic movement and advocates of specialized vocations. Not only does the modern metropolis stimulate the development of these two ideals (as well as provide obstacles to their realization) but it is the function of the metropolis to provide an arena for the *conflict and shifting relations between these two great ideals*, a struggle which constitutes much of the 'external as well as the internal history of our time' (1971: 339).

III

If Simmel was content simply to analyse these contradictory tendencies of the modern order in the first years of this century, by 1916 he was ready to diagnose the modern situation as that of a persisting, chronic state of crisis. Summing up its main symptoms, Simmel wrote in 'The Crisis of Culture':

> That mere means count as final purposes, thus completely distorting the rational order of inner and practical existence; that objective culture develops in a degree and tempo which leaves farther and farther behind the cultivation of subjects, which alone provides meaning for all perfection of objects; that the individual branches of culture grow apart in divergent directions and mutual alienation, such that the totality of culture hastens toward the fate of the tower of Babel and its deepest value, which exists precisely in the coherence of its parts, seems threatened with its annihilation . . . all this threatens to lead culture to ruin. (1968a: 235)

To limit one's attention to this stark diagnosis of cultural anomie and alienation, however, is to forget the other side of Simmel's invariably 'dialectical' mode of understanding. His late writings also indicate a number of bases for resistance against those negative tendencies. These consist of a renewed appeal to the creative energies of the life process; the articulation of a modern ideal of personal development; and a set of prescriptions for educational practice.

Indeed, in the very same essay Simmel went on to observe that 'the fundamental, dynamic unity of life continually offers resistance to [this crisis of culture], and forces the alienating objectivity to return back to the source of life itself' (1968a: 235). Although in that piece Simmel could only appeal to the energizing effects of the First World War as an instance of this reunifying process, in other writings he leaves open the ways in which this return to basic, vital roots might manifest itself.

At this point we should take note of the centrality of the concept of life in Simmel's thought more generally. The prominence of Kantian motifs in Simmel's work has tended to obscure the equally prominent role of vitalistic motifs. Far from being an afterthought inspired by Bergson, the notion of life process played a foundational role throughout Simmel's career. Some of his early writings, including the doctoral essay on music and the paper on 'evolutionary epistemology' of 1896, were clearly inspired by Darwinian theory. Throughout his middle years he was engaged with the figures from the German tradition who focused on vitalistic principles — with Goethe, Schopenhauer and Nietzsche. With his culminating philosophic work, *Lebensanschauung* (1918), Simmel explicitly articulated a series of notions about the life process.

Viewed from the perspective of his philosophy of life, the contradictions of modern culture represent no more than an intensification of that conflict between life process and generated forms which represents a constitutive feature of life at the symbolic level. If the cultural forms, with their fragmenting and oppressing demands, seem to be out of control, that imbalance is bound, sooner or later, to evoke a reaction, because the life-related 'positive and meaningful elements of culture always produce counterforces' (1968a: 235). And the energy of the life process is essentially a force that animates individual lives:

> Life is a stream whose [individual] drops are its essence. Life does not pass through them; rather, its flowing is nothing other than their existence. . . . The more that life manifests itself at the psychic level, the more we perceive its greatest concentration, its highest vitality, as it were — and precisely here [we find] the highest individuality of the single being. (1968a: 205-6)

Moreover, just as human reality exists in the form of individualized beings, so moral obligation, in Simmel's mature view, must be understood as flowing from the character of the individual. The categorical imperative cannot take the form of a universal maxim, because universals are external to the ethical person and not an expression of the individual's own authentic being. Moral obligation does not express some external content, but flows from the idealization of the life process. Reality and value remain two irreducibly different modes of categorizing all the contents of life, but the distinction does not correspond to that between individuality and generality; rather, the distinction falls within each individual existence. The ethical moment relates not to some external purpose, but 'is determined by the developing life out of its own roots' (1919: 239, 1968a: 226). A further implication of this 'vitalization and individualization of ethics' is that one's moral imperative does not remain fixed for all time, but changes in accord with the integration of emerging ethical decisions; for just as each increment of warranted knowledge subtly changes the entire configuration of our cognitive sensibility, so each new ethical decision affects our entire moral personality. In consequence, 'the responsibility for our entire history lies in the emerging duty of every single action' (*Schon in dem Gesolltwerden jedes einzelnen Tuns liegt die Verantwortung für unsere ganze Geschichte* (1919: 243, 1968a: 228).

To hold this position is not to espouse a doctrine of egoism or even of individual self-perfection, Simmel advises us. That one's ideal conception should flower forth from the roots of one's individual life does not entail that its contents must necessarily turn back to that source. Those contents could just as readily be turned into social, altruistic, spiritual or artistic directions. What matters is simply that the ideal stems from the inner resources of the individual person.

With this formulation of a doctrine of an individualized ethics, which he terms *das individuelle Gesetz* (the Individual Law), Simmel consummated his life-long quest to represent the liberation of individual personality in the modern order. He has supplemented his delineation of ways in which the modern individual has become liberated from external social constraints with an argument for liberation of individuals from external ideal norms. He has proclaimed a novel doctrine which makes the ethically free individual as well as the empirically liberated individual the foundation for interpreting the modern human order.[3]

IV

The cultivation of individual autonomy and integrity as an antidote to the crisis of modern culture was not the only thing Simmel analysed in his abstract speculations. He also devoted considerable thought to the ways in which such individuality could be promoted. The main vehicle of this concern was his analysis of appropriate educational practices.[4] In fact, in the very year in which Simmel published his 'Crisis of Culture' essay, he offered a course of lectures on educational theory at the University of Strassburg. Since wartime conditions had converted the main university building into a hospital, he delivered these lectures in the Botanical Institute. They were published posthumously, in 1922, as *Schulpädagogik*. No less than Comte, Spencer, Durkheim, Dewey and Mead, Simmel complemented his social theory with systematic attention to the problems of pedagogy.

Schulpädagogik sets forth a rich array of pedagogical principles and practices, but it is informed by the core intention of helping students develop as complete, individual personalities. Simmel's sense of the critical tension between objective and subjective culture pervades its argument. He looks continually for ways to promote the process of *Bildung*, the cultivation of subjective powers through the utilization of objective contents.

The old-fashioned view of the student as a vessel into which information is to be dumped has given way to the modern ideal of engaging the student actively in a learning process. But the contemporary school system, Simmel notes, has not departed very much from that old-time 'objectivism'. Rather than indulge in fruitless criticism, Simmel (1922: 12) says he will ask simply: 'Taking schools as they are, how can one become the best possible teacher?'

The best approach is to follow a 'genetic method', bringing instructional materials to the students in accord with the stages of their organic development. Since objective knowledge figures here as a means to the end of developing the student as a complete human being, the point is not to amass a certain amount of information, least of all by rote memorization. 'Nothing should be learned which does not in some way contribute to the life of the student — be it through a strengthening of the energy for a certain function which this learning carries, or through the farther-reaching significance which this content wins for the depth, clarity, breadth, and moral constitution of the student' (1922: 22).

Acknowledging the individuality of the student means that the unconditional authority of the teacher must be renounced, since mastery of a certain subject-matter now forms only part of the teacher's relevant qualifications. Attending to the differing interests and capacities of students means that *patience* must become one of the most essential qualifications of a teacher, as well as the ability to take stock of the student's total personality through *non-judgemental* observation. Successful teaching in this mode involves appealing to the experience of the students, engaging their interest in the subject by showing its connections to their own lives, and evoking a certain mood in the class that is appropriate to the subject-matter being discussed.

Moral education, like every other instructional domain, should be subordinated to the broader ideal of cultivating one's full humanity, an ideal that encompasses 'power, spiritual meaning, pride, and *joie de vivre*' (1922: 114). Moral development should be enhanced neither through didactic exposition of ethical principles nor through mechanistic reinforcement of moral conduct. Instead, Simmel calls for a third approach, one which encourages students to engage in moral practices in ways that lead them to reflect on the moral principles they embody. He urges teachers to help students appreciate moral practices, not on the basis of external pressures like belief in authority but out of inner conviction. Indeed, his pedagogical approach emphasizes the importance of appealing to the students' inner motivations and eliciting responses that proceed from their own free will. Thus, while advising teachers frankly to acknowledge differences in students' capacities, he recommends that they reward students on the basis of their effort, industry and attentiveness, not on the basis of their natural gifts.

Time and again, Simmel presents ideas for how to make the materials of objective culture pertinent to the individual student's development as a complete human being. Decrying the current atomization of disciplines, he advocates a curriculum which offers the student a coherent sequence of learning experiences — and makes the student aware of that coherence. He defines the teacher's goal as that of making himself superfluous as students come to learn for themselves and to internalize a schema of intellectual connections flexible enough to facilitate the acquisition of new knowledge. The task of the good teacher, in short, is to provide a continuous setting for overcoming the crisis of modern culture.

Although Simmel's lectures on pedagogy were aimed at pre-collegiate teachers, we should also take note of the ways in which he adhered to their principles in his role as a university teacher. Indeed, his prowess as a lecturer was legendary; no other eminent figure in sociology earned so dazzling a reputation as a classroom teacher. What counts here, of course, is not his reputation but the practices he followed in using his teaching to stimulate the independent thinking of his listeners. Both from his many published lectures and from the reports of former students we can discern the working of the principles Simmel articulated in *Schulpädagogik* — the way he prodded listeners to think by laying down a certain line of thought, then abruptly challenging the assumptions he had just elaborated; his frequent use of analogies to connect insights on particular topics to diverse domains of culture; his appeal to the life experiences of listeners as a basis for deriving or exemplifying quite abstract notions. What he said of his great treatise on money — that its point was to demonstrate 'the possibility . . . of finding in each of life's details the totality of its meaning' (1978: 55) — was true of a good many of his expository efforts. And that work contains a number of passages with profound curricular and pedagogical implications.[5] That Simmel's ability as a teacher weighed on his mind appears from a reminiscence conveyed by one of his many distinguished former students, Martin Buber.[6] Before leaving for Strassburg, Buber recalled, Simmel asked him with some trepidation just what, finally, he had given to his students in Berlin. Buber's reply — 'you taught them how to think' — seemed to leave him satisfied (Gassen and Landmann, 1958: 223).

In this light Simmel's famous testamentary statement, that he was leaving behind no disciples, but a legacy like cash — 'distributed to many heirs, each transforming his part into use according to *his* nature' (1919: 121) — takes on a special meaning. The author of that statement had of course produced an acute analysis of the significance of money for personal growth: that it maximizes the freedom of individuals to pursue their own interests and develop their personalities in accord with their innermost dispositions and aspirations. Consistent to the end, Simmel evinced a radical respect for the individuality and developmental capacities of every person.

V

Recalling now the interpretive schema presented at the beginning of this article, we may summarize its argument as follows. For Simmel, the most salient effects of the factors which produced the modern order — the enlargement of societies and the concentration of populations in large cities, the extended division of labour and the widespread use of money as a generalized medium of exchange — produced a number of transformations which benefit humanity. These take the form of an unprecedented liberation of individuals from social constraints, and the opening up of unprecedented opportunities for their individual development. At the same time, these same forces have introduced new kinds of human problems, represented by phenomena which others have described as anomie and alienation, changes which seriously threaten the moral integration and cultural development of individuals. The threats to subjective culture have become so acute that Simmel came to describe the modern order as marked by a chronic state of crisis.

As an antidote to this crisis, Simmel appealed, by precept and example, to a kind of educational process that focused on the development of the potentialities of the individual person. His programme is familiar to us today under the name of 'liberal education'. In the key elements of the crisis which Simmel diagnosed, we may recognize some central motifs of the philosophy of liberal education in our time: to counter the fetishism of techniques and methods with a return of attention to ultimate human purposes; to counter the atomization of the disciplines with a sense of the connectedness of the different domains of culture; and to counter the alienation of objectified culture by connecting knowledge with the cultivation of human powers, and with its roots in the ongoing flow of the life process.

In the repertoire of models and metaphors about modernity we inherit from the classic tradition, Simmel's distinctive contribution remains timely. We continue to experience the chronic crisis he depicted so acutely; we continue to need the antidotes he outlined so thoughtfully. And, as we pursue our quest to make sense of the modern order by considering the other great theories in that repertoire, we shall find ourselves returning again to Simmel, securing stimulation from those evocative glosses on what he calls 'the deepest mystery of our world view. Individuality — this unanalyzable unity, which is not to be derived from anything else, not subsumable under any higher concept, set within a world otherwise infinitely analyzable, calculable and governed by general laws — this individuality [which] stands for us [moderns] as the actual focal point of love' (1971: 244, 242).

Notes

An earlier version of this article was presented at the conference, 'Culture, Eros and Modern Society: Contemporary Potentialities in Georg Simmel's Sociological and Cultural Theories', Bergen, Norway, 21–22 May 1990.

1. The following few pages draw on Levine (1981).

2. This misreading is promoted by the way certain passages are rendered in the English translation. Thus, Frisby misleadingly translates what Simmel intends as 'de-rooting of the personality' (*Entwurzelung der Persönlichkeit*), the destabilization that ensues under some conditions of emancipation, as 'extirpation of the personality', and mistranslates the passage where Simmel argues that diffuse personal relations are dissolved in the segmental transactions of monetarized relationships as: 'such a personality is almost completely destroyed under the conditions of a money economy' (1978: 400, 296, 1989: 1, 393).

3. With his doctrine of the Individual Law, which began to take shape in the early years of this century, Simmel thus emerged as the first systematic philosopher to propound some of the central tenets of what became known as existentialism. As a system of normative ethics, of course, it remains vulnerable to the various objections which have been levied against existentialist ethics generally.

4. Rüdiger Kramme has independently provided convergent documentation of Simmel's stance as an actively engaged philosopher, with an analysis of Simmel's efforts to promote the humanistic development of modern individuals through his

work for the journal *Logos,* in 'Fragments of Life/The Enclosure of Being — Simmel's Philosophy of Culture, 1908-1918', a paper presented at the conference, 'Culture, Eros and Modern Society: Contemporary Potentialities in Georg Simmel's Sociological and Cultural Theories', Bergen, Norway, 21-22 May 1990.

5. 'No one speaking his mother tongue senses the objective law-like regularities that he has to consult, like something outside of his own subjectivity, in order to borrow from them resources for expressing his feelings — resources that obey independent norms. . . . In the same way, people who know only one uniform style which permeates their whole life will perceive this style as being identical with its *contents.* Since everything they create or contemplate is naturally expressed in this style, there are no psychological grounds for distinguishing it from the material of the formative and contemplative process or for contrasting the style as a form independent of the self.'

'Intelligence definitely requires fusing with general life-energy. However, the more it coalesces with specific forms of that energy, for example, religious, political, sensual, etc., the more it is in danger of being unable to develop its own independent direction. Thus, artistic production at the levels of particular refinement and spirituality depends on a higher degree of intellectual training; but it will be able to profit by that development, or even to bear it, only if the straining is not too specialized but rather unfolds its range and its depth only in more general fields of knowledge.' (Simmel, 1978: 462, 314).

6. The roster of Simmel's former students includes such luminaries as Ernst Bloch, Ortega y Gasset, Georg Lukács, Robert Park, Max Scheler, Herman Schmalenbach and Albert Schweitzer.

References

Ferguson, A. (1966) *Essay on the History of Civil Society.* Edinburgh: Edinburgh University Press.

Gassen, K. and M. Landmann (eds) (1958) *Buch des Dankes an Georg Simmel.* Berlin: Duncker & Humblot.

Green, B. (1988) *Literary Methods and Sociological Theory: Case Studies of Simmel and Weber.* Chicago: University of Chicago Press.

Levine, D.N. (1981) 'Sociology's Quest for the Classics: The Case of Simmel' in B. Rhea (ed.), *The Future of the Sociological Classics.* London: George Allen & Unwin.

Levine, D.N. (1985) *The Flight from Ambiguity: Essays in Social and Cultural Theory.* Chicago: University of Chicago Press.

Simmel, G. (1890) *Über soziale Differenzierung.* Leipzig: Duncker & Humblot.

Simmel, G. (1908) *Soziologie.* Leipzig: Duncker & Humblot.

Simmel, G. (1918) *Lebensanschauung.* Munich and Leipzig: Duncker & Humblot.

Simmel, G. (1919) 'Nachgelassenes Tagebuch,' *Logos* VII.

Simmel, G. (1922) *Schulpädagogik.* Osterwieck/Harz: A.W. Zickfeldt.

Simmel, G. (1968a) *Das Individuelle Gesetz: Philosophische Exkurse.* Edited by M. Landmann. Frankfurt: Suhrkamp Verlag.

Simmel, G. (1968b) 'On the Concept and Tragedy of Culture', in *The Conflict in Modern Culture and Other Essays.* Translated by K.P. Etzkorn. New York: The Teachers' College Press.

Simmel, G. (1968c) 'The Conflict in Modern Culture', in *The Conflict in Modern Culture and Other Essays*. Trans. K.P. Etzkorn. New York: Teachers' College Press.

Simmel, G. (1971) *On Individuality and Social Forms*. Edited by D.N. Levine. Chicago: University of Chicago Press.

Simmel, G. (1978) *The Philosophy of Money*. Translated by T. Bottomore and D. Frisby. London: Routledge & Kegan Paul.

Simmel, G. (1989) *Philosophie des Geldes*, Vol. 6, in *Georg Simmel: Gesamtausgabe*. Edited by D.P. Frisby and K.C. Köhnke. Frankfurt: Suhrkamp.

Smith, A. (1965) *The Wealth of Nations*. Edited by E. Cannan. New York: Modern Library. (Originally published 1776.)

Donald N. Levine is Professor of Sociology at the University of Chicago. He is author of *The Flight From Ambiguity* and editor of *Georg Simmel: On Individuality and Social Forms*, both published by the University of Chicago Press.

The Body

Social Process and Cultural Theory

Edited by **Mike Featherstone** *Teesside Polytechnic* **Mike Hepworth** *University of Aberdeen* and **Bryan S Turner** *University of Essex*

Traditionally the social sciences have worked within dichotomies which have profoundly influenced western thought: body/soul and nature/culture. Whereas anthropology has recognised the importance of human bodies, sociology has tended to treat the individual as a disembodied decision-making agent. Yet contemporary societies exhibit a profound concern over bodily practice. This is expressed not only through pervasive concepts of bodily health, fitness and beauty, but also in relation to sexuality - exemplified in particular by concerns with female sexuality, homosexuality and AIDS.

This challenging volume, drawing in part on papers published in *Theory, Culture & Society,* reasserts the centrality of the body within social theory as a means to understanding the complex interrelations between nature, culture and society. At a theoretical level, the volume explores the origins of a social theory of the body in sources ranging from the work of Nietzsche to contemporary feminist theory. The importance of a theoretical understanding of the body to social and and cultural analysis of contemporary societies is demonstrated through specific case studies. These range from the expression of the emotions, romantic love, dietary practice, consumer culture, fitness and beauty, to media images of women and sexuality.

November 1990 · 352 pages
Cloth (8039-8412-X) · **£27.50**
Paper (8039-8413-8) · £12.95

SAGE Publications Ltd
6 Bonhill Street
London EC2A 4PU

The Berlin Trade Exhibition

Georg Simmel

In his *Deutsche Geschichte* Karl Lamprecht relates how certain
medieval orders of knights gradually lost their practical purpose
but continued as sociable gatherings. This is a type of sociological
development that is similarly repeated in the most diverse fields. The
double meaning of the word 'society' symbolizes this twin sense.
Alongside the very process of sociation there is also, as a byproduct,
the sociable meaning of society. The latter is always a meeting-point
for the most diverse formation of interest groups, thus remaining
as the sole integrating force even when the original reasons for con-
sociation have lost their effectiveness. The history of world exhibitions, which originated from annual fairs, is one of the clearest
examples of this most fundamental type of human sociation. The
extent to which this process can be found in the Berlin exhibition
alone allows it to be placed in the category of world exhibitions.
In the face of the richness and diversity of what is offered, the
only unifying and colourful factor is that of amusement. The way
in which the most heterogeneous industrial products are crowded
together in close proximity paralyses the senses — a veritable hyp-
nosis where only one message gets through to one's consciousness:
the idea that one is here to amuse oneself. Through frequency
of repetition this impression overwhelms countless no less worthy
impressions, which because of their fragmentation fail to register.
The sense of amusement emerges as a common denominator due to
a petty but psychologically subtle arrangement: every few steps a
small entry fee is charged for each special display. One's curio-
sity is thus constantly aroused by each new display, and the enjoyment derived from each particular display is made to seem greater
and more significant. The majority of things which must be passed
creates the impression that many surprises and amusements are in
store. In short, the return to the main motif, amusement, is more

Theory, Culture & Society (SAGE, London, Newbury Park and New Delhi), Vol. 8
(1991), 119–123

effectively achieved by having to make a small sacrifice, which overcomes one's inhibitions to indulge, than if a higher entry price, giving unrestricted access, was charged, thereby denying that continuous small stimulation.

Every fine and sensitive feeling, however, is violated and seems deranged by the mass effect of the merchandise offered, while on the other hand it cannot be denied that the richness and variety of fleeting impressions is well suited to the need for excitement for overstimulated and tired nerves. While increasing civilization leads to ever greater specialization and to a more frequent one-sidedness of function within an evermore limited field, in no way does this differentiation on the side of production extend to consumption. Rather the opposite: it appears as though modern man's one-sided and monotonous role in the division of labour will be compensated for by consumption and enjoyment through the growing pressure of heterogeneous impressions, and the ever faster and more colourful change of excitements. The differentiation of the active side of life is apparently complemented through the extensive diversity of its passive and receiving side. The press of contradictions, the many stimuli and the diversity of consumption and enjoyment are the ways in which the human soul — that otherwise is an impatient flux of forces and denied a complete development by the differentiations within modern work — seeks to come alive. No part of modern life reveals this need as sharply as the large exhibition. Nowhere else is such a richness of different impressions brought together so that overall there seems to be an outward unity, whereas underneath a vigorous interaction produces mutual contrasts, intensification and lack of relatedness.

Now this unity of the whole creates a stronger impression and becomes more interesting when one considers the impossibility of surveying the objects produced in a single city. It is only as a floating psychological idea that this unity can be apprehended since in its origins the styles and emerging trends receive no clear expression. It is a particular attraction of world fairs that they form a momentary centre of world civilization, assembling the products of the entire world in a confined space as if in a single picture. Put the other way round, a single city has broadened into the totality of cultural production. No important product is missing, and though much of the material and samples have been brought together from the whole world they have attained a conclusive form and become part of a single whole. Thus it becomes clear what is meant by a 'world city' and that Berlin, despite everything, has become one. That is, a single city to which the whole world sends its products and where all the important styles of the present cultural world are put on display. In this sense perhaps the Berlin exhibition is unique, perhaps it has never been so apparent before how much the form of modern culture has permitted a concentration in one place, not in the mere collection of exhibits as in a world fair, but how through its own production a city can represent itself as a copy and a sample of the manufacturing forces of world culture.

It is a point of some cultural historical interest to follow how a particular style for such exhibitions has developed. The specific exhibition style is seen at its clearest in the buildings. An entirely new proportion between permanence and transience not only predominates in the hidden structure but also in the aesthetic criteria. In doing this the materials and their intrinsic properties have achieved a complete harmony in their external design, so satisfying one of the most fundamental demands of all art. The majority of the buildings, in particular the main ones, look as if they were intended for temporary purposes; because this lack of permanence is unmistakable they are absolutely ineffective as unsolid buildings. And the impression of lack of solidity works only where the temporary can claim permanence and durability. In the exhibition style the imagination of the architect is freed from the stipulation of permanence, allowing grace and dignity to be combined in their own measure. It is the conscious denial of a monumental style that has produced a new and positive shape. Elsewhere it is the meaning of art to incorporate the permanence of form in transient materials, and the ideal of architecture is to strive to give expression to the permanent, whereas here the attraction of the transient forms its own style and, even more characteristically, does this from material that doesn't appear as if it was intended for temporary use. And in fact the architects of our exhibition have succeeded in making the opposition to the historical ideal of architecture not a matter of absurdity or lack of style; rather they have taken the point last reached in architecture as their starting-point, as if only this arrangement would allow its meaning to emerge fully against a differently coloured background and yet be seen as part of a single tradition.

It is on the architectural side that this exhibition reaches its acme, demonstrating the aesthetic output of the exhibition principle. From another point of view its productivity is at least as high: and here

I refer to what could be termed the shop-window quality of things, a characteristic which the exhibition accentuates. The production of goods under the regime of free competition and the normal predominance of supply over demand leads to goods having to show a tempting exterior as well as utility. Where competition no longer operates in matters of usefulness and intrinsic properties, the interest of the buyer has to be aroused by the external stimulus of the object, even the manner of its presentation. It is at the point where material interests have reached their highest level and the pressure of competition is at an extreme that the aesthetic ideal is employed. The striving to make the merely useful visually stimulating — something that was completely natural for the orientals and Romans — for us comes from the struggle to render the graceless graceful for consumers. The exhibition with its emphasis on amusement attempts a new synthesis between the principles of external stimulus and the practical functions of objects, and thereby takes this aesthetic superadditum to its highest level. The banal attempt to put things in their best light, as in the cries of the street trader, is transformed in the interesting attempt to confer a new aesthetic significance from displaying objects together — something already happening in the relationship between advertising and poster art.

Indeed it strikes one as curious that the separate objects in an exhibition show the same relationships and modifications that are made by the individual within society. On the one side, the depreciation of an otherwise qualified neighbour, on the other, accentuation at the expense of the same; on the one side, the levelling and uniformity due to an environment of the same, on the other, the individual is even more accentuated through the summation of many impressions; on the one side, the individual is only an element of the whole, only a member of a higher unity, on the other, the claim that the same individual is a whole and a unity. Thus the objective relation between social elements is reflected in the impression of things in unison within a single frame yet composed of interactively excited forces, and of contradictions, yet also their confluence. Just as in the exhibition the contours of things in their interactive effects, their moving to and fro undergoes an aesthetic exploitation, so in society the corresponding patterns allow an ethical use.

German, in particular north German, exhibitions could compete only with difficulty with French ones where the ability to accentuate by all means possible the stimulus of appearance has a much longer history and wider applicability. Nevertheless this exhibition shows the attempt, often successful, to develop aesthetic opportunities which through display can contribute to their attractiveness. Certainly the qualities of taste are mostly lacking in the individual items of the exhibition. Aside from the practical motive of Berlin's exhibition, it is to be hoped at the least that the aesthetic impulse is encouraged beyond the exhibition itself and becomes part of the way products are presented.

Translated by Sam Whimster.

Note

This article is a translation of 'Berliner Gewerbeausstellung', *Die Zeit* (Wien) 7 (91): 204ff., 1896. The translator, Sam Whimster, thanks Ralph Schroeder for reading through the final draft of this translation.

The British Journal
of Aesthetics

Editor: T.J. Diffey, University of Sussex

The British Journal of Aesthetics is one of the leading journals for philosophical discussion on the international scene. Its main purpose is to provide a medium for study of the philosophy of art and the principles of aesthetic judgement, in the context of all the arts. In addition to general aesthetics, experience of both fine and applied art is examined from the point of view of the psychologist, and the general critic.

Forthcoming articles will include:
Ole Martin Skilleås Anachronistic Themes
and Literary Value: *The Tempest*
M.R. Haight Conditional Essences
Margaret A. Rose Post-Modern Pastiche
George Pattison Kierkegaard: Aesthetics and
'The Aesthetic'
M.A.R. Habib Horace's *Ars Poetica*
and the Deconstructive Leech
Peter Abbs From Babble to Rhapsody:
On the Nature of Creativity
Jerome Stolnitz On the Historical Triviality of Art
Cheryl Foster Schopenhauer's Subtext on Natural Beauty

Subscription rates Volume 31 (4 issues)
UK & Europe: £42.00; Elsewhere: US$90.00

To subscribe, obtain further information
or a *free* sample copy of this journal, please write to:
Journals Marketing Dept. (X), Oxford University Press,
Southfield Road, Eynsham, Oxford OX8 1JJ, UK

Oxford Journals

On Simmel's Aesthetics: Argumentation in the Journal Jugend, 1897-1906

Otthein Rammstedt

'To be perfectly frank about it, I am not very enchanted with the fact that this casual joke should continue living in any consciousness. I ask you in any case to treat my authorship with absolute discretion,' Georg Simmel wrote to William Stern in 1902. Heinrich Rickert had referred Stern to the essay, 'Metaphysics of Laziness' [Metaphysik der Faulheit] (1900c), which had appeared in *Jugend* — signed 'G.S.'. The author's plea for discretion can hardly keep those of us in later generations from investigating this essay as a Simmel text.

But this request for discretion was probably not meant so seriously by Simmel, either. For it can be asked why he signed this contribution 'G.S.' like many others in the same journal, why he introduced himself in the articles as a scientist, a philosopher, why he gave the fictitious son in the articles the name of his real son Hans, why he spontaneously 'reacted' to personal experiences in the essays, without fictionalizing them. All this would have to have made it appear improbable to Simmel that his 'authorship would remain absolutely confidential', for many of his literary acquaintances were also contributors to *Jugend*, including Dehmel and Paul Ernst, von Hofmannsthal and Keyserling, Mühsam and Rilke, Gleichen-Russwurm (and later also) Sombart. And for them it would have been easy enough to identify the initials 'G.S.'.

Additionally, Simmel himself contributed to the indiscretions by circulating his contributions among his circle of friends, or talking about them, as his son Hans still reports. Thus one can ask whether the joke was really considered so 'casual' by Simmel, as he would have had Stern believe. Would he then have sent a copy to Rickert, who at the time, around 1900, was not yet among Simmel's closest

Theory, Culture & Society (SAGE, London, Newbury Park and New Delhi), Vol. 8 (1991), 125-144

friends; would he then have handed this 'Satire on the Tragedy of Philosophy', as its subtitle reads, from one philosopher to another? The 'Metaphysics of Laziness' is no more a casual joke than are any of the other contributions to *Jugend*.

On the one hand, the 'Metaphysics of Laziness' is aimed at Paul Lafargue's 'The Right to be Lazy' (1887). Lafargue had been familiar to Simmel for some time. He was after all a prominent contributor to Karl Kautsky's *Die neue Zeit*, in which Georg Simmel also occasionally published, although always anonymously. In addition, Simmel had occupied himself extensively with Marxist thinking when he wrote his *Die Philosophie des Geldes* (1900a) as one can see from the introduction to that work. And the circle around *Die neue Zeit* was the centre of contemporary Marxism: Bebel, Bernstein, Engels, Lafargue, Liebknecht, Mehring, Schippel, and Sorge are explicitly listed on the cover of this 'review of intellectual and public life'.

On the other hand, the 'Metaphysics of Laziness' gets stuck on the methodological admonition that too much generalization can bring about banality.

Simmel's publications in *Jugend* are strikingly different from his other publications in periodicals and newspapers. After hearing attacks against writings of this type in connection with his subsequently unsuccessful nomination to a professorial post in Heidelberg, Simmel writes in a letter to Georg Jellinek of 11 September 1909, of his publications in such outlets:

> As far as I can recall, I have never written *for* a newspaper; everything I have published in them were suitable parts from my larger works. I actually consider it a cultural task not unworthy of a philosopher to present to the broadest possible public a certain intellectual opinion on and absorption in precisely the most superficial and everyday phenomena. *This* is the reason I have accepted the form of a feature article or a periodical piece, which I do not particularly care for in and of themselves. That form always takes something to overcome, but I hope to have contributed my bit to intellectual culture with it.

Simmel's contributions to *Jugend* are indebted to the spirit of this 'Illustrated Munich Weekly for Art and Life', which after 1896 soon became an organ against artists and authors who considered their narrow themes surpassed by the 'Jugendstil' conceptions of the work of art, and who joyfully joined in with the credo that Georg Hirth had intoned in the preface to the third volume of *Jugend*:

Our times are not old, not tired! We are not living among the last gasps of a dying epoch. We are at the dawn of a thoroughly healthy time. It is a joy to be alive!

There was no actual agenda for *Jugend*. 'We wish to present everything that is beautiful, good, characteristic, jaunty – and genuinely artistic', Hirth had proclaimed. But what came together in *Jugend* was in fact connected by more than the 'genuinely artistic'.

People rebelled against clericalism and aristocracy, pilloried the reviving conservatism and emphasized the hypocritical and anachronistic aspects of decadence of the *fin de siècle*. As in *Pan*, in *Das Narrenschiff* or in *Simplizissimus*, political and social satire was cultivated, but *Jugend* deliberately wished to distinguish itself from those others. It did not wish to emphasize criticism so exclusively; it wanted to aim generally at art and life, to thematize 'art, ornamentation, decorating, fashion, sports, politics and literature' (Hirth). The first issues accordingly contained musical supplements with original compositions by Richard Strauss, August Bungert and other composers. *Jugend* was more interested in being a springboard than a net, and thus in being more open to young people.

Until the First World War, *Jugend* represented the emancipatory aspect of art nouveau and an intellectual commitment to Ibsen and Nietzsche. A quarter century later, Walter Benjamin even stated:

> One can say that Munich's *Jugend* was the central organ of that mysterious 'emancipation movement', which resides in the mood of those verses, 'Place the fragrant mignonettes upon the table, Bring forth the final red asters . . .

Georg Simmel in *Jugend* seems to be a different, a 'casual' Simmel, by comparison to the Simmel familiar to us from 'Über Soziale Differenzierung' (1890c) to the *Lebensanschauugen* (written 1918, pub. 1922). Thirty contributions to *Jugend* by Simmel have been identified so far: poems, collections of aphorisms, fairy-tales, a joke and then the small stories and collections of thoughts, eight of the latter under the title 'Snapshots *sub specie aeternitatis*'.[1]

All these Simmel publications in *Jugend* display a directness that distinguishes them from his other philosophizing newspaper articles, which otherwise strive for popularization. While some of the themes addressed are familiar, they remain separated in their substantive treatment. Thus 'Beyond Beauty' (*Jugend*, 1897a) versus 'Sociological Aesthetics' (1896a), or 'Theistic Fantasies of a Fin-de-siècle Man' (*Jugend*, 1898a) versus *Sociology of Religion* (1898b), thus 'Only a Bridge' (*Jugend*, 1901c) versus *Bridge and Door* (1909b), or 'Money Alone Does not Bring Happiness' (*Jugend*, 1901b) versus *The Philosophy of Money* (1900a), or 'Flirtation' (*Jugend*, 1901d) versus *The Psychology of Flirtation* (1909a). One can consider his apparently final contribution in *Jugend*, 'Fragments from a Philosophy of Love' (1907a) an exception. It reappears in part in the posthumously published 'Fragment on Love' (1921).

Simmel took up themes in *Jugend* which must seem marginal to empirical science. By problematizing aesthetics, religion or love as a relativizing assessment of theories and methods, he appeared to be subordinating his own 'modern' sociological, Darwinist-evolutionary, theoretical approach. Indeed, when treating these themes, he consciously declined to build upon that which he had already discussed; instead, he started afresh each time. And the results — whether presented as a moral philosophical quintessence or ironically alienated in the manner of Heine — do not overlap. The connection is in almost all cases the author's own involvement, the personal aspect of the problematic under discussion.

Simmel's 'Sociological Aesthetics', which had appeared in *Die Zukunft* (1896a), was written in the scientific manner that he like many other, mostly younger, scholars considered 'modern and progressive', as Simmel put it in a letter to the publisher of his *Einleitung in die Moralwissenschaft* [Introduction to the Moral Sciences] (1892/93).[2] The starting-point for the considerations is a Darwinistic interpretation of beauty, which on the one hand, appeals to the 'material utility of objects' (Simmel, 1896a: 212). On the other, it interprets perception as the resonance 'in the individuals' of the 'adaptations and feelings of utility of the species' (Simmel, 1896a: 213). If Simmel generally sees the essence of the aesthetic in the fact that 'the type appears in the individual, the law in the contingent, and the essence and significance of things in the superficial and fleeting' (Simmel, 1896a: 205), then that which is peculiarly aesthetic is subject to evolutionary changes, which are said to become tangible in a respective 'dualism of tendencies in thought and life' (Simmel, 1896a: 204). For the present era, such a dualism is addressed formulaically in the confrontation of the socialistic and the individualistic tendencies; this dualism is irreconcilable, in fact it is becoming fruitful, since it takes effect 'in one species of beings, indeed in the individual psyche' (Simmel, 1896a: 207).

Almost a year after this aesthetic article which pointed the way for Simmel, the brief article 'Beyond Beauty' appeared in the second volume of *Jugend* (1897a). He proceeded playfully from the thesis 'that the beautiful does not have value and dignity'. The ideal of beauty, he writes, carries within itself 'the secret promise of full attainability and thus draws a bill on reality which reality will never honor'. Therefore, the 'ideal of ugliness' should be made the standard and measure of all things, as an 'organic adaptation of psyches to their world'.

Beauty and ugliness are posited antagonistically by Simmel here; there is no connection between them. In this respect he distinguishes himself from the 'Sociological Aesthetics'. In the latter he had alleged that aesthetic consideration can even draw a 'charming significance' from that which is 'lowest and ugliest in and of itself'. And additionally, Simmel was convinced there of the psychological rule that 'our feelings are connected to distinctions' so that the beautiful is only conceivable by comparison with the ugly — and vice versa.

This mutual and natural dependence, however, is precisely what he denied in the *Jugend* article. For here he claimed that 'the beautiful' has 'value and dignity in itself', no matter 'by what convoluted baroque paths the ugly grows into the beautiful'. Indeed, in a first attempt he removed beauty from any empirical accessibility, which is natural for the Darwinistic, evolutionary approach, by stating:

> And it is also really not as if just a little bit were missing so that things would be beautiful; just *one* more breath and glimmer, *one* redeeming word, a final rousing and culmination, as if beauty were always hidden right behind things, and they and we only needed to reach out for it. (Simmel, 1897a: 234)

Now it is also possible to call 'Beyond Beauty' a 'casual joke' — and this time in the argumentation of Nietzsche. The very title points to Nietzsche's *Beyond Good and Evil: Prelude to a Philosophy of the Future* (1886). And it is indeed the question of dualism which Nietzsche places at the turn to a new philosophy.[3]

And superficially, Simmel plays the simple-minded 'dualist' here, by which he himself slips into the role of Nietzsche's 'new philosopher'. This role can also be interpreted as a joke. If one reads Simmel's slightly earlier article 'Friedrich Nietzsche: A Moral Philosophical Profile' [Friedrich Nietzsche. Eine moralphilosophische Silhouette] (1896b), then it is not only the scholarly commitment to Nietzsche which is striking. An identification by Simmel with the philosopher also seems to come into view, which brings about a stylization of Nietzsche in the essay.[4]

Nietzsche's *Beyond Good and Evil* refers to morality, but Simmel's 'Beyond Beauty' to aesthetics, a tentative application of Nietzsche's argumentation. And that is no ironic plagiarism for Simmel — which is probably why the title does not read 'Beyond Beauty and Ugliness' — it is rather a continuation of Nietzsche.

Already in the Nietzsche essay, Simmel had sensitively remarked that the starting-point for the latter's theory of value, the 'theory of the natural distance of people from one another', provided evidence of the 'influence of aesthetic feeling'.[5]

In contrast to that, Simmel had always favoured a sociological interpretation of art, as he mentioned for the first time in his reflection 'On Art Exhibitions' [Über Kunstausstellungen] in 1890. On the relationship of modern art to the 'public spirit' he wrote:

> The activities of the mass, it is said, are more and more taking the place of the great individualities; the problems of modern culture can be solved less by the strength of the individual personality than by the cooperation of the many, and it is rather collective achievements than original productions of individuals which give the creations of our time their character. Originality has passed from the individual to the group to which he belongs, and from which he receives the type of his activity in fief. Perhaps this also applies to art. (Simmel, 1890a)

In his 'Sociological Aesthetics', he then proceeds from the distance between the socialistic and the individualistic tendencies in art. Only one aspect is taken up in 'Beyond Beauty', and specifically that one which is appropriate to the Nietzsche interpretation. Art as a product of individual genius (in conscious separation from the mass) also conditions a different understanding of aesthetic value, of beauty, for Simmel. For now, beauty no longer appears conceivable in direct social terms, becoming rather something objective for him, in the absolute sense.

Accordingly, different, even seemingly contradictory concepts of aesthetics are found in Simmel's contributions to *Jugend*. In 'Beyond Beauty' (1897a) he questions for the first time his sociological, evolutionary, Darwinistic thoughts on the functionality of aesthetics. He speaks here of the 'ideal' of beauty and articulates the possibility of viewing beauty as 'something objective in the absolute sense' (c.f. Simmel's 1895b view of truth). Two years later, two pieces appeared in *Jugend* in which he came to discuss aesthetic problems. In 'Sound, Little Song of Spring — A Snapshot' [Klinge kleines Frühlingslied — Ein Momentbild] (1899b), he closes with the opinion that the beautiful is perhaps not recognized, and that what is accepted as beautiful is perhaps not the beautiful. Simmel varies these thoughts in a fairy-tale ('On Fulfilled Wishes: Two Very Similar Fairy Tales' [Von erfüllten Wünschen. Zwei sehr ähnliche Märchen] (1899b), in which he places beauty in — tragic — dependence on the perception of beauty, by using the Fichtean relationship of 'I' and 'Thou' as a framework.

This thought is further pursued along two strands. First, he proceeds more and more rigidly in what follows from the 'ideal of beauty', connected explicitly to Plato's 'idea of reality', in which the 'meaning of the world rests' (see Simmel, 1901g, 1902a). Second, there is beauty as experienced by people. The experiencing of beauty ultimately always remains deficient for people, as already mentioned ironically in 'Beyond Beauty': these deficiencies are perceived as an inability of mankind to prove itself worthy of the ideal. Here, Simmel (1901b: 300, 1901a, 1902a) mentions above all the money economy, which altered relationships to things. The money economy is also mentioned in order to relativize the psychic condition that distinction is required in order to perceive something. The enhancement of attraction through the contrasting of perceptions becomes virtually the sign of modernity for Simmel. This condition had been a ubiquitous rule of human perception for him in 'Sociological Aesthetics' and the first contributions to *Jugend* (Simmel, 1897b).[6] Yet in 1899 he reflected: 'Is it not the actual curse of everything human that we can enjoy each thing only by distinction to its other?' And he concludes this thought with the question: 'Have not purity and unity become an unattainable ideal for even our deepest joys, because all our feeling is a feeling of differences?' (Simmel, 1899a: 92).[7] But just as Simmel distinguished in those years around the turn of the century between the ideal of 'beauty' and the 'beauty' that could be experienced by people,[8] he also distinguished between distance as a necessity of the human perceptive ability, distance as a factor for enhancing attraction, and distance as reality.[9]

The knowledge of the necessity of distance, as a means of

knowledge and as a constitutive part of tangible beauty,[10] does not seduce Simmel into cancelling the distance by overcoming binarity, but rather by elevating distance to an end in itself, as he believes he has found in Nietzsche's work.[11] Simmel also sees this end in itself in the aesthetic realm, by denying the predominance of the substantive aspect.[12] The work of art cannot be adequately grasped by intellectual means; rather, it can only be experienced sensorily (emphasized in many places in *Jugend*, e.g. Simmel, 1900c). Thus the form acquires a decisive meaning, which can be heightened through self-referentiality. With his idea of 'detachment', 'self-referentiality' in modern terms, Simmel does justice to the growth in importance of aesthetics in society.[13] Additionally, the idea of detachment results for Simmel in the possibility of being able to dispense with Darwinism in his argumentation — at least for the aesthetic realm — without breaking with the Darwinist theory.

Simmel had begun his sociological career in the 1890s by believing he was modernizing Kant; in view of evolution, Darwinism and socialism as determining factors of modernity,[14] Kant would have to be reformulated in that sense: 'since we can no longer twist things around our ideals, we must conversely attempt to modify our ideals according to reality as it has been recognized', and he demands new 'standards of value' (Simmel, 1891). Simmel had addressed this in *Social Differentiation* [Über Sociale Differenzierung] (1890c), and energetically advocated it in *Introduction to the Moral Sciences* [Einleitung in die Moralwissenschaft] (1892/3) for the educated middle classes, as well as for workers in several articles in the social-democratic newspapers *Vorwärts* and *Die neue Zeit*. The neo-Kantian as a Darwinist socialist — this was probably identical to sociology for Simmel at that time.[15]

After 1896, this changed. Sociology, once (around 1892) the modern science per se, now becomes secondary for Simmel.[16] Indeed, he even claimed to Bouglé that he was the only representative of his sociology. Now materialism and Kantianism had become opposites for him, (see Simmel, 1900a: Introduction) and this man, the great relativist, drew close to Plato.[17] Simmel emphasizes of Plato 'that the impersonal idea, the objectively good is realized', and 'in contrast to all anthropological ethics' (a passage in which Simmel [1896b: 207] sees Nietzsche as a successor of Kant and Plato).

This change begins in the theory of values. The period around the turn of the century, the same time Simmel often published in *Jugend*, was when he often questioned his relativism and flirted with

Platonism. He now spoke of the absolutely good as well as the absolutely true and the absolutely beautiful, and the same aspect also played a part in his reflections on individualism, just as it marked the first considerations of religion. All these themes were often addressed by him in *Jugend*, always with a hint of irony. That permitted him to maintain an apparent distance, which is often supported by the self-ascribed role of the 'old philosopher'. The distancing irony leaves it uncertain how Simmel personally stands on the absolute under discussion, but allows him, almost unnoticed, to speak of absolute values.

While this aspect was only touched upon in discussions of the problem of individuality in *Jugend* — the dependency of *ego* on *alter* was regretted — it points the way towards Simmel's future interests in the religious question and in aesthetics. Both topics occupied him his whole life long after the period of publication in *Jugend*.

He treated religion twice in 1898. His 'Theistic Fantasies of a Fin-de-siècle Man' (Simmel, 1898a) were published in *Jugend* (p. 508). Here he ironically forces God to be God by negating the Enlightenment interpretation of religion as a creation of imperfect mankind. Even if one would subject God scientifically to teleology, forcing him to seek 'the end of his being in the being of the world', one would only reach the result: 'God exists for the sake of the world, which exists for his sake.' Simmel's (1898b) 'On the Sociology of Religion' [Zur Soziologie der Religion] was published the same year. In that article he analysed the social function of religion,[18] discussing the evolution of belief systems, only to distinguish clearly in the end between the social conditionality of all religions and their objective truth.[19] Indeed he stressed explicitly that a sociological derivation of religion does not strip away the 'attraction of an ideal', does not degrade 'the dignity of a feeling', even though the fiction of an 'unexplainable miracle' or a 'creation from nothing' might vanish. 'Understanding the origin' does not call 'the value of what has come into being into question'.

This becomes even more tangible in Simmel's reflections on aesthetics. Publications on this subject suddenly begin in 1895-6, with no connection to his 'Psychological and Ethnological Studies of Music' [Psychologische und ethnologische Studien über Musik] (1882, trans. Simmel, 1968), nor to Gerber's *Sprache als Kunst* (Language as Art), which Simmel had reviewed in 1885. Neither are they akin to his anonymously published 'On Art Exhibitions' [Über Kunstausstellungen] (1890a), nor to his review of *Rembrandt als*

Erzieher [Rembrandt as an Educator] (1890b), which was already similarly sociological in orientation. The 'The Alpine Journey' [Alpenreisen] (trans. in this issue) and 'Böcklin's Landscapes' [Böcklins Landschaften] (1895a), as well as the anonymous 'Berlin Letter on Art' [Berliner Kunstbrief, 1896d] and the 'Sociological Aesthetics [Soziologische Ästhetik] (Simmel, 1896a) prepared the way for the contributions to *Jugend*. When he wrote in that journal: 'You walked like a great question on the beauty of things through a world that gave no answer . . .' (Simmel, 1901c: 200), he addressed beauty as an objective thing to which the perception of beauty is contrasted. Indeed, Simmel made a further differentiation: 'Certainly, the work is pure — but what of our soul? When we think of Plato and St. Francis, of Fra Angelo and Spinoza — don't we see then that our soul, which we offer to the idea, lost its sanctity when it ran into its animalistic double, the ego of egoism, on the way of sacrifice, when it brushed past money, which can touch no one without leaving a stain' (Simmel, 1902a: 446).[20]

He not only pursues the thought of whether aesthetic value is superior to all others, since it can be more generally addressed (see Simmel, 1898d), now he also questions the distance factor. On the one hand, Simmel is aware of the necessity of 'distance' for the process of perception, but on the other hand, 'distance' separates subject and object for him, which, given his sociological orientation, must appear tragic to him in a platonic interpretation. If he follows Nietzsche in the emphasis on 'distance' as a sign of modernity, then he is probably referring to Marx and Hegel in the normative value of 'distance', because it has resemblance to the concept of 'alienation' (see Simmel 1900a, trans. 1990, where he takes up aesthetic arguments in relation to modernity). The fundamental structures of aesthetic argumentation are set for roughly a decade starting from 1895-6, and in that sense, the publications in *Jugend* are no different from such other works as 'Stefan George: An Aesthetic Consideration' (1898d), 'Rome: An Aesthetic Analysis' [Rom. Eine ästhetische Analyse] (1898c), 'Kant and Goethe' [*Kant und Goethe*] (1899/1906b), 'The Aesthetics of Heaviness' [Ästhetik der Schwere] (1901h), 'The Aesthetic Significance of the Face' [Die ästhetische Bedeutung des Gesichts] (1901), 'The Picture Frame: An Aesthetic Essay' [Der Bildrahmen. Ein ästhetischer Versuch] (1902c), 'Rodin's Sculpture and the Intellectual Tendency of the Present Day' [Rodins Plastik und die Geistesrichtung der Gegenwart] (1902d), 'Kant and Modern Aesthetics' [Kant und die moderne Ästhetik] (1903b) or 'On Aesthetic Quantities' (1968) [Über ästhetische Quantitäten] (1903). Beside their continual attempts to draw the limits of this argumentation, what distinguishes the contributions to *Jugend* is their emphasis on tragedy, which is not resumed until years later (Simmel, 1911/12, trans. 1968).

The privileged position of aesthetics in Simmel's reflections is also heightened in the contributions to *Jugend* by his distinguishing of aesthetics from science. For aesthetics can indeed explain beauty, but it cannot make beauty comprehensible.[21] For Simmel, art becomes an alternative world, in which he attempts to establish himself. And apart from his work on *The Philosophy of Money*, published in 1900, his attention and commitment belong to that other world. Simmel's literary forms of expression are probably not a concession to *Jugend*, rather, he probably chose *Jugend* as an organ of publication because he could produce himself literarily there. If Simmel emphasized Nietzsche's linguistic and literary abilities at this time, he also tried to prove himself in the same vein. During this period he saw Nietzsche as the value-setting philosopher, consciously distancing himself from the anaemic scribes who taught philosophy at universities, and Simmel attempted to slip into the same role.

'Snapshots *sub specie aeternitatis*' − these are what Simmel intended to produce literarily − creating values and destroying them. At the same time this title is an affront to academic philosophy. Accordingly, he stressed the limitations of current science in a poem on the turn of the century,[22] aired his views on the 'miracle of banality',[23] as well as on the sense of nonsense,[24] and claimed that every theory is 'only a form' in which the individual's 'personal nature' expresses itself (Simmel, 1897d).

In this phase, Simmel relies on the directness of the access to art. That is why 'distance' is and remains a problem, that is why the 'perspective' one has for something becomes the decisive category (he even demanded this for sociology, see letter to Celestin Bouglé, 22 November 1896 where he emphasizes 'the sociological perspective . . . on which everything depends . . .'). That is why one finds the first reflections on holistic theories (for example, he states '. . . I learned to feel the things, which are much, and do not include the few' (Simmel, 1902b: 446). This phase should therefore be interpreted as a transition, because Simmel's thoughts on the theory of art follow without interruption, and remain almost unchanged from the 'Picture Frame' (1902c) to *Rembrandt* (1916) (see, for example, Utitz, 1920). It can also be interpreted as a dead end, an uncompleted attempt, a phase that Simmel denies having lived through ex post facto in his unfinished autobiography. For there, he claims to have started from the basic concept of sociology (1894) and hit upon the concept of interaction (*Wechselwirkung*), which became 'gradually an all-encompassing metaphysical concept for me:'

> The temporal dissolution of everything substantial, absolute and eternal into the flow of things, into historical mutability, into merely psychological reality, seems to me assured against a groundless subjectivism and skepticism, only if one replaces those substantially solid values with the living interactions of elements, which in turn are subject to the same dissolution into the infinite. The central concepts of truth, value, objectivity and so on arose for me as interactions, as contents of a relativism, which now no longer means the skeptical loosening of all solidities, but precisely the assurance against this by means of a new concept of solidity. (Simmel, 1958: 9–10)

That is the understanding of value which is maintained throughout his contributions to *Jugend*. For there one is ultimately always concerned with the objectivity of value, truth and beauty.

Why this phase remained an intermezzo only seems answerable if it is known in advance how it came about and why it came to an end. Why did Simmel consciously seek a change that can be labelled as the abandonment of sociology, the turn to aesthetics and art and the change from the equation to the opposition of materialism and neo-Kantianism? This may have to do with Simmel's academic career, which he appeared to have cancelled. With the onset of the Stumm period and the forced arch-conservative higher education policies of Althoff (see Rammstedt, 1988), the opportunities for a Berlin *Privatdozent* from Schmoller's circle with a specialization in sociology to obtain a full professorship declined to nil.[25] Simmel seemed to need a professorial position, since his sources of financial support were exhausted.[26] His hope of taking over the Nietzsche archives in Weimar also remained a dream. This may make it understandable why the emphasis on Nietzsche soon dissipated, and why he opportunistically cancelled his activism as a sociologist, and abandoned the attempts to reconcile Marx and Kant.

But all of that still does not yet explain the intention to become a poet, or at least a philosopher and a poet in one. He had stood up for naturalism and been a part of it while a young *Privatdozent*, but like his circle of literary acquaintances, he moved away from naturalism or into opposition to it in the mid-1890s. Stefan George, Rainer Maria Rilke and Paul Ernst were probably the most prominent representatives of a new literature with whom Simmel came into close contact in these years. For them, art was at least as valuable as science. In addition to this there is an 'amour fou', the stations of which can be pursued naively and directly, though slightly elevated in the literary sense, in Simmel's contributions to *Jugend*. Art was another world for him, where he believed he could go into exile as a poet.

But he soon came to learn that this avenue was barred to him. He was no poet, and 'No Poet' [Kein Dichter] was also the title of the little story published in 1900 in *Jugend*. There he confesses that he could not 'break up' a particular concrete situation, 'in order to form an artistic object out of its parts. Then I saw: *reality is too strong for me* — I was not a poet — not a poet!' This confession is not only submitted in the first person, it also seems to have exerted effects on Simmel's publications, for after 1900, he published no more fairy-tales, and poems are scarcely found, and if so, they are topically oriented, not literary; he no longer dares to approach the small 'snapshots', which really make no statement, but are only intended to be beautiful. 'Reality is too strong for me — I am not a poet — not a poet!' Here, Simmel is probably describing his own situation, and perhaps the assessment goes back to Paul Ernst (1937: 119), who denied he had 'creative power', despite all his admitted perspicacity in thinking, because 'a good measure of stupidity is needed for creativity.'[27]

If this signals the premature end of his career as a poet, then it also marks a change in this phase characterized by the contributions to *Jugend*. In addition, Simmel received a readership (*Extraordinariat*), his great love affair became ordinary, and his rebellion against the bourgeois world gave way to a purportedly unpolitical opposition in the name of modernity.

If Simmel had discussed current painting in *Jugend* at various times, and not hesitated to issue criticism against specific figures — as an artist among artists — he played an officious role in 1902–3 as committee member of the 'Kulturleben-Klub' in Berlin. He writes to Ricarda Huch (letter of 5 March 1903):

Since art has nothing to do with the division of labor, but always creates a totality, the artist will never have a fundamental relationship to 'associations', in which a totality can only come about through the cooperation of the many.

Though Simmel does not present himself to her as an artist, he does establish his closeness to art by naming the committee members ('Liebermann, L. von Hofman, Vandevelde, Count Kessler') and the list of the remaining members hints at exclusivity ('Klinger, Richard Strauss, Dehmel, Gerhard Hauptmann, Mommsen, Wölfflin'), so that Simmel can (must?) formulate it in his letter to Huch as follows:

> I myself confess openly that I only joined . . . the organization against resistance and second thoughts. But the artistic and cultural state of emergency in Berlin — where the major forces in public life crush us with barbarism and the worst art — is so great that I was not able to resist the plan to support the scattered initiatives for something better, no matter how imperfectly it may be realized.

This association bogged down in the preparatory stages. Count Kessler, the actual driving force, left for Weimar, Vandevelde followed and Simmel lost contact with this group of cultural policy activists. From then on, he viewed reality only from his study; he had no more opportunity to intervene in the world of art and artists.

He notes resignedly in his last contribution to *Jugend*: 'There is nothing more deceptive than so-called reality, and that is of course the only thing which could reconcile me with it' (Simmel, 1906a: 309). This is situated at the end of his aesthetic efforts in *Jugend*. His efforts for aesthetics continued; he remained loyal to an unsociological, ultimately elitist interpretation in Nietzsche's sense. The holistic theory approach is then the gateway for the thoughts inspired by the philosophy of life that came to assume an ever greater importance in Simmel's thinking after 1904-5.

Translated by Mark Ritter.

Notes

1. In 'Böcklin's Landscapes', Simmel (1895a: 272) writes: 'Spinoza demands of the philosopher that he view things *sub specie aeternitatis*. That is to say, purely according to their inner necessity and significance, divorced from the contingency of their here and now.'

2. Letter to Wilhelm Hertz (of the Cotta publishing house), dated 18 December 1891. Simmel suggests as an abstract of his *Einleitung in die Moralwissenschaft*: 'The work is directed against the validity of the general concepts and principles with which ethical systematics tends to work. By proving the ambiguity and empty formalism of the latter on the basis of psychological and sociological experience, it forms the critical foundation for the adaptation of ethics (*Moralwissenschaft*) to the demands of modern scientific standards. Those standards are not allowed to consider moral

life explained by mere combinations of abstract generalities, but only by its psychological dissolution into individual events and by the historical derivation of those events.'

3. Friedrich Nietzsche introduces *Beyond Good and Evil* (First section: 'On the Prejudices of Philosophy') as follows:

How *could* anything originate out of its opposite? for example, truth out of error? or the will to truth out of the will to deception? or selfless deeds out of selfishness? or the pure and sunlike gaze of the sage out of lust? Such origins are impossible: whoever dreams of them is a fool, indeed worse: the things of the highest values must have another, *peculiar* origin — they cannot be derived from this transitory, seductive, deceptive, paltry world, from this turmoil of delusion and lust. . . . The fundamental faith of the metaphysicians is *the faith in opposite values*. It has not even occurred to the most cautious among them that one might have a doubt right here at the threshold where it was surely most necessary. . . . It might even be possible that what constitutes the value of these good and revered things is precisely that they are insidiously related, tied to, and involved with these wicked, seemingly opposite things — maybe even one with them in essence. Maybe!

But who has the will to concern himself with such dangerous maybes? For that, one really has to wait for the advent of a new species of philosophers, such as have somehow another and converse taste and propensity from those we have known so far — philosophers of the dangerous 'maybe' in every sense.

And in all seriousness: I see such 'new' philosophers coming up. (Nietzsche, 1968: 199–201).

4. This concept is reserved for later development. Just how serious this interpretation of Nietzsche was to Simmel (1907b, 1987) can be gauged not only by his adoption of these theses in his book *Schopenhauer and Nietzsche: A Series of Lectures* [Schopenhauer und Nietzsche: Ein Vortragszyklus], but is already mentioned in a letter on 1 January 1896. There he asks Hugo Münsterberg for information whether Rickert had already 'read my Nietzsche' and for advice whether he should 'give it to Prof. Weber'. The 'urgent invitation' to Weimar from Frau Förster-Nietzsche, about which Simmel reports in a letter to Münsterberg on 10 March 1897, should also be evaluated as a reaction to his article as well as to his review of her biography of Nietzsche. It is to be assumed that this invitation is connected with the fact that Elisabeth Förster-Nietzsche had discharged Koegel and Steiner as coeditors of the Nietzsche edition in the spring of 1897 and was intending to initiate a Nietzsche foundation (cf. Karl Schlechta, 1984).

5. 'For in art,' Simmel comments in a footnote (1896b: 206), 'the value of an epoch is not decided by the height of the average achievements, but solely by the height of the greatest achievement. It is not the sum of admirable works, but only the distance of the most outstanding work from these merely admirable ones which measures the significance of an artistic period, whereas in all other eudaemonistic, ethical and cultural relationships it has so far been precisely the average, the degree of distribution of desirable conditions that determined the value of the epoch.'

6. He writes (1897b: 390–1): '. . . peculiar property of the human psyche, rooted so deeply in it and so intertwined in its experiences of every day, that it has only been recognized at all after thousands of years of reflections on our mind. The psyche cannot sense anything other than the difference between its momentary motion and stimulation and those preceding it. The difference echoes in the psyche in a

mysterious way and forms the background on which the present moment gains and measures its contents and its significance.'

7. It is probably not by accident that the concepts of 'purity' and 'unity' are frequently applied by Simmel in the same context: 'We create beauty and knowledge, and believe in the absolute purity with which we serve the ideal, if the inner aspect of the work shows no influence of the will for money which stands at its beginning and its end. Certainly, the work is pure, but what of our mind?' (Simmel, 1902a: 446). See also Simmel's 'Snapshots . . . Only Everything' [Momentbilder . . . Nur Alles] (1902b); 'Snapshots . . . Anima candida' (1903a: 573–4).

8. Cf the description of beauty when Simmel (1901c: 326) says with respect to Eleonora Duse: 'And thus the unique quality of this artist became clear to me: that she is inconceivably beautiful in every moment we separate out of her movement, which we may wish to hold onto as a lasting image indifferent to any particular mind — and that *she* is at the same time, in the sum of all these moments, in her motion, the most perfect, complete expression of the soul and all its tendencies. Because the psychic meaning of life becomes the visible beauty of an image for her, she permits us to sense that what we call beauty is the unity of those struggling powers.' The relativism with respect to the scientific method that can be located in Simmel at the period is found in the concluding sentence: 'But no one until Duse has taught it to me in such a way that the entire human being and not just the philosopher comprehended it.'

On this description of beauty and the problematizing of form and motion addressed in it, (See Kutzbach, 1973/4: 36ff.).

9. All three aspects are clearly addressed in 'Snapshots . . . Heaven and Hell' [Momentbilder . . . Himmel und Hölle] (Simmel, 1901f.: 300). Here one reads: 'When I read Dante, I must often think how much more elastic nerves the people of the 14th century must have had; the horrors of Hell strung together just as uninterruptedly as the ecstasies of Paradise! A modern poet would surely have alternated shadow and light. We are only stimulated by rapid distinctions any more, we have to *alternate* between Heaven and Hell, if we wish to feel both of them.' If one could draw conclusions on concepts on the basis of perceptions, then the cancellation of the binarity of Heaven and Hell could be demanded here. But Simmel characterizes that very conclusion as wrong-headed.

10. 'Perhaps the deepest attraction of beauty lies in the fact that it is always the form of elements which are of themselves indifferent and alien to beauty, and which achieve aesthetic value only through their coincidence' (Simmel, 1898c: 137).

11. 'For the first time in modern ethics, the criterion itself becomes something different here; the heightening of strength, beauty, the distancing between one person and another, becomes an *end in itself*, here, and does not derive its dignity only from the fact that this heightening benefits others than its agents themselves' (Simmel, 1907b: 211).

12. Thus Simmel attests with respect to Stefan George: 'that the very part of a poem which is a pure work of poetic art makes up the totality more than anywhere, with a strict elimination of all secondary effects that might flow into its content from its other relationships and meanings. Here it appears with the greatest decisiveness: it is not that some meaning or other should be presented in a poetic form, but rather that a poetic work of art is to be created, for which the content has no more meaning than does marble for a statue. Certainly even the most spiritualized work of art is not indifferent to its material; what one can say in marble can not be expressed

equally well in bronze or in fayence. It is an ideological error, now fortunately overcome, to fantasize that the value and essence of a work of art lie in its "idea" and behave quite indifferently to the material in which this idea was to be realized' (Simmel, 1898d: 394).

13. See on this point *Sociological Aesthetics*, and also 'Stefan George . . .' (Simmel, 1898d: 234), where we read: 'Certainly, since the aesthetic values are not at all the only ones in life, but coexist alongside intellectual, ethical, sensory, religious and many other interests, then a product which shares in many of them, will represent a particularly high overall value. But beyond that lies the special charm of the structures which embody *one* of the ideas from our value system in pure detachment.'

14. Thus, Georg Simmel (1891) reproaches Rudolf Eucken in 1891 for not having understood these 'three most modern philosophies of life' and therefore treating them unfairly. 'Darwinism and socialism are only individual, but significant stages on this path of world history, which is leading what had been obscurely amalgamated into clear separation.' And he proceeds from the fact that 'in the great process of differentiation' the 'movement of modern culture' had split between the 'materialist and the mechanistic character of the modern world view' into two special areas: 'the external nature for the mechanism, and the human world for the drive of the psyche, to find something spiritual outside itself'. As a parallel to that, see also Georg Simmel 'On a Relationship of the Theory of Selection to Epistemology' [Über eine Beziehung der Selectionslehre zur Erkenntnistheorie] (1895b).

15. The conceptualizations used by Simmel between 1890 and 1895/6 should probably also be interpreted accordingly. As one example, let us point out 'form/content', a central terminological element in Simmel's sociology. Content means for him, e.g. in 'The Problem of Sociology' [Das Problem der Soziologie] (1894) — probably referring to Marx, 'the economic situation and the industrial-technical development', and form means interaction (*Wechselwirkung*) or the social-psychological relationships between people. Kistiakowski (1899: 77, 79) had already pointed this out and emphasized the parallels to Rudolf Stammler's *Wirtschaft und Recht nach der materialistischen Geschichtsauffassung* (1896). Simmel was familiar with this work by Stammler, since he discussed it in 'On the Methodology of Social Science' [Zur Methodik der Sozialwissenschaft] (1896c).

16. Thus he writes: 'Who knows whether there are particular laws for society in general, uniform formulae which would permit us to derive each social status from the preceding one? All of modern sociology views its task as the search for such laws, for the fact that they do exist and prevail at all seems to result from the axiom of the natural regularity of all events, including social ones. And yet one can deny the existence of social laws while maintaining this regularity in its full extent . . . There cannot be social laws in the sense of physical laws, because society consists of very many elements, each of which is controlled by natural laws in its own right, so that the movement of the totality obeys only the complex of these natural laws, not a superordinated, specifically social law' (Simmel, 1897c).

17. Under the title 'Ten Details' [Zehn Einzelheiten] (1897e) Georg Simmel published aphorisms, of which the third reads: 'Skepticism, which now appears as the great liberator and guide to life, acts something like magic bullets. Nine out of ten times we can hit whatever we want, but the Devil directs the tenth one where he wants, often enough into the heart of our beloved.'

18. 'The social role of this faith has not yet been investigated at all, but this much is certain: without it, society would disintegrate', is prominently stated (1898b: 116).

19. 'Even if one succeeds in understanding the origin of a religion as an event in the life of humanity from the inner conditions of that very life, that has not even touched upon the problem of whether objective reality, outside of human thought, contains the counterpart and the confirmation of that psychic reality or not' (Simmel, 1898b: 122).

20. Simmel persists here in a sociological approach with his reference to money. 'Life has drawn us diverse people of the present so much into its confusion, its anticipations, its secret greed, that we can no longer present a flower to a saint without first having sniffed it.'

21. 'Only beauty can come both to the one [the body] and to the other [the soul]; it is the point where the two meet, elevated beyond themselves. Philosophers may have already figured that out otherwise. But no one until Duse has taught it to me in such a way that the entire person and not only the philosopher comprehended it' (Simmel, 1901e).

22. 'A Longing' [Eine Sehnsucht] (Simmel, 1900b) 'We, who had seen so much, we did not see all that plenitude which surrounds us, did not hear what fell silent for us. The spirit first had to pour so much light through the worlds, before it uncovers the darkness that carries our brightness. No, not only the sun shows us where we belong: Deep into the darkness, its root sends being! Teach us, shining day, the rights of mysteries anew. Give us, o coming age, give us back reverence'.

23. 'Snapshots . . . Money Alone Does not Make one Happy' (Simmel, 1901b) 'First of all, the miracle of banality became clear to me: that one need only elevate the most disparate points of view to absolute banality in order to defend them with equal strength. At this altitude the demand of the intellectual lowlands disappears, the demand that one must be in error if one's opposite is in the right.'

24. He writes in 'Snapshots . . . Animation' [Momentbilder . . . Beseeltheit] (1901g): 'For me it has always been one of the purest joys, when in that way a plummet was dropped from the surface of thoughtless words into the depths of things, and the nonsensical provided the frame for a sense of which it would never have dreamed. That is not malicious arrogance, but modesty. For in it, there is something like consolation and hope that even our wisdom, whose wisdom we so often have to doubt . . .'

25. That is why Schmoller's first attempts to get Simmel an appointment as Associate Professor were condemned to failure from the start.

26. The best source of information on this to date have been Simmel's few extant letters from these years.

27. See also Max Dessoir (1947: 164f.), who extends this assessment to Simmel's philosophy. He claims that 'Simmel lacks naiveté, the simple wisdom which is so well-suited to a philosopher.'

References

Dessoir, M. (1947) *Buch der Erinnerung*. Stuttgart.

Ernst, P. (1931) *Jünglingsjahre*. München: Georg Müller.

Kistiakowski, T. (1899) *Gesellschaft und Einzelwesen*. Berlin.

Kutzbach, K.U. (ed.) (1973/4) 'Paul Ernst und Georg Lukács. Dokumente zu einer Freundschaft'. Special issue of *Wille zur Form, Jahresgabe der Paul-Ernst-Gesellschaft*.

Rammstedt, *On Simmel's Aesthetics* 143

Nietzsche, F. (1968) 'Beyond Good and Evil' in *Basic Writings of Nietzsche*. Translated by Walter Kaufmann. New York: Modern Library.

Rammstedt, O. (1988) 'Wertfreiheit und die Konstitution der Soziologie in Deutschland', *Zeitschrift für Soziologie* 17: 264–72.

Schlechta, K. (1984) *Nietzsche-Chronik*. München: dtv.

Simmel, G. (1882) 'Psychologische und ethnologische Studien über Musik', *Zeitschrift für Völkerpsychologie und Sprachwissenschaft* 13: 261–305.

Simmel, G. (1890a) 'Über Kunstausstellungen', *Unsere Zeit* 26(2): 474–80.

Simmel, G. (1890b) 'Rembrandt als Erzieher', *Vossische Zeitung*, Sunday supplement, June.

Simmel, G. (1890c) *Über Sociale Differenzierung*. Leipzig: Duncker & Humblot.

Simmel, G. (1891) 'Rudolf Euckens Lebenschauungen, Part III', *Vossische Zeitung*, Sunday supplement, 28 June.

Simmel, G. (1892/3) *Einleitung in der Moralwissenschaft*. Berlin.

Simmel, G. (1894) 'Das Problem der Soziologie', *Jahrbuch fur Gesetzegebung* 18: 257–65. (English translation, 'The Problem of Sociology', *Annals of the American Academy of Political and Social Science* 6(3): 412–23).

Simmel, G. (1895a) 'Böcklins Landschaften', *Die Zukunft*, 12: 272–7.

Simmel, G. (1895b) 'Über eine Beziehung der Selektionslehre zur Erkenntnistheorie', *Archiv für Systematische Philosophie* 1: 34–45.

Simmel, G. (1896a) 'Soziologische Ästhetik', *Die Zukunft* 17: 204–16. (English translation in Simmel, 1968.)

Simmel, G. (1896b) 'Frederich Nietzsche. Eine moralphilosophische Silhouette', *Zeitschrift für Philosophie und philosophische Kritik* 107: 202–15.

Simmel, G. (1896c) 'Zur Methodik der Sozialwissenschaft', *Jahrbuch fur Gesetzgebung, Verwaltung und Volkswirtschaft im Deutschen Reich* 20: 575–85.

Simmel, G. (1896d) 'Berliner Kunstbrief', *Die Zeit* 21 March.

Simmel, G. (1897a) 'Jenseits der Schönheit', *Jugend* 2: 234–5.

Simmel, G. (1897b) 'Rosen. Eine soziale Hypothese', *Jugend* 2: 390–2.

Simmel, G. (1897c) 'Über Massenverbrechen', *Die neue Zeit*, 2 October: 4–5.

Simmel, G. (1897d) 'Das Gleichgiltigste. Ein moralisches Dilemma', *Jugend* 2: 774–5.

Simmel, G. (1897e) 'Zehn Einzelheiten', *Jugend* 2: 176.

Simmel, G. (1898a) 'Theistische Phantasien eines Fin-de sièclisten', *Jugend* 3: 508.

Simmel, G. (1898b) 'Zur Soziologie der Religion', *Neue Deutsche Rundschau* 9(1): 111–27.

Simmel, G. (1898c) 'Rom: eine aesthetische Analyse', *Die Zeit*, (Wein), 191, 28 May: 137–9.

Simmel, G. (1898d) 'Stefan George: Eine kunstphilosophische Betrachtung', *Die Zukunft* 22: 394.

Simmel, G. (1899a) 'Momentbilder. . . .Gegensatz', *Jugend* 4: 92.

Simmel, G. (1899b) 'Von erfüllten Wünschen. Zwei sehr ähnliche Märchen', *Jugend* 4(2): 630.

Simmel, G. (1900a) *Die Philosophie des Geldes*. Leipzig. (English translation, *The Philosophy of Money*, Routledge: 1990.)

Simmel, G. (1900b) 'Eine Sehnsucht', *Jugend* 5: 30.

Simmel, G. (1900c) 'Metaphysik der Faulheit', *Jugend* 5: 337–9.

Simmel, G. (1901a) 'Momentbilder Sub Species Aeternitatis. Gelbe Kühe', *Jugend* 6: 672.

Simmel, G. (1901b) 'Geld allein macht nicht glücklich', *Jugend* 6: 300.

Simmel, G. (1901c) 'Nur eine Brücke', *Jugend* 6.

Simmel, G. (1901d) 'Koketterie', *Jugend* 6: 672.

Simmel, G. (1901e) 'Momentbilder. . . . die Duse', *Jugend* 6: 326.

Simmel, G. (1901f) 'Momentbilder . . . Himmel und Hölle', *Jugend* 6: 300.

Simmel, G. (1901g) 'Momentbilder . . . Beseeltheit', *Jugend* 6: 92.

Simmel, G. (1901h) 'Ästhetik der Schwere', *Berliner Tageblatt*, 10 June.

Simmel, G. (1902a) 'Momentbilder sub specie aeternitas. Reinheit', *Jugend* 7: 446.

Simmel, G. (1902b) 'Momentbilder . . . Nur Alles', *Jugend* 7: 446.

Simmel, G. (1902c) 'Der Bildrahmen. Ein ästhetischer Versuch', *Der Tag* 541.

Simmel, G. (1902d)'Rodin's Plastik und die Geistesrichtung der Gegenwart', Berliner Tageblatt 29 Sept.

Simmel, G. (1903a) 'Momentbilder. . . . Anima candida', *Jugend* 8: 573–4.

Simmel, G. (1903b) 'Kant und die moderne Ästhetik', *Berliner Tageblatt* 12: (19 Oct.).

Simmel, G. (1906a) 'Strandgut', *Jugend* 11: 309.

Simmel, G. (1906b) *Kant und Goethe*. Berlin: Bard, Marquard.

Simmel, G. (1907a) 'Fragmente aus einer Philosophie der Liebe', *Jugend* 12: 242–4.

Simmel, G. (1907b) *Schopenhauer und Nietzsche: ein Vortragszyklus*. Leipzig. (Translation see Simmel, 1987.)

Simmel, G. (1909a) 'Psychologie der Koketterie', *Der Tag* 109, 11 May and 110, 12 May.

Simmel, G. (1909b) 'Brücke und Tür, *Der Tag* 15 Sept.

Simmel, G. (1911/12) 'Der Begriff und die Tragödie der Kultur', *Logos* 2: 1–25.

Simmel, G. (1916) *Rembrandt*. Leipzig: Kurt Wolff.

Simmel, G. (1921) 'Fragment über die Liebe Aus dem Nachlass Georg Simmels', *Logos*, 9: 1–54. (English translation 'A Fragment on Love' in G. Simmel *On Women, Sexuality and Love*. New Haven: Yale University Press.)

Simmel, G. (1958) 'Anfang einer unvollendeten Selbstdarstellung', in K. Gassen and M. Landmann (eds), *Buch des Dankes an Georg Simmel*. Berlin: Duncker & Humblot.

Simmel, G. (1965) 'The Aesthetic Significance of the Face', in G. Simmel et al. *Essays on Sociology, Philosophy and Aesthetics*. Edited by K. Wolff. New York: Harper.

Simmel, G. (1968) *The Conflict in Modern Culture and Other Essays*. Translated by K.P. Etzkorn. New York: Teachers' College Press. (Contains translations of Simmel, 1896 'Sociological Aesthetics' and Simmel, 1911–12 'The Concept and Tragedy of Culture' and 1903, 'On Aesthetic Quantities'.)

Simmel, G. (1987) *Schopenhauer and Nietzsche*. Translated by H. Loiskandi, D. Weinstein and M. Weinstein (translation of Simmel, 1907b). Amherst: Massachusetts University Press.

Simmel, G. (1990) *The Philosophy of Money*, second edition. Translated by Tom Bottomore and David Frisby. London: Routledge. (Translation of Simmel, 1900a.)

Utitz, E. (1920) 'Georg Simmel und die Philosophie der Kunst', *Zeischrift für Ästhetik und Allgemeine Kunstwissenschaft* 14: 1–14.

Otthein Rammstedt teaches Sociology at the University of Bielefeld, Germany.

Georg Simmel

Georg Lukács

Georg Simmel was undoubtedly the most significant and interesting transitional figure in the whole of modern philosophy. This is why he was so exceptionally fascinating for all the really talented philosophers of the younger generation of scholars (who are more than clever or diligent specialists in special philosophical disciplines), so that there is almost no one among them who did not for a shorter or longer time fall under the spell of his thought. But, for the very same reason, this fascination was only in the rarest cases a lasting one. Simmel has had no 'students' as Cohen or Rickert or Husserl did; he was a great stimulator, but neither a great educator nor — and this takes us immediately nearer to the centre of his nature — one who brought matters to a close.

Simmel is often called brilliant — both as a term of praise and of disparagement. But this characterization, however correct it may be, in no way reaches the heart of his philosophical personality. Simmel was also brilliant in the normal sense of the word and one could quote pages of his sayings which would stand comparison with the greatest masters of wit — but the essence of his spirit lies deeper: his was a philosophical spirit in the truest and purest sense, spirit as only the greatest possess it. 'Brilliance' means his lightning grasp and striking expression of a yet undiscovered philosophical matter, his ability to see the smallest and most inessential phenomenon of daily life so sharply *sub specie philosophiae* that it becomes transparent and behind its transparence an eternal formal coherence of philosophical meaning becomes perceptible.

Simmel possessed in outstanding measure this highest gift of the philosopher. Why is it then that in spite of this he became only a dazzling, 'brilliant' stimulator and not a really great, really epoch-making philosopher? The basis of this failure at the greatest things reveals at the same time the point where Simmel's richest and

Theory, Culture & Society (SAGE, London, Newbury Park and New Delhi), Vol. 8 (1991), 145–150

most fertile abilities were anchored: stressing the positive aspect, one could call it his boundless and unrestrained sensibility; but one must also speak of a missing centre, of an inability to make ultimate, absolute decisions, if one defines the limits of his nature brought to light here. Simmel is the greatest transitional philosopher of our age — to condense his greatness and his limits in a sentence, he is the genuine philosopher of Impressionism. This does not mean that he simply brought to a conceptual level what the Impressionist development of music, of the visual arts and poetry expressed; his work is much more than a conceptual formulation of the Impressionist *weltanschauung*; rather, it brings into philosophical form that feeling for the world out of which come the greatest works of this tradition. It shapes the nature of the period directly behind us in just as problematic a fashion as characterizes the works of a Monet or Rodin, a Richard Strauss or Rilke.

Each Impressionism is by its very nature a transitional form: it refuses completion, the fateful and fate-creating definitive form, on principle and not out of an inability to attain it. (This characterization of course fits only the highest representatives of Impressionism; with the epigones and camp-followers, it is always a matter of cleverly masked impotence.) Impressionism experiences and assesses the great, solid and eternal forms as doing violence to life, to its richness and its colours, its fullness and polyphony; it is always a celebration of life and puts all form in its service. With this, however, the very essence of form becomes problematic. The heroic and tragic undertaking of the great Impressionists consists precisely of this: unable to escape form — the only possible medium of their essential existence — they always demand of it and impose on it something which contradicts its meaning, which annuls form. For, if form ceases to be self-contained, sovereign and complete in itself, it ceases to be form. There can be no form which serves and is open to life.

In spite of this permanent problematic, there arose in the works of the great Impressionists of the nineteenth century a profusion of eternally imperishable values. For, however self-contained and turned away from life the eternal forms must be in their perfection, still they must always again and again refer back to life, and try to absorb it in its full manifoldness so that the work which now is sovereign and complete in itself can be a true work, a self-sufficient world, a microcosm. And every great Impressionist movement is nothing other than the protest of life against forms which have become too rigid and in this rigidity too weak to shape and incorporate its fullness. But because Impressionisms stop short at this intensified apperception of life, they are essentially transitional phenomena, preparing for a new classicism which renders eternal the fullness of life, which has become perceptible through their sensibility, in new, hard and severe but all-inclusive forms. Simmel's historical place can be formulated from this point of view thus: he was a Monet of philosophy who has not yet been followed by a Cezanne.

The situation Simmel came upon in philosophy was the dullest imaginable: the great tradition of classical German philosophy seemed lost; the important outsiders of that time (Nietzsche, Hartmann) stood without roots or following in a floodtide of the most desolate and soulless materialism and positivism. For a philosophical receptiveness, no other way seemed open than the heightening of the sensibility through historical empathizing with past epochs and men (in the manner of Dilthey), for even the beginnings of neo-Idealism, which is flowering now, must have given the impression that its strong emphasis on the eternally a priori must mean violence to the fullness of life, that its triumph could become only the triumph of formal, methodological monism over the substantive monism of the philosophy that was dominant then; Simmel's historical significance lies in this. From the beginning he was the pithiest representative of methodological pluralism; the pathos of his philosophy stems from his marvelling recognition of the endless diversity of the possibilities of philosophical approaches and topics. 'There are too few categories, just as there are too few sexes', he once said in conversation. Of course, this remark also captures the distinctive limits of his nature. The discovery of the plurality of philosophical approaches is for him the final goal, the end in itself, not a means for finding a complexly organized and yet unified system.

Because of the pluralistic-unsystematic tendency of his thought, Simmel has often been called a relativist. In my view, this is incorrect. For relativism means the doubt about the unconditional validity of the various possible approaches (for example, science and art), and it is therefore wholly independent of the question of whether our world image has a monist or a pluralist character. Simmel, on the contrary, holds firm to the absoluteness of every single positing; he considers each as indispensable and unconditional — only he does not believe that there can be any a priori point of view concerning the world which would really embrace the totality of life. Each affords only an aspect, an a priori and essential aspect, but only an aspect and not the totality itself. What here separates Simmel from the pluralist and yet unified system of philosophy that is being striven for today is exactly this stopping at the recognition of the individual aspects.

In part, this is connected with his joy at the qualitative and unique, with his pleasure at being able to discover various original subject areas where the dullness of others had seen an undivided unity, probably also with a geniune Impressionistic delight at his own sensibility; but its decisive reason is that for Simmel the last resort was always something beyond all positing: life — of which approaches can offer no more than aspects. (Here rests the affinity of his thought to Bergson's.) Among these various aspects there are the most manifold and intricate connections which Simmel devotes the full sensitivity and sharpness of his thought to unravelling. But since — because of his basic attitude — this net of interrelations must remain a labyrinth and cannot become a system, Simmel's sagacity which uncovers, unravels and reties ever new threads and snarls, takes on the appearance of playfulness, and his hypersensitivity to always newly discovered qualities, that of a dependable virtue. Still, no matter how decisively it may reject his ultimate position, the new philosophy will never disregard his formulations of philosophical matters.

The character of Simmel's talent makes it understandable that his most enduring contributions are in sociology and philosophy of history. The peculiarity of these two disciplines rests on the reciprocal penetration of heterogeneous standpoints to form a new unity, on the interaction of the conditioned and the unconditional. If sociology before Simmel, especially Marxist sociology which was important for his own position, too, had the tendency to resolve everything timelessly unconditional (religion, philosophy, art) into the temporally conditioned, then the one-sidedness and weakness of the greatest conceptions of philosophy of history of the classical epoch, such as Hegel's, was the attempt to incorporate the temporality of history wholly and completely into the unconditionality of a purely a priori relation. Simmel's significance for sociology — I am thinking in the first instance of his *Philosophy of Money* — lies in this, that he pushes the analysis of conditioning factors so far and sharpens it to such finesse, unlike his predecessors, and yet at the same time makes visible with inimitable acuity the reversal of the limitations, their self-containment, their stopping before that which cannot be conditioned. A sociology such as is undertaken by Max Weber, Troeltsch, Sombart and others has become possible only on the ground laid by him, however much all of them may differ from him methodologically.

Certainly, this sociology of Simmel's is only an 'experiment' and nothing complete; his 'sociology' bears the stamp of his Impressionism even more strongly than the great essay on money; and his efforts in the philosophy of history were clearly conceived as fragments. The innovation of his attitude shows itself much less in his work on the theory of history than in his efforts to consider particular historical individuals philosophically. The manner in which Simmel comprehends Goethe, Kant, Michelangelo, Rembrandt and Rodin is neither that of the historian who inserts them into a temporal continuity of development or considers them as phenomena of a certain epoch, nor that of the systematizer who dissects their work in its a priori normativity, detached from everything temporal; but rather that of the philosopher of history for whom each of these great figures is at the same time something unique and an a priori category. Simmel's Impressionism sees in each of these geniuses a uniquely determined but at the same time eternal and a priori possibility of an attitude towards the totality of life: his pluralism refers not only to the particular kinds of positing matters but also to the individual realizations within each kind of positing. The world image of Goethe is different from that of Kant in exactly as a priori and necessary a manner as is the way of forming concepts in history from that in the natural sciences. But because Simmel's Impressionism is a genuinely and deeply philosophical one, each of these world images becomes something absolute. Just as the plurality of positions cannot obliterate the unconditional validity of each individual one in its sphere, nor does any relativisim result from this multiplicity: the 'category' of Rembrandt is just as absolute as the 'category' of Michelangelo. It is the metaphysical nature of the world not only to allow but to demand the multiplicity of such 'categories'. How fruitful this approach is for the philosophy of history can unfortunately not be indicated here; much less the relation between Simmel and the efforts which have followed him in this area. But here, too, the essence of his personality shows itself in his effect: no one has pursued his path directly, but no one could nor can undertake anything essential in the philosophy of history without having examined this perspective.

Translated by Margaret Cerullo.

Note

This is a translation of an article which first appeared in the German Hungarian newspaper *Pester Lloyd*, 2 October 1918. This was reprinted in Kurt Gassen and Michael Landmann (eds), *Buch des Dankes an Georg Simmel: Briefe, Erinnerungen, Bibliographie* (1958, Berlin: Duncker and Humblot, pp. 171–6).

Reference

Simmel, G. (1990) *The Philosophy of Money* (second edition). Translated by T. Bottomore and D. Frisby. London: Routledge (German original 1900).

Georg Simmel: Sociological ~~Flâneur~~ Bricoleur

Deena Weinstein and Michael A. Weinstein

Raising questions about the intellectual character of famous thinkers, creative artists, and even scientists, who have worked in the twentieth century, has become fashionable. One need only think of the Heidegger–Nazi affair to grasp the shift in attention from critiquing the status and validity of propositions to criticizing the character of those who formulate them. To a lesser degree the character issue has been raised about many, if not most, of the leading figures of twentieth-century humanities.

There is no need to deplore the change in focus from validity to virtue, but only to insist that the criticism of character be done with perspicuity. The current concern about character is based most deeply on an awareness that although it may not be possible to determine the truth about such things as human nature or the meaning of Being, it is still necessary to reflect on one's engagement with one's circumstances. With what attitude, disposition, or manner of being-in-the-world should one engage in the humanities and, by extension, the social sciences? This is a serious question, especially if one agrees with Nietzsche and Heidegger that thinking is grounded in mood or manner of attunement (*stimmung*). As Simmel understood, temperament becomes of primary importance when the objectivity of truth claims is thrown into doubt. One finds the only truth that one is capable of discerning is one's manner of participating in the struggles of one's life. Criticism of intellectual character, lifestyle, virtue, temperament, sensibility, mentality, taste and personality becomes the path of Socratic reflexivity for the contemporary intellect.

Of course, the character issue can be and is raised in other than Socratic ways. Character assassination parades comfortably in the mask of aesthetic and moral criticism. It may be actuated by *ressentiment*, a devaluation of intellectual values in terms of

Theory, Culture & Society (SAGE, London, Newbury Park and New Delhi), Vol. 8 (1991), 151–168

conventional social and personal morality. It may function as mere name-calling in inter-perspectival debate. It may reveal that the humanities have been permeated by the standards and sensibility of the gossip column and the scandal sheet. Whether criticism of intellectual character is high minded or a low blow is not always easy to determine. But it must be treated as if it were serious, just in case it is.

Georg Simmel has come in for his share of character criticism. In his major work on Simmel, *Sociological Impressionism*, David Frisby (1981: 68–101) discusses the question of whether or not Simmel is a sociological *flâneur*, in the sense that Walter Benjamin used that term. The term *flâneur* certainly has pejorative connotations and was not one that Simmel chose to describe himself. The following discussion considers the question of Simmel's intellectual character, with the aim of presenting an alternative vision of it to Frisby's. Rather than being Benjamin's *flâneur*, Simmel is seen to be more like Claude Lévi-Strauss's *bricoleur*. The discussion proceeds by examining the Benjamin/Frisby definition of *flâneur* and how Frisby applies it to Simmel's sociological practice. Then a Simmelian analysis of the form of the *flâneur* is worked up as a prelude to contrasting the *flâneur* to the *bricoleur*. Finally, 'The Metropolis and Mental Life', Simmel's well-known and influential essay on the sociocultural matrix of urban mentality, will be read as the self-reflexive analysis of the modern urban scene as a bricolage, calling for the virtues of the *bricoleur*. That is, the metropolis is the site of postmodernity, and the intellectual character most appropriate for describing it is developed in postmodernist discourse, not in the gallery of human types received from the first half of the nineteenth century.

For Frisby, Simmel is an escapist to an earlier period of urban development to the one in which he wrote. In the present writing, Simmel is an anticipator of postmodernism, presenting a thought contemporaneous to that of postmodernism. That is, Simmel is a postmodernist in advance of the discourse. The recent wave of interest in his work, then, would reflect, at least in part, the relevance of that work to clarifying current circumstances, even when that interest is in discrediting his thought. Otherwise the Simmel boom would simply be an internal development of the academic scholarship industry. Perhaps it is partly that, but the presumption here will be that Frisby, at least, takes on Simmel because he believes that Simmel's thought has significance beyond some

Simmel industry. Implied here is that the issue of Simmel's character is keyed to the culture war between modern progressivism and postmodern criticism, between diachrony and synchrony. There is no essential Simmel, only different Simmels read through the various positions in contemporary discourse formations. Yet the aim of criticism is to make one of the accounts more compelling than its competitors, to rely on plausibility rather than a proof that is impossible in this field.

The *Flâneur*

The foundation of criticism of intellectual character for Benjamin and Frisby is a neo-Marxist version of the sociology of knowledge. That is, the intellectual character of someone who does not hold to some variant of a broadly defined Marxist world perspective is a victim of class bias. More specifically, those who break with progressivism of a Marxist sort place themselves outside history, in some class-protective fantasia or *imaginaire*. The Benjamin/Frisby critique of character is a critique of ideology.

In essence, the critique is simple, at least as applied by Benjamin to Baudelaire and by Frisby to Simmel: those who de-totalize modernity, who have no coherent account of the whole of modern society, are retreatists from the great historical conflicts. Could they help themselves? Benjamin and Frisby are equivocal. But at least some intellectuals (like Benjamin and Frisby) join the progressive forces, so one might be tempted to think that some weakness in moral fibre or intellectual competence might help to account for the presence of de-totalizing intellectuals. Some character flaw. Benjamin and Frisby do not want to come right out and say 'character flaw', partly, perhaps, because it would conflict with their sociological approach, which minimizes voluntarism. So, they compromise by using the rhetorical technique of innuendo. In summary, they explain the de-totalizer as a victim of class bias who has, perhaps, contributed to his victimization by having a weak character. That the de-totalizer does not have the guts to commit himself to the historical struggle (at least reactionaries take a stand) is the more visceral message that Benjamin and Frisby sublimate. Too timid to mix in. Prone to escapism. Holds himself aloof from others and has fantasies of superiority that mask his feelings of inferiority. That is the diagnosis/indictment. The next move is to see how it is presented.

The rhetorical imagery providing the aesthetic dimension of Benjamin's and Frisby's critique of retreatism is the figure of the *flâneur*, a Parisian type, a kind of metropolitan persona of the mid-nineteenth century. When he associates, indeed, identifies Baudelaire with the *flâneur*, Benjamin is deprecating him. However, he may end up spiritualizing and embroidering the term so that it becomes applicable to an artist or intellectual, *flâneur* is at root and in its received connotations a term of opprobrium referring to someone who is not serious, indeed, someone who is socially superfluous, an idler, and, worse, a supercilious idler. Benjamin (1973: 54) quotes Paul Ernest de Rattier's 1857 utopia, *Paris n'existe plus* to the effect that the *flâneur* is a 'nonentity', a 'constant rubberneck' and an 'inconsequential type', who is 'always in search of cheap emotions' and knows about 'nothing but cobblestones, fiacres, and gas lanterns'. The *flâneur* was the kind of person who, around 1840, would take a turtle for a walk around the Paris arcades, letting the turtle, of course, set the pace (Benjamin, 1973: 54). In 1845 Ferdinand von Gall says that the *flâneur* provides 'the strollers and the smokers' with their chronicler and philosopher (Benjamin, 1973: 37). One gets the idea of what the *flâneur* is at the cobblestone level. To respectable opinion he is a social waste product. To the morally sensitive he is a fraud, a tin-horn aristocrat. Facetious. Fatuous. Making sport of the city's serious business. The term cannot help but retain these associations when it is used to characterize an artist like Baudelaire or an intellectual like Simmel. They are, of course, not really *flâneurs* in the strict sense, but somehow they are like *flâneurs*, spiritually.

For Benjamin, the point in drawing an analogy (homology?) between the *flâneur* and Baudelaire is that both epitomize the mentality and sensibility of the nineteenth-century petty bourgeoisie. That class was, according to Benjamin (1973: 59), passing its time until its members would have to 'become aware of the commodity nature of their labour power'. In the meantime the petty bourgeoisie could seek enjoyment not *in*, but *from* the society, as semi-detached spectator of the spectacle of urban capitalism: 'If it wanted to achieve virtuosity in this kind of enjoyment, it could not spurn empathizing with commodities' (Benjamin, 1973: 59). Baudelaire, then, is the virtuous *flâneur*, someone who makes it a self-conscious practice to perfect the stroller's art of observing the urban spectacle. He empathizes, for example, with the prostitute, enjoying her damage and decay at a distance. He owes his enjoyment of society to having 'already half withdrawn from it' (Benjamin, 1973: 59).

In Benjamin's hands, Baudelaire's *disponibilité* of the imagination becomes empathy with the commodity, which means identification with it: Baudelaire speaks as/for the commodity. Says Benjamin (1973: 55), the 'soul' of the commodity, mentioned in jest by Marx, 'would be the most empathetic ever encountered in the realm of souls, for it would have to see in everyone the buyer in whose hand and house it wants to nestle'. Poor commodity, which does not want to be homeless. Poor *flâneur*/Baudelaire, by extension, who doesn't want to stroll aimlessly, semi-detached from society, superfluous. More, perhaps, to be pitied than scorned. Benjamin's (1973: 58) intent is captured when he quotes approvingly Engels's indictment of the metropolis as a place where people 'crowd by one another as though they had nothing in common, nothing to do with each other, and their only agreement is the tacit one, that each keep to his own side of the pavement, so as not to delay the opposing stream of the crowd, while it occurs to no man to honour another with so much as a glance'. Engels's sentimentalism is what rules Benjamin's critique of Baudelaire as *flâneur*. Simmel, in 'The Metropolis and Mental Life', provides a functional explanation of the urban phenomena that Engels emotes about. That does not concern Benjamin, who pities/scorns Baudelaire's failure (a failure from Benjamin's, but, perhaps, a strength from another viewpoint) to become solidary with others (the proletariat).

No one will deny the difference between the sensitivity of Baudelaire and the superficiality of the standard-issue *flâneur*. But that sensitivity only makes the pathos of retreatism more acute; the sense of a wasted life that knows itself to be such is more pathetic than the sense of a wasted life that veils its impotence in a supercilious mystique. Pitied and scorned. When Frisby takes up Benjamin's image of the *flâneur* and applies it to Simmel, he also takes up Benjamin's spirit.

Frisby on Simmel is more elusive than Benjamin on Baudelaire. Ironically, Frisby (1981: 77), who makes a point of noting Simmel's reputation as 'the philosopher of the "perhaps" ', introduces his discussion of Simmel/*flâneur* by suggesting that an examination of 'Simmel's manner of working and his relation to his subject matter might prompt comparison with Benjamin's analysis of the *flâneur*. It might raise the question of how far Simmel himself is a "sociological *flâneur*".' Simmel was rarely that provisional. Indeed,

Frisby never answers the question that titles his chapter: 'A Sociological *Flâneur*?' But it's probably safe to say that he wouldn't have brought up the issue if he didn't see a Simmel–*flâneur* connection.

Frisby makes that connection when he recurs to Benjamin's judgement that Baudelaire had 'half withdrawn' from society. He (Frisby, 1981: 79) remarks: 'Such a judgment could equally apply to many of Simmel's essays. Simmel, too, could extract from the seemingly most insignificant details of social life the most interesting connections. In this respect, we might see Simmel as a *flâneur* for the intelligentsia, providing them with the most subtle analyses of all manner of social phenomena without disturbing any of them.' 'Might' again, but all right. The association is there. Simmel is similar to the *flâneur* because he observes the details of life without disturbing them. His works, indeed, are 'harmless'. That is, they do not indicate, promote, or prescribe a commitment to and programme of action, but are simply collections of intellectual miniatures catering to the refined tastes of the salon. Rather than being the chronicler and philosopher of the strollers and smokers, Simmel is provisioner and panderer to the intellectual diversions of the haute bourgeoisie.

Whether or not Frisby's description of Simmel's work is accurate (its accuracy will be disputed below), it is the description of the practice of a sociological *flâneur*. Frisby does not ground his judgement in any scrutiny of Simmel's texts, but supports it with quotes from Simmel's contemporaries and later commentators. Koppel, for example, calls Simmel 'the intellectual neurasthenic', which Frisby (1981: 80) finds 'most remarkable of all' because Simmel singled out neurasthenia as a condition in which 'reality is not touched with direct confidence but with fingertips that are immediately withdrawn'. Simmel's theory of social pathology is a symptom of his own disease. By the same reasoning Frisby might turn out to be a *flâneur* himself.

Frisby follows Benjamin's example by making Simmel a victim of class bias in addition to revealing a personality defect (neurasthenia) in him. Unlike Baudelaire, Simmel cannot be called a petty bourgeois, so the analogy with the *flâneur* is more tenuous in his case. For Frisby, the most proximate social type to Simmel is the salon intellectual who values the interesting fragment or charming vignette higher than the systematic totalization. Simmel, indeed, ran a salon, and it is pointless to deny that the norms of polite conversation impacted on his writing style. Whether they governed the content of his thought is another question. The salon intellectual is made by Frisby the bourgeois equivalent of the *flâneur*. Both of them are innocuous and, finally, superfluous. In this light Simmel's sociological works become 'images of a section of the bourgeoisie that is no longer confident, that feels the need to distance itself from a reality it no longer controls' (Frisby, 1981: 83). That is, just like Benjamin's petty bourgeoisie, the educated bourgeoisie in imperial Germany had nothing to do but pass its time, and it was enabled to do so by aestheticizing its reality.

The critiques of Simmel's character and of the class bias of his thought come together in Frisby's notion that Simmel is a retreatist. Alluding to Simmel's idea that the objective and subjective dimensions of culture are in conflict in modern life, Frisby (1981: 88) asserts: 'The response to this tragic contradiction is the inward retreat to subjectivism, the retreat to the *intérieur*.' There is no need to deny the cogency of a class analysis to explain aspects of Simmel's thought in order to question the characterization of him as a retreatist. Indeed, the term retreatist does not seem adequate to characterize even the *flâneur*, who makes a point of going out in the world, if only to observe it. It certainly does not provide the complexity necessary to account for why someone would study intensively that which they are determined to hold at a distance.

What is a *flâneur*, if not a retreatist? To answer this question it might first be advisable to sketch a Simmel-style formal analysis of the *flâneur* along lines consistent with Benjamin's definition of the type, though not necessarily with his interpretation of it. Although the *flâneur* does not appear in Simmel's own gallery of social forms, the type is amenable to Simmelian analysis because it shares boundary-crossing and mediating attributes with such figures as the stranger and the adventurer. The *flâneur*, according to Benjamin, takes the urban scene as a spectacle, strolling through it as though it were a diorama, that is, detached from involvement with its practical concerns and purposes. In making public places into playgrounds, the *flâneur* takes advantage of the systems of public order and control, and of production, which permit him to stroll safely and be entertained by the human comedy. He does not contribute to the maintenance or alteration of these systems, but has a parasitical relationship with them. The *flâneur* could not exist on a desert island or in the state of nature. He might be called a 'surplus value' of the city, a type made possible by industrial capitalism and

inconceivable beyond the protected environment that it provides to the bourgeoisie in periods of relative stability. The *flâneur*
de-historizes the city, breaking it apart into a shower of events,
primarily sights. He emphasizes synchrony over diachrony, and has
no interest in systematizing the fragments of urban life. Each one
is an aesthetic object to him, existing to titillate, astonish, please,
or delight him. He appropriates the city as performance art, not
seeking to know it and certainly not trying to reform it; but merely
enjoying it.

The *flâneur's* supercilious manner, so despised by respectable
society, is necessary to protect him from being taken seriously by
others. The *flâneur* is an observer, a spectator, a gazer; and, as both
Simmel and Sartre have shown vividly, the glance has powerful
effects on the psyche and in constituting social relations (Weinstein
and Weinstein, 1984). The *flâneur* would be met with antipathy and
in some cases would even be endangered if he adopted the pose of
surveillance. By playing the fop he shows everyone that he is not
concerned with getting the goods on them, but, indeed, deems them
unworthy of all but superficial and momentary attention. In order
not to provoke fear he risks provoking scorn. He must be innocuous
in order that society be innocuous for him. Too detached to be a
gossip, he is not above listening to gossip as another emanation of
the urban scene. The *flâneur* is an idler, but he passes his time in
the midst of the world of affairs.

Benjamin is astute when he identifies the *flâneur* with Poe's 'man
of the crowd', who cannot exist apart from the presence of other
human beings, but has no positive relations with them. He seeks out
others with desperation, because he panics at being by himself. The
flâneur is, perhaps, a sublimation of the man of the crowd, able at
least to hold himself a bit aloof from the society that provides him
with the *raison d'être* of his life. Rather than suffering from a
psychosis, an implosion of self, like the man of the crowd, the
flâneur shows signs of neurosis, of life lived as a compromise.
Perhaps the term 'neurasthenia' applies well here, since the *flâneur*
does not seem to touch reality with direct confidence but with
'fingertips that are immediately withdrawn'. It is like the game that
the moth plays with the flame and it might be a way of neutralizing
the overload of urban stimuli, of coping with a fear of others or
with a fear of one's own inadequacy in relation to others, or, more
fundamentally, of coping with an ambivalence toward others, a
need of and a loathing for them, the hallmark of Kant's 'unsociable

social being', the empirical self. If Simmel is called a *flâneur*, perhaps what is meant most deeply is that he has this ambivalence in an acute form, that he must toy with his fellow human beings but does not have the strength of humanity to commit himself to them. In terms of psychology, the *flâneur*/Simmel would, according to this view, be determined by inferiority feelings which had blossomed into the classical inferiority complex. Airs of superiority. Unwillingness to risk himself for fear of revealing his inferiority. Abstention from the struggles of the community. Perhaps there is some truth to this, both as a psychology of the *flâneur* and as a diagnosis of Simmel. Some truth, because there is an alternative to this character criticism.

In his treatment of the *flâneur* Benjamin quotes Simmel, not to criticize him, but for theoretical support. According to Simmel (Benjamin, 1973: 37–8), 'Someone who sees without hearing is much more uneasy than someone who hears without seeing. . . . Interpersonal relationships in big cities are distinguished by a marked preponderance of the activity of the eye over the activity of the ear.' Simmel then goes on to argue that in systems of public transportation people are thrown into the position of having to look at each other for extended durations without speaking to each other. Perhaps, using one of Simmel's favourite terms, the *flâneur* should be considered the 'play-form' of the practice of refraining from verbal and gestural communication when one cannot help gazing at others and being gazed at by them. The *flâneur* perfects this restraint and makes it into a style of urban living that produces pleasure. From this viewpoint the *flâneur*'s practice would be play in the Foucauldian panoptic society, the neutralization or deconstruction of the scrutinizing gaze of commerce and administration, a subversion of the official society, perhaps even a kind of situationist *détournement*. As *détournement* it would not be motivated by feelings of inferiority but by recognition that the community had been eclipsed by systems of planned organization, so that there was no more community to commit oneself to, not even a progressive class.

Here is the core of the matter between Benjamin's and Frisby's modern-progressive criticism of character, and a postmodernist alternative: does the *flâneur* seek to escape from a commitment or is the kind of commitment that Benjamin and Frisby imply questionable itself? It is a problem of the strategies and tactics of engagement in modern/postmodern society, which in turn depends upon the intellectual question concerning the general form of that 'society'. That is, it is not a problem of engagement and retreat, but of different forms of engagement. It would not be so damaging to Simmel's character if it was associated with the play-form interpretation of the *flâneur* presented above. But even in that sense, Simmel is not a *flâneur*. The *flâneur* does not study society, but wanders through it, going, as Benjamin quips, 'botanizing on the asphalt', that is, collecting experiences. Simmel is more than a collector. He seeks knowledge of his milieu, not merely diversion from it. Even Frisby admits that.

The *Bricoleur*

In the most philosophical moment of his critique of Simmel's intellectual character, Frisby defines the structure of Simmel's thought process and relates it to a fundamental issue in theoretical sociology. For Frisby (1981: 81), 'It is through the examination of the particular and the fragmentary that Simmel hopes to grasp what is universal.' Here Frisby's characterization breaks away from the model of the *flâneur*. While both Simmel and the *flâneur* are concerned with the fragment, no *flâneur* would be interested in trying to grasp what was universal about it. Simmel is at no distance from the object of knowledge; he is thoroughly engaged with it, seeking to make it yield universal significance. He lets that object be only insofar as it is necessary to do so in the interest of objectivity. Beyond that the object is put into a disciplined conceptual play, the cognitive yield of which is chains of significance connecting diverse cultural objects. The task is to seek whatever orders of homology and analogy can be discerned in what initially appears to be radically heterogeneous. As Frisby (1981: 81) notes, 'Simmel, as the astute wanderer, can connect seemingly isolated fragments with other apparently unrelated fragments.' Promoted from *flâneur* to astute wanderer (very near to where he belongs).

But Frisby (1981: 81) also remarks that although, 'through sensitive reflection upon each of life's fragments one can arrive at an understanding of some aspect of society as a totality . . . society conceived as a totality is an absent concept in Simmel's thought'. Here is the issue of the culture war on its philosophical plane. Can one credibly conceive of modern/postmodern society as a totality, or is it wiser to conceive of that society as a tangle of tightly and loosely coupled syntagmatic chains? As astute wanderer, Simmel chooses the latter, postmodernist, alternative. Which of the alternatives is the truer is not directly in question here. But if Simmel has some truth on his side, he might not be a *flâneur* or a neurasthenic, but simply sane and lucid. He is mapping the heterogeneous rather than revealing a deeper homogeneity, a common nature that would make diverse appearances a totality. For Simmel, it is a victory to understand 'some aspect of a society' *as a totality*, that is, to construct a totalization of society from one of the aspects in terms of which it can be totalized. There is no totalization of totalizations for him, no meta-narrative, and no deep structures. Such forms simply do not seem to him to be immanent to the complexes of modern culture that are his primary objects of study. Conflicts and stalemates are what seem to be immanent to them. In the absence of system there is the systematization of conflict, postmodern bricolage.

The practice of seeking generality through particularity recalls the *bricoleur* that Lévi-Strauss described in *The Savage Mind* (1966). The meaning of *bricoleur* in French popular speech is 'someone who works with his hands and uses devious means compared to those of a craftsman' (Lévi-Strauss, 1966: 16–17). That is, the *bricoleur* is a sly handyman, who accumulates a stock of items and takes from it whatever might seem to be useful to complete the job that he is presently doing: 'His universe of instruments is closed and the rules of his game are always to make do with "whatever is at hand", that is to say with a set of tools and materials which is always finite and is also heterogeneous because what it contains bears no relation to the current project, or indeed to any particular project, but is the contingent result of all the occasions there have been to renew or enrich the stock or to maintain it with the remains of previous constructions or destructions' (Lévi-Strauss, 1966: 17).

The result of the *bricoleur*'s method is a bricolage, a construction that arises from interrogating 'all the heterogeneous objects' of which the *bricoleur*'s 'treasury is composed to discover what each of them could "signify" and so contribute to the definition of a set which has yet to materialize but which will ultimately differ from the instrumental set [of the craftsman or engineer] only in the internal disposition of its parts' (Lévi-Strauss, 1966: 18). The *bricoleur* is practical and gets the job done, but it is not always or even usually the same job that was initially undertaken and is uniquely structured by the set of 'preconstrained' elements that are selected from the treasury. A substitution of one element for another would change the form of the construction. The *bricoleur* works and plays with the stock. His parts are not standardized or invented; they are appropriated for new uses.

An intellectual *bricoleur* does not do hand work with tools and materials, but brain work with signifiers and significations. As an intellectual *bricoleur*, Simmel deploys a fixed stock of signifiers, the cultural and mental forms that social life has taken. That is, his treasury is the stock of culture that is given to him in his social environment, and the psychological and existential responses that are generally made to it. He does not interpret culture through a utopia, nor does he develop a special technical language to describe its deep structure or to explain its dynamics. Rather, he constructs syntagmatic chains out of the stock, each of which reveals 'some aspect of a society as a totality'. These claims connect, as Frisby noted, 'seemingly isolated fragments with other apparently unrelated fragments'. Simmel's totalizations are constructions of the culture as received, not reintegrations of it. His constructions suggest order within a field of heterogeneous contents. He 'makes do' with 'whatever is at hand'.[1]

Not only is the 'set' with which Simmel works finite; it is also heterogeneous. The cultural and mental forms that compose his stock are the 'contingent results' of life's precipitation of culture, which he uses for the new purpose of aspectival totalization. These forms were not created and are not maintained, altered or destroyed for the project of totalization, but are the very ways in which society is constituted. If they all happened to fit within a logically coherent system, if they could be described adequately in terms of homology and logical equivalence and negation, all the better. But they cannot be so described, and the intellectual *bricoleur* is constrained to apply such thought forms and processes as analogy and qualitative opposition to the task of construction. Conceived as sociological *bricoleur*, Simmel is on a mission of cultural mapping, tracing the affinities and ruptures among the cultural complexes of the modern/postmodern metropolis. Renouncing transcendence over the cultural stock in his capacities of sociologist and cultural theorist, he finds as much order in that stock as he can wrest from it by using his intellectual imagination.

Simmel as *bricoleur* is a practitioner of a demystified savage mind, a post-structuralist before the advent of structuralism. The mystified savage mind, the one that Lévi-Strauss devoted himself to describing, works with a finite and heterogeneous stock of signs, but feels compelled to reconcile the heterogeneity through metonymical and metaphorical mediations, which do not provide logical coherence, but which somehow offer satisfaction to the mind, which enjoys the symbolic reconciliation. The demystified savage mind is, in contrast, a postmodern critic, unmasking the reconciliations of the mystified savage mind, showing connections where there was supposed to be separation, and identifying rupture where mythic reconciliation was supposed to have occurred. By pointing out where the ruptures and oppositions appear in structurally based cultural complexes, the sociological *bricoleur* becomes a social diagnostician (not a shaman), who identifies the sites at which myth is most likely to arise. His surprising connections disturb the taboos of hierarchy and of seriousness ('sociability', for example, becomes indicative of how society is fundamentally constituted), and his disconnections disturb the myths of identification. The *bricoleur* is only innocuous if people cannot or will not attend to him. Of course, he cannot compel them to entertain a better map of their circumstances. He does not have any 'divisions' to deploy, not even a holy office — only signifiers. He cannot, like Lévi-Strauss, even plead the cause of a future positive science of deep structures, since his rules of the game constrain him to describing the forms that characterize the apparent cultural complexes (within themselves, in relation to each other, and in relation to psychological/existential responses to them). That is, he constructs a bricolage from his stock.

Metropolis: Bricolage
About a third of the way through 'The Metropolis and Mental Life' Simmel (1950: 413) pauses from his main discussion and reflects on the import of his method: '. . . the general conclusions of this entire task of reflection become obvious, namely, that from each point on the surface of existence — however closely attached to the surface alone — one may drop a sounding into the depth of the psyche so that all the most banal externalities of life finally are connected with the ultimate decisions concerning the meaning and style of life'. Here is confirmation, expansion and explanation, in Simmel's text, of Frisby's point that Simmel 'can connect seemingly isolated fragments with other apparently unrelated fragments'. Those fragments can be related to each other intelligibly because all of them are somehow also related to 'ultimate decisions concerning the meaning and style of life'. That does not mean that the psyche generates the appearances, as idealism would hold; nor that the appearances are

merely organized in the unconscious mind, as Lévi-Strauss seems to hold; but that there is a relation between the surface and the interior, if only metaphorical. As *bricoleur* Simmel connects the banal externalities of life to each other, and then to what would later in the century be called existential concerns.[2] His relations are meaningful, not causal, but they do not provide a meaning for the totality: they reveal aspects of a totality that shows certain comprehensive patterns of order that answer to the problems posed by the ego-centred discourse of the existential self. But that self is de-centred by the sociological discourse of 'The Metropolis' (Simmel, 1971), which does not privilege, causally or ontologically, the existential self; rather, that self appears, not as the protagonist, but as an interlude in a sociocultural bricolage.

As bricolage 'The Metropolis and Mental Life' displays a structure of analogy and opposition, metaphor and metonymy; that is, a structure of similarity in difference, and of difference in similarity. Cutting through and yet constituting the chain of discourse is the opposition between the *blasé* and intellectualized self, which is interpreted as a defensive action of the self against being overwhelmed by the diverse and often adverse stimuli of the metropolitan environment; and the interior self, associated with romanticism and in rebellion against the metropolis and the defensive adaptations of the psyche to it, which demands expression and acknowledgment of, if not submission to, its unique contents. That is, the metropolis is not productive of one form of mental life, but conditions two irreconcilable, yet intelligible, mental responses to it. One of them, the protective, nurtures the calculative freedom of the rational ego (Enlightenment freedom) and the other, the expressive, is the romantic freedom to determine one's life according to one's inner nature.

The most comprehensive structure of 'The Metropolis' is metonymic. The totality of metropolitan life is first viewed under the aspect of the defensive self and then under the aspect of the expressive self. Neither one is allowed to claim victory; they stalemate each other, and their stalemate is the synchronic analogue to diachronic theories of meaning and direction in history.[3] There is no meaningful totality: 'The metropolis reveals itself as one of those great historical formations in which opposing streams which enclose life unfold, as well as join one another with equal right' (Simmel, 1950: 423). But there is an intelligible opposition between two versions of and responses to totality, indeed, to the same totality, but with differences. (Enter Derrida and undecidability.) 'The Metropolis' is a bricolage in which the form of the 'metropolis' mediates between two alternative totalizations of itself. It cannot unify them, but it can bring them together by placing them on a common ground.

Although that common ground cannot be defined apart from the two aspectival totalizations of it, it is indicated metaphorically by a series of structural analogies between levels of metropolitan life that cut across the opposition between the defensive and expressive responses to the metropolis. Especially in the division of the chain devoted to the defensive self, Simmel composes a fugue, showing how the intellectualization of life, as a protection against sensory and emotional overload, corresponds to the depersonalized and calculating mentality of the money economy, which in turn corresponds to the calculative precision of the natural sciences and the need for a uniform system of mechanical time to coordinate the disparate practical activities of the metropolis. Then he does a reprise, showing how the defence mechanism of the *blasé* attitude corresponds to the devaluation of the objective world and, finally, of the self in a 'completely internalized money economy', which in turn corresponds to the psychological reserve, masking mild antipathy, which is required for people to pursue their particular affairs without mutual interference. Thus, Simmel moves from the more superficial to the deeper, using successive sets of analogies between the same three levels, creating a tight weave among the elements he has taken from his stock to place in his bricolage.

When he turns to the expressive self, Simmel follows the same strategy of moving from periphery to core, tracing the drive to be unique and different from others first to the sheer size and specialized fragmentation of the metropolis, which makes people strive to be distinguished by each other; and then to the unmasterable 'overgrowth' of objective culture, which threatens to overwhelm individuals and provokes their efforts to summon 'the utmost in uniqueness and particularization', in order to preserve their most personal cores. Here analogous external structures (size/specialization and cultural-mass/complexity) are related to analogous personal responses (the need to be distinguished by others and the need to distinguish oneself to oneself). Again the relations are analogical and meaningful — a bricolage — not homological and causal.

The 'metropolis' is, for Simmel (1950: 409), a structure 'set up between the individual and the super-individual contents of life',

that is, a mediation between the objective culture of institutionalized pursuits, each with its autonomous standards, and the subjective culture of personal character. But in an 'overgrown' objective
culture the metropolis is capable only of mediating opposition to
the individual. The stock of the *bricoleur* that is appropriate
to defining the most comprehensive social structure, the context
of modern life, its physical and sociocultural site, does not
allow for a single and consistent totalization. One form of life, the
modern(postmodern) metropolis, gives rise to opposing responses,
through which that form of life is interpreted, but neither of which
is sustainable as an organizing principle for personality because
it excludes what is cogent, intelligible, perhaps, justifiable in the
alternative.

The detached and intellectualized ego, void of emotional
response, confronts the expressive self, void of calculative reason. Each is an intelligible response, illuminating an aspect of the
totality; but neither is a sufficient response, just because it is aspectival (presents an aspect of totality). The preferred contemporary
mythology, advertising, is in large part an exercise in merging these
responses, without being able to synthesize them; that is, it identifies
circumspective calculation with expressive emotion, the purchase of
a commodity with the core of personality. But in the absence of
models of character, appropriate to mediating engagement in a
coherent objective culture, the reflective and self-critical individual
is forced by the duplicitous mediation of the metropolis to become
a *bricoleur*. The incoherence of the stock of signifiers indicates a
built-in incoherence to modern life. The individual must cobble
together whatever meaning can be wrested from the irreducible
and irreconcilable fragments of reality. Even the most fateful
and existential decision, that between the two forms of self and
of freedom, is made within this sociocultural horizon of elusive,
unrationalizable totality. Simmel has constructed the bricolage that
makes intelligible the strategy of being the *bricoleur* of one's own
personality.

A *bricoleur*, not a *flâneur*. Simmel (1950: 423–4) concludes 'The
Metropolis' by asserting that in the process of the struggle between
and changing entanglements of the two responses to (post)modern
life, 'the currents of life, whether their individual phenomena touch
us sympathetically or antipathetically, entirely transcend the sphere
for which the judge's attitude is appropriate. Since such forces of
life have grown into the roots and into the crown of the whole of

the historical life in which we, in our fleeting existence as a cell, belong only as a part, it is not our task either to accuse or to pardon, but only to understand.' Sociological progressives (and reactionaries) want to judge, and in order to do so they need to hold that society is a describable totality. Postmodernism, by negating modern historicist sociology, also negates its humanism. There is nowhere that 'man' stands to define 'himself'. Each individual is a cell in an overwhelming organism, which is divided in itself. This is not a 'tragic' view, as Frisby would have it, but something even worse from his viewpoint, a destiny or fatality. But fatality appears only from the form of sociology. For the individual there is liberation to gratuity, which can take up sacrifice or commitment as easily as it can observational play.

It is doubtless that the modern self is afraid of the gratuity of any commitment with reference to its historical meaning, that is, of not knowing which side will win or even if the struggle has yet to be decided. But historical gratuity is the grace of the postmodern condition, the opportunity to be a *bricoleur*, to construct a self and strategy of living from the shards of objective culture.

Notes

1. In the process of making chains of meaning from cultural stock Simmel is often a *bricoleur* of the second order, using the same element in more than one chain, sometimes to different effect. For example, Simmel (1950: 154–62, 232–4) uses the form of *tertius gaudens* to illuminate the structure of the triad and that of subordination. An element is sometimes detachable from any specific perspective and, thus, fit to function in more than one perspective.

2. The following interpretation of 'The Metropolis and Mental Life' as bricolage is a supplement to interpretations of 'The Metropolis' as the deconstruction of community that are presented in previous work by the authors (Weinstein and Weinstein, 1989, 1990).

3. The stalemate is one of Simmel's favourite forms of argumentation. See *Schopenhauer and Nietzsche* (Simmel, 1986) for his uses of the stalemate in philosophical discourse.

References

Benjamin, Walter (1973) *Charles Baudelaire: A Lyric Poet in the Era of High Capitalism*. Translated by Harry Zohn. London: New Left Books.

Frisby, David (1981) *Sociological Impressionism: A Reassessment of Georg Simmel's Social Theory*. London: Heinemann.

Lévi-Strauss, Claude (1966) *The Savage Mind*. Chicago, IL: University of Chicago Press.

Simmel, Georg (1950) *The Sociology of Georg Simmel*. Translated and edited by Kurt Wolff. New York: Free Press.

Simmel, Georg (1971) 'The Metropolis and Mental Life', in G. Simmel, *On Individuality and Social Forms* (ed. D. Levine). Chicago, IL: University of Chicago Press.

Simmel, Georg (1986) *Schopenhauer and Nietzsche*. Translated by H. Loiskandl, D. Weinstein and M.A. Weinstein. Amherst, MA: University of Massachusetts Press.

Weinstein, Deena and Michael A. Weinstein (1984) 'On the Visual Constitution of Society: The Contributions of Georg Simmel and Jean-Paul Sartre to Sociology of the Senses', *History of European Ideas* 5(1): 349-62.

Weinstein, Deena and Michael A. Weinstein (1989) 'Simmel and the Dialectic of the Double Boundary: The Case of the Metropolis and Mental Life', *Sociological Inquiry* 59(1): 48-59.

Weinstein, Deena and Michael A. Weinstein (1990) 'Dimensions of Conflict: Georg Simmel on Modern Life', pp. 341-55 in Michael Kaern et al. (eds), *Georg Simmel and Contemporary Sociology*. Boston, MA: Kluwer.

Deena Weinstein teaches Sociology at De Paul University, Chicago, Illinois, USA.

Michael A. Weinstein teaches Political Science at Purdue University, West Lafayette, Indiana, USA.

Individualization, Exaggeration and Paralysation: Simmel's Three Problems of Culture

Birgitta Redelmann

The Triadic Frame of Reference

The relationship between culture and the individual is a central research topic within the field of the sociology of culture. It has entered into sociological discourse in various semantic and theoretical disguises. As a consequence, a range of complementary and contradictory conceptualizations have been generated. One prominent example is Margaret Archer's approach (1988). She conceptualizes the relationship between culture and agency in systemic terms, adopting a dualistic approach. She examines both the influence of the cultural system (CS) upon human agency (or the sociocultural level), and the influence of human actors upon the cultural system. The principle of analytical dualism allows her to distinguish between three different problems.

The first one concerns the question of how human beings make culture. The cultural system is analysed as originating from the sociocultural level, and human agents as producers of the cultural system.

The second problem relates to a discussion of long-term changes. Archer explores how the cultural system, after having become autonomous, influences the sociocultural level and acts back on subsequent generations of people. Cultural systems which have become autonomous from their immediate creators have in their turn an influence upon subsequent generations as 'receivers' of those cultural products which previous generations have created.

The third question raised by Archer (1988: 144) concerns the problem of cultural change: How do 'new items enter the CS

Theory, Culture & Society (SAGE, London, Newbury Park and New Delhi), Vol. 8 (1991), 169–193

and [how are] old ones . . . displaced'? Human agents are again conceptualized as producers of culture, but, in contrast to the first problem, now those cultural changes are emphasized which are brought about by human agents adding new cultural items to the already created and autonomized CS and displacing old ones. This then entails an exploration of the impact which human agencies have upon the cultural system in their role as cultural transformers.

These three problems of the sociology of culture raised by Archer can be situated within a triadic frame of reference:

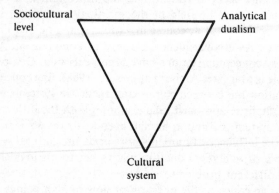

Sociocultural
level

Analytical
dualism

Cultural
system

This triadic scheme is a most fruitful heuristic device for generating theoretically interesting and empirically relevant problems within the field of the sociology of culture. In this article I show that there is a further way of generating such problems by adopting a similar triadic frame of reference. Its point of departure is Georg Simmel's sociology of culture, itself a highly complex and somewhat incoherent body of thought. Rather than talking about Simmel's 'theory of culture' (as some Simmel scholars do — see Levine, 1971: XV and Scaff, 1990a: 284), I prefer to talk about Simmel's *theories* of culture. It is precisely the plurality of his theories from which the present discussion in the field of the sociology of culture can profit. The richness of Simmel's thought results from the different ways in which he defines the basic concept of culture, the different ways in which he conceptualizes the role of the individual in the cultural process, and the different analytical principles he uses when analysing the relationship between cultural level and individual level. It is hoped that a re-analysis and re-formulation of his contribution, could help to stimulate the theorization of this field, and sharpen our understanding of ongoing cultural problems in contemporary societies.

Simmel's Triadic Frame of Reference

Simmel's work offers different points of departure for the analysis of culture. Within the limitations of this article, I draw attention to three different approaches. They have a common basis in a triadic frame of reference, yet differ from each other with regard to their underlying analytical principles and analytical definition of the two main poles, culture and the individual. According to the first version, the individual pole is conceptualized in terms of cultural *creativity*, and culture as a social system. In the second version individuals are analysed from the point of view of social actors consciously *consuming* cultural goods, and culture as the social sphere in which processes of cultural exchange and lifestyle management take place. In the third approach individuals are analysed in their role as *receivers* of cultural objects and culture as social structure. The analytical principle underlying the first type of approach is the principle of *antagonism*. In the second version Simmel uses the principle of *ambivalence* in order to define the relationship between individuals as cultural consumers and the sphere of culture. In the third version it is the principle of *dualism* which is responsible for the tensions between individuals as receivers of cultural objects and the cultural structure. Accordingly, we will speak of the first version as the model of *cultural antagonism*, of the second version as the model of *cultural ambivalence*, and of the third version as the model of *cultural dualism*.

There is yet another decisive way in which these three analytical approaches differ from each other. They can be interpreted as analytical tools with the help of which Simmel identifies three different problems of modern culture. The first one he refers to via the concept 'cultural malaise', the second 'exaggerated subjectivism' (or stylelessness), and the third, 'tragedy of culture'. The latter is perhaps one of the most well-known Simmelian concepts, but at the same time it is often misunderstood. I will explore in more detail the kind of cultural phenomena Simmel had in mind when talking about these problems. Table 1 gives an overview of the main dimensions for discussing the three Simmelian models of culture.

Table 1
Simmel's Three Models of Culture

	I. Model of cultural antagonism	II. Model of cultural ambivalence	III. Model of cultural dualism
Individual pole	Individuals as creators of culture ('life')	Individuals as consumers of culture or lifestyle managers	Individuals as receivers of culture ('subjective culture')
Cultural pole	Culture as social system ('forms')	Culture as aesthetic sphere	Culture as social structure ('objective culture')
Analytical principle	Antagonism between 'life' and 'form'	Ambivalence of action orientation	Dualism between subjective and objective culture
Cultural problem	'Cultural malaise' (individualization)	'Exaggerated subjectivism' (stylelessness of modern culture)	'Tragedy of culture': paralysation (incommensurability of subjective and objective culture)

I. Cultural Antagonism

The first model refers to Simmel's essay, 'The Conflict of Modern Culture', written in 1918 (Simmel, 1976). As other scholars have already remarked, Simmel uses a somewhat 'exotic language' (Scaff, 1990a: 287) which needs clarification and specification. The two poles of culture and the individual are conceptualized here as an opposition between 'form' and 'life'.[1] This vocabulary is easier to understand if we recall the Marxian terminology of an opposition between productive forces and relations of production, frequently quoted by Simmel himself. In a similar way to the Marxian notion of the forces of production as the ultimate driving force of the process of social change, Simmel defines 'life' as the ultimate driving force of the process of cultural change. 'Life' can be translated as the creative potential on the individual level, as the productive forces of culture. It is important to emphasize that Simmel uses this concept from a macrosociological point of view. In the context of the model, he is not concerned about the creative activity of each single individual, but of cultural creativity as resulting from human agents' collective cultural efforts.

The analogy between Marx and Simmel's terminology holds also true for the concept of relations of production and social forms. Cultural creativity (the forces of production) have to struggle against social forms (relations of production) in order to realize themselves. In contrast to the dynamics of cultural creativity, cultural forms are relatively fixed and timeless and therefore constitute a relatively rigid institutional context for the realization of individuals' creative potential. Hence Simmel refers to '. . . culture when the creative dynamism of life produces certain artefacts which provide it with forms of expression and actualization, and which in their turn absorb the constant flow of life, giving it form and content, scope and order; e.g. civil laws and constitutions, works of art, religion, science, technology and innumerable others' (Simmel, 1976: 223).

Simmel's concept of cultural forms comes very close to our understanding of culture as a system. This becomes obvious when Simmel explains, that it is 'a peculiar quality of these products of the life-process (. . .) that from the first moment of their existence they have fixed forms of their own, set apart from the febrile rhythm of life itself, its waxing and waning, its constant renewal, its continual divisions and reunifications' (Simmel, 1976: 223). Cultural forms are transformed into social systems when they develop 'their own logic and laws, their own significance and resilience arising from a certain degree of detachment and independence vis-à-vis the spiritual dynamism which gave them life' (Simmel, 1976: 223). Due to these systemic properties cultural forms can achieve a certain degree of autonomy from the cultural forces which have created them. But the greater the autonomy of cultural forms as social system, the greater the antagonistic tension between them and the creative forces of culture ('life').

We can now proceed to specifying the relationship between cultural system and cultural creativity as a *mutually interdependent* and *antagonistic* relationship. This again reminds us of the type of relationship that Marx assumes for the forces and relations of production. The cultural system and cultural creativity, form and life, are mutually interdependent because: a) cultural creativity can only become social reality in certain forms, and b) cultural forms can only survive in the long run if they receive the creative inputs from the individual level. We can now look more closely at the two sides of this interdependent, antagonistic relationship.

With regard to the first side of this relationship (the dependence of cultural creativity ['life'] upon cultural forms), Simmel explains:

. . . life must either produce forms, or proceed within given forms. What we *are* is, it is true, spontaneous life, with its equally spontaneous, unanalyzable

> sense of being, vitality and purposiveness, but what we *have* is only its particular form at any one time, which, as I have stressed above, proves from the moment of its creation to be part of a quite different order of things. (Simmel, 1976: 240)

As human creativity can only express itself in and through cultural forms, it necessarily has to create its own antagonistic counterpart.

> Life is ineluctably condemned to become reality only in the guise of its opposite, i.e. as *form*. (Simmel, 1976: 240)

It is this built-in paradox which gives rise to the intrinsic dynamic in the relationship between cultural creativity and the cultural system. In producing cultural forms, individuals not only create the opposite of their spontaneous needs and desires, but also the motives for continuous cultural change.

> It is the nature of life to produce within itself that which guides and redeems it, and that which opposes, conquers and is conquered by it. (Simmel, 1976: 236)

What concerns the other side of this relationship, the cultural forms, is that they are equally dependent upon its antagonistic counterpart, cultural creativity. Without such inputs like ideas, desires, motives and needs, cultural systems could not survive in the long run. They have therefore necessarily to associate themselves with those cultural forces which change, and, in the end, destroy them. The very moment of their construction is at the same time the beginning of their destruction. Simmel describes this process of cultural change metaphorically as a process 'between the poles of death and rebirth, rebirth and death' (Simmel, 1976: 224).

This metaphor reminds us again of the Marxian model of social change. Firstly, like Marx, Simmel assumes that there is a latent opposition between the creative forces and the cultural system. This opposition increases in strength, the more the latter becomes autonomous and the more the former cannot realize itself within the fixed context of existing cultural institutions.

> . . . it is the essence of form to lay claim, the moment it is established, to a more than momentary validity not governed by the impulse of life. . . . That is why there is from the very outset a latent tension between these forms and life, which subsequently erupts in various areas of our lives and activity. (Simmel, 1976: 224–5)

Secondly, like Marx, Simmel argues that human creativity and cultural institutions develop at a different speed. The forces of cultural creativity develop quicker than the cultural institutions they have created. The cultural system thus lags behind the development of human creativity. In Simmel's words, there is a

> perpetual struggle between life, with its fundamental restlessness, evolutions and mobility, and its own creations, which become inflexible and lag behind its development. Since, however, life can take on external existence only in one form or another, this process can be clearly identified and described in terms of the displacement of one form by another. (Simmel, 1976: 224)

This Simmelian model of cultural change can be understood as a model of intrinsic cultural dynamics, pushed forward by the necessity of cultural creativity to produce its own contradiction, i.e. cultural institutions, on the one hand, and the necessity of the cultural system to integrate cultural inputs into its systemic boundaries, on the other. This necessity to associate themselves with their antagonistic counterparts is responsible for the autonomous dynamics of cultural change which, according to Simmel, in principle has no end.

There is however an important difference to the Marxian dialectics of societal change. According to Simmel, there is no definite solution of this endless cultural antagonism. 'It is . . . pure philistinism to assume that all conflicts and problems are meant to be solved' (Simmel, 1976: 241), as he says. Cultural conflict and permanent change according to the pattern of 'death and rebirth, rebirth and death' are constitutive elements of the first model of cultural antagonism.

The Cultural Malaise: Individualization

At the outset I claimed that Simmel's sociology of culture helps to generate new problems and sharpen our awareness of actual cultural conflicts. What does Simmel's model of cultural antagonism and intrinsic cultural change add to our understanding of contemporary cultural problems?

In order to answer this question it is helpful to return to Simmel's analysis and to see how he applied this antagonistic model for the analysis of the cultural problems at the beginning of the twentieth century. According to his diagnosis the antagonism between cultural institutions and individual creativity had reached a climax and been transformed into what he calls a general *Kulturnot*, a cultural malaise (translation of the term by P.A. Lawrence). Simmel illustrates his diagnosis with examples drawn from different cultural spheres — philosophy, arts, religion, science. They had in common the fact that culturally productive individuals no longer contented themselves with changing existing cultural institutions according to their needs, but that they started to revolt against existing cultural institutions, against forms as such. So, for example, Simmel describes the problems individuals of his time had with such traditional institutions like marriage and prostitution, which they found equally inappropriate for realizing their erotic desires. It is worth quoting this example at length:

> The theme of the critique is, fundamentally, that erotic life is striving to assert its own authentic, inmost energy and natural proclivity against the forms in which our culture has in general imprisoned it, robbed it of its vitality and caused it to violate its own nature. Marriage is contracted in innumerable cases for other than actual erotic reasons, and thus, in innumerable cases, the vital erotic impulse either stagnates or perishes when its individuality comes up against inflexible traditions and legal cruelty. Prostitution, which has almost become a legalized institution, forces young people's love life to take on a debased form, a caricature which transgresses against its inmost nature. These are the forms against which authentic spontaneous life is in revolt. (Simmel, 1976: 237)

This example shows that the dynamic pattern of cultural change, described above as a continuous process of substituting old institutions by new ones ('death and rebirth, rebirth and death'), has been broken: within the sphere of erotic relationships, the antagonism between cultural institutions and cultural creativity has given rise to neither innovation of institutions, nor to 'merely licentiousness and anarchistic lust', that is, to destruction of traditional forms and formlessness (Simmel, 1976: 237). The cultural malaise expresses itself in still another way:

> Authentic erotic life flows along wholly individual channels, and the above forms arouse hostility because they trap this life in institutionalized patterns and thus do violence to its special individuality. Here, as in many other cases, it is the struggle between life and form which, in a less abstract, metaphysical way, is being fought out as a struggle *between individuality and standardization* [*zwischen Individualisierung und Verallgemeinerung*]. (Simmel, 1976: 237, my italics)

It is this process of *individualization of cultural creativity* which Simmel is so deeply concerned about. The cultural malaise is not limited to the erotic sphere, but is characteristic of all cultural spheres in modern societies. For Simmel, individualization of cultural creativity, the escape from the cultural system as a whole, is a fundamental dilemma of modern society.

> This, however, goes against the essence of life itself, its surging dynamism, its temporal fortunes, the inexorable differentiation of all its elements. Life is ineluctably condemned to become reality only in the guise of its opposite, i.e. as *form*. (Simmel, 1976: 240)

Religious, erotic, ethical, scientific or artistic creative needs 'can, from the outset, only become articulate in *forms*. Its *freedom* likewise can only be actualized in forms, even though they also immediately restrict that form' (Simmel, 1976: 239).

The more the cultural process progresses, the more this cultural malaise is transformed into an acute dilemma:

> This paradox becomes more acute, more apparently insoluble, to the degree that the inner being which we can only call life *tout court* asserts its formless vitality, while at the same time inflexible, independent forms claim timeless legitimacy and invite us to accept them as the true meaning and value of our lives — i.e. the paradox is intensified, perhaps, to the degree to which culture progresses. (Simmel, 1976: 240)

The more cultural institutions claim autonomy, the less individuals will find their cultural demands represented, and the more they will react with retreatism from the cultural system as a whole and with individualistic responses. On the other hand, the more cultural creativity finds individualistic channels of expression, the more the cultural system is cut off from the individuals' creative energy, and, as a consequence, the more it develops in orientation to its own systemic needs. If this development of individualization continues, the cultural system will be more and more composed of lifeless artefacts. The level of individual creativity, on the other hand, will become more and more disintegrated and finally consist of nothing else but unrelated idiosyncratic acts. As a consequence, it will become increasingly difficult to identify *social* patterns of individual cultural behaviour. The mania for originality (Simmel, 1976: 233), the most extreme expression of this tendency towards individualization, does not give rise to socially patterned individual culture. Therefore, increasing individualization not only destroys cultural institutions as a system, but also individual culture understood as macrophenomenon.

It is important to emphasize that the acute cultural dilemma diagnosed by Simmel is *not* identical with formlessness or cultural anarchy as so many contemporary critiques of modern culture would like to make us believe. Increasing individualization means increasing disentanglement of the relationship between the cultural system and the level of individual creativity, the cultural system becoming more and more devitalized, and cultural creativity becoming more and more individualized (idiosyncratic). In terms of systems analysis, Simmel's diagnosis could be reformulated as increasing self-referentiality of both the cultural system and of the system of individual creativity, resulting in gradual self-destruction of both systems. Individualization of cultural energy and devitalization of cultural institutions are two parallel processes which have as a consequence not only to loosen the relationship between these systems, but also to destroy the social life characteristic of these systems.

II. Cultural Ambivalence

In the second model the two poles of the triadic frame of reference are conceptualized in terms of actors, individuals as strategically calculating consumers of cultural goods or lifestyle managers, and culture as the market-place in which processes of cultural exchange take place. The analytical principle underlying this model is the principle of ambivalence, more precisely, of ambivalent action orientation.

There are many writings of Simmel which invite such a kind of re-interpretation; his essay on 'The Problem of Style' written 1908 is perhaps best suited to illustrate this type of cultural ambivalence (Simmel, 1908). In this essay, Simmel presents himself as a deeply engaged critique of modern man as cultural consumer. He accuses him for his 'exaggerated subjectivism', which for Simmel is an expression of his deep misunderstanding of the idea of individuality. In order to understand this criticism we have to develop Simmel's somewhat complex type of thought step by step. Firstly, I must specify what Simmel means when talking about the concept of individuality. I then reconstruct his view of the relationship between individuals as cultural consumers and the cultural sphere, and explain how he uses the principle of ambivalence to analyse this relationship. Finally, I introduce what might be called Simmel's functionalist approach to the analysis of the sphere of aesthetics for the development of individuality.

Simmel's Concept of Individuality

In his sociological analyses, Simmel implicitly uses a normative concept of individuality, which he derives from the social norms with which modern man is confronted. Wherever human beings interact with each other, they are guided by a double and contradictory normative requirement to develop a unique and differentiated personality *and* to find social recognition for this uniqueness. In Simmel's concept of individuality both normative requirements are integrated. It can therefore also be understood as the ethical standard guiding human interaction in all social spheres of modern society.[2] Modern man is also confronted with this normative standard in his role as cultural man, that is, both in his role as cultural consumer and in the way he structures his relationship to the elements of his cultural environment. Therefore, the cultural environment can not only be interpreted merely in functional terms as the social sphere in which he can satisfy his cultural needs, but also as the field in which he can demonstrate his capability to fulfil the double task of becoming a social subjectivity (Popitz, 1987: see note 2). How does he manage to fulfil this task and how does he structure his relationship to the objects in his cultural environment when being oriented towards the normative requirement of developing his individuality?

Simmel repeatedly uses the metaphor of the circle in order to describe the relationship between the individual and his or her environment (Simmel, 1982: 472). He has an image of the self as being in the centre of various concentric circles. This metaphor is used to conceptualize the relationship between the self and the elements of the cultural environment in terms of difference in distance. Simmel situates those objects which belong to the intimate sphere within the inner circle; the outer circle comprises those elements which belong to the individual's social sphere.

However, this is not to say that the relationship between the individual and the cultural environment is fixed. Cultural objects do not have a given distance to the individual, but they can be brought at different distances from him by using social strategies of taking distance (*Distanzierung*). Among those social strategies aesthetic perception is one of the most important strategies by which the distance between the cultural objects and the self can be manipulated. Therefore aesthetic perception has to be considered a crucial social technique for handling the problem of individuality.[3] The management of this strategy, however, is a highly risky enterprise. This is not only connected to the contradictory norms cultural man is exposed to when trying to conform to the ideal of social subjectivity, but also to a more fundamental conflict underlying human interaction and action in general.

According to Simmel, our lives are governed by the opposing poles of generality (*Allgemeinheit*), on the one hand, and individuality (*Individualität*), on the other. These principles represent two essential poles of human existence which are equally important. To use his words from his essay on fashion, Simmel sees social life as a 'battle ground, of which every inch is stubbornly contested by both principles' (Simmel, 1986: 40). In social interaction these opposing poles can manifest themselves as oscillation between contradictory needs or goals, such as the need for rest *and* movement, integration *and* isolation, opposition *and* obedience, freedom *and* obligation, to name only some of the examples mentioned by Simmel. It is the very tension between the two poles of this ambivalent structure of action orientation that gives human life in general, and life within the different social spheres in particular, its specific *social* character (see Nedelmann, 1990).

How does this general ambivalence of human interaction orientation manifest itself in the cultural sphere? In the essay under consideration here, Simmel is particularly concerned about the aesthetic sphere as the 'battle ground' of the ambivalence between the principles of generality and individuality.

The Dualistic World of Aesthetics

In the aesthetic sphere the ambivalence between generality and individuality manifests itself in two contrasting principles of aesthetic perception,[4] in the principles of *style* and *art*. Whereas the principle of generality is expressed in style, the principle of individuality is expressed in art. To perceive an object according to the principle of *style* means that the observer is oriented towards common laws of form and design. He or she is only attracted by those elements of the artistic object which it has in common with other objects belonging to the same category. So, for example, Simmel explains, we classify a rose as a stylized rose if it shows the typical features of a rose, the generality of the rose as a type.[5]

According to this definition, we can speak about *stylization* as a social technique of aesthetic perception with the help of which the individual as art consumer manages to put a distance between himself and the artistic objects under observation; it is a strategy which permits realizing the *social* pole and the principle of generality in the ambivalent structure of his orientation.

Simmel conceptualizes *art* in contrast to style. To perceive or to create an object according to the principle of art means to focus our attention on the singularity of the artistic work, on its uniqueness and individuality.[6]

A work of art does not appeal to us because it represents a specific style, but because it is something *unique*. Works of art created by Michelangelo, Rembrandt or Velasquez usually involve our total personality because they appeal to us as exceptional artistic works. For Simmel, to have a total artistic experience means to surrender oneself totally to the uniqueness of the work of art. The observer feels as if he or she were alone in the world with the work of art (Simmel, 1908: 280).

To perceive aesthetic objects as objects of art means creating an intimate relationship between the art consumer and the objects of the aesthetic sphere. We can therefore speak of *aestheticization* as a special technique with the help of which individuals can structure an intimate relationship with the objects of the aesthetic sphere and him- or herself. By aestheticizing objects the cultural consumer can realize the personal pole of his or her ambivalent action orientation and the principle of individuality.

The ambivalence between individuality and generality not only expresses itself in these two techniques of aesthetic perception, in stylization and aestheticization, but also in a division of the world of art into two types of artistic objects. Simmel makes a clear distinction between 'works of art' (*Kunstwerke*), on the one hand, and 'objects of craft' (*Kunstgewerbe*), on the other.

Objects of craft represent the principle of generality, that is, *style*. Stylized objects usually have a specific pragmatic function in everyday life. A chair, for example, is for sitting on, a glass should be filled with wine and held in the hand, or jewellery should function as adornment (Simmel, 1908: 310). The fact that people have a common understanding of the utility of these objects is materialized in the stylish form of these objects, which allows for reproducing them without destroying the nature of their substance. Utility, reproducibility and style thus go hand in hand.

In contrast to objects of craft, works of art have no external pragmatic function. They are means in and for themselves, they are *l'art pour l'art*. Works of art are not submitted to any general law of form or style; they create a world of their own and define the law of their existence by and with reference to themselves. In contrast to objects of craft, works of art are excluded from the pragmatic functions of everyday life (Simmel, 1908: 310). They are, as Simmel says, superfluous but essential (*überflüssige Hauptsache*). This characteristic also manifests itself in the way we behave towards them. In contrast to stylized objects, works of art are usually given a special place in our lives, separated from objects of craft. Whereas the use-value of works of craft manifests itself in the fact of their reproducibility, works of art are destroyed in their uniqueness the moment they are reproduced. Accordingly, works of art cannot exist in great numbers without losing their essential nature.

The Functions of Aesthetic Objects for Individuality

Simmel's analysis lends itself to a functionalistic re-formulation. Aesthetic objects are given a precise function in cultural man's effort of becoming a socially recognized individual and to maintaining an equilibrium between the poles of generality and individuality in his ambivalent orientation towards the cultural environment. Works of art have the function of realizing the principle of individuality, objects of craft of fulfilling the principle of generality.

This functionalist perspective allows us to describe the aesthetic sphere in modern societies as being highly differentiated in both its material manifestations in the areas of art and style and in its functional specificity for the development of individuality. Whereas art supports the development of the unique aspects of the individuality, craft supports the development of its social aspects. Cultural man has to integrate both types of aesthetic objects into his individuality and to give them an equally strong representation in his personal aesthetic world.

The following diagram summarizes the discussion we have made so far on the second model of culture:

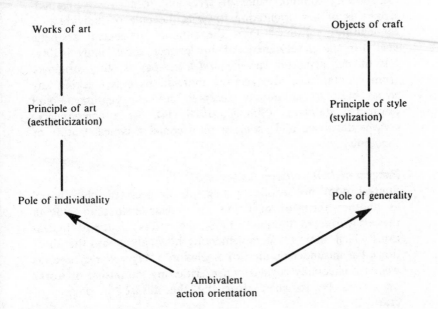

Exaggerated Subjectivism

We can now better understand what Simmel means when he criticizes modern man for his tendency towards 'exaggerated subjectivism'. Perceiving objects of craft as if they were works of art and perceiving works of art as if they were objects of craft means aestheticizing craft and stylizing art. In doing so, he creates disorder in the aesthetic sphere. He mixes up the principles of aesthetic perception and reverses the functional meaning the two types of aesthetic objects have for the development of his individuality. This, however, is the most 'caricaturing misunderstanding of modern individualism'.[7]

To admire a chair, a glass, or jewellery as if they were works of art deprives these objects of their immediate use-value. The chair which is admired as a work of art no longer functions as a seat; the glass which is put behind locked doors can no longer be used to offer a drink; and the jewellery which is created as a work of art functions for itself, but not for others. Aestheticization of craft results in de-differentiating the material areas of craft and art and in perverting the function of craft for strengthening the development of the social aspect of individuality.

Aestheticization of craft has another implication. It means disregarding common rules of style and form. In overemphasizing his or her orientation towards the pole of individuality, the cultural consumer loses the support of general aesthetic laws for the development of his or her *social* individuality. His or her activities become *styleless*, that is, they originate from spontaneous, idiosyncratic motivations only, lacking any social basis of commonly accepted aesthetic sentiments and normative standards (Simmel, 1908: 314). As a consequence, style is destroyed and stylelessness becomes a typical feature of modernity.

Exaggerated Objectivism

Simmel does not explicitly talk of 'exaggerated objectivism' as another form of deviation and misunderstanding. But in the essay quoted (Simmel, 1908), he offers plenty of indications which allow for complementing his analysis into the direction of a misunderstanding of 'sociation' (*Vergesellschaftung*) as well. He is equally engaged when criticizing the misuse of works of art as he is when criticizing the misuse of objects of craft:

> To sit on a work of art, to handle it or use it for any practical purpose is tantamount to cannibalism, of reducing the master to the status of a slave. . . . (Simmel, 1908: 310)

Works of art are functionally perverted if they, instead of being used as a means for differentiating one's personality, are 'mis'-used for purposes of sociation. When works of art are not perceived in orientation to the principle of individuality, but in orientation to the principle of generality, then the main criterion of art observation becomes *style*. Stylization of works of art has as a consequence that the aesthetic world of art is destroyed and *artlessness* becomes dominating.

If both types of 'exaggerations' are practiced at the same time, the world of aesthetics is turned upside down. Instead of a balance between style and art, between objects of craft and works of art, artlessness *and* stylelessness coexist. In such a world full of paradoxes, the norm of attaining a balanced individuality has finally been transformed into an unrealizable ideal (see Nedelmann, 1988).

III. Cultural Dualism

Simmel's third model of culture is based on his essay 'On the Concept and the Tragedy of Culture' published in 1911 (Simmel, 1968a). It is perhaps the most well-known piece of Simmel's sociology of culture, but, at the same time, it has often been misunderstood and even obscured. This is especially true for the key concept Simmel introduces here, 'the tragedy of culture'.

Cultivation

It is important to emphasize from the outset, that the concept of culture underlying this model differs from the other models presented so far. Simmel talks here of culture in the sense of *cultivation*. Formally speaking, cultivation can be understood as a feedback process between the individual level and the cultural level, starting from individuals and going back to them after having passed the system of 'objective culture'. The general insight underlying this concept of cultivation as a feedback process refers to Simmel's conviction of the human being's unique capacity to complete his or her personality by assimilating and internalizing influences external to his or her personal sphere. Cultural objects function as means for his or her goal to develop and perfect his or her individuality.[8] The concept of 'cultivated individuality' differs from the concept of 'individuality' discussed above insofar as it is only concerned with the individual's capacity to receive and integrate elements of his or her cultural environment into his or her personality structure, but not with utilizing them strategically for his or her lifestyle management. When talking about individuals as cultural consumers, Simmel investigates the impact of the individual upon culture; when talking about individuals from the point of view of their chances to become cultivated, he analyses the impact of culture upon the individual.

Looking at the feedback process from the point of view of the cultural level, one could say that what Simmel calls 'objective culture' functions as the intermediary station between the not yet cultivated subject and the cultivated subject.[9] As a consequence, Simmel gives a definition of culture in which these dynamic and goal-oriented elements are included:

Culture is the way that leads from closed unity through the unfolding multiplicity to the unfolded unity. (Simmel, 1968a: 28)[10]

In spite of the evolutionary bias of this formulation, it becomes clear that culture in the sense of cultivation has the effect of transforming subjects from being 'closed unities' in the beginning of the process of cultivation and proceeding to the stage of increasing differentiation when assimilating objects from the cultural environment ('unfolding multiplicity'), until finally becoming 'unfolded unities' after having succeeded in internalizing and absorbing the external cultural influences into the structure of their personalities. Simmel reserves the concept of *subjective culture* in order to describe the degree in which individuals have absorbed the elements from the objective culture and integrated them into their personality structure. To use Levine's words: 'Culture in the proper (i.e. subjective) sense of the term, exists only in the presence of the self-development of a psychic centre, provided that this self-development relies on external, objective means' (Levine, 1971: xix).

Ideally speaking, the feedback process of cultivation is terminated if objective culture and subjective culture correspond with each other. In this ideal case, culture has become the synthesis of the subjective and objective poles.[11] The ideal feedback process of cultivation could therefore also be described as a process of 'subjectification of objective culture' and 'objectification of subjective culture'. We do not have to repeat the reasons why objective culture has to pass a process of 'subjectification' in order to survive in the long run. Like cultural forms, objective culture also has to associate itself with its counterpart in order to survive in the long run. There is another reason why objective culture has to become subjectified. For Simmel it is the meaning of cultural objects to be internalized by individuals.[12] The value of objective culture consists precisely in the contribution it makes to human self-perfection. The moment it can no longer fulfil the function of cultivation, objective culture loses its specific meaning and cultural value.

Dualism between Subjective and Objective Culture

The chances for realizing the ideal feedback process of cultivation are, however, according to Simmel, limited under the conditions of modern society. It is typical of these societies, that the feedback process between subjective and objective culture is blocked. Objective culture can no longer fulfil the function of cultivating modern man. After having lost its instrumental function for cultivation, objective culture has become a means in and for itself constituting an autonomous world, separate from and in opposition to subjective culture. Instead of being a chance for modern man's possibility to cultivate himself, it is a threat to the development of his personality. Why does Simmel tend towards such an attitude of *Kulturpessimismus*, cultural pessimism? What are the reasons he gives for his negative evaluation of objective culture in modernity?

There are mainly two reasons. The first one refers to the development of objective culture under the conditions of modernity, the second one to the limitations inherent in subjective culture. There is no need to repeat the reasons why objective culture tends towards becoming more and more autonomous and transforming itself into a self-reflexive social system. Simmel adds another observation of importance for explaining the increasing dissociation of subjective culture from objective culture. Objective culture has a 'voracious capacity for accumulation' (*unorganische Anhäufbarkeit*) (Simmel, 1968a: 44; German version: Simmel, 1968b: 143); there is no limit to its quantitative growth.[13]

There is no cultural field which would be able to escape this seemingly endless process of quantitative accumulation: art, law, custom, technology, science etc. are more and more transformed into 'mass' cultures, developing their own immanent logic and criteria of division of labour and specialization. The more the overall societal development proceeds, the faster this process of quantitative accumulation and internal specialization of objective culture develops.

Why does subjective culture not succeed in developing at the same speed and size as objective culture does? Simmel's answer refers to the receptive capacity of the single individual; in contrast to objective culture, the capability to accumulate is limited not only because of scarcity of time and energy of each individual life, but also because of the degree of unity and closure each individual already has attained (see Levine, 1971: xx). To put it in other words: as the process of cultivation is directed to each single individual and has to be filtered through the limited scope of the receptive capacity of each single individual, subjective culture is not able to produce effects of micro-macro-aggregation. As subjective culture refers to another level of aggregation than objective culture, it cannot produce macro-effects. Objective culture, on the other hand, produces such macro-effects due to its systemic properties, and, as a result, is more and more transformed into a *Übermacht*, a superpower (Simmel, 1968a: 46), the more it grows in scope.

The effects of this incommensurable development of subjective culture and objective culture are immediately felt for the single individual. His life is burdened with thousands and thousands of superfluous objects from which he cannot liberate himself. Modern man, the *Kulturmensch*, is in a permanent state of overstimulation (*Angeregtsein*), without however being able to transform these stimuli into cultural creativity; he knows and perhaps enjoys a lot of things, but they appear to him as nothing else but ballast, too heavy and too great to be capable of assimilating and integrating them into his personality structure. Simmel concludes:

> Thus, the typically problematic situation of modern man comes into being: his sense of being surrounded by an innumerable number of cultural elements which are neither meaningless to him nor, in the final analysis, meaningful. In their mass they depress him, since he is not capable of assimilating them all, nor can he simply reject them, since after all, they do belong potentially within the sphere of his cultural development. (Simmel, 1968a: 44)

Confronted with the cultural superpower, modern man becomes paralysed in his capacity to select elements from the objective culture. The stimuli he permanently receives from the objective culture give rise to feelings of incapability and helplessness and block his capacity to instrumentalize them for the purpose of cultivating his personality. Instead of becoming a cultivated man, he becomes a powerless and alienated man. Quoting Marx, Simmel characterizes the *Fetischcharakter* of economic products 'only a special case of this general fate of contents of culture' (Simmel, 1968a: 42). Cultural products are more and more submitted to the paradox, that they, although having been created by and for individuals, develop according to their own immanent logic of development. 'In so doing they estrange themselves from their origin as well as from their purpose' (Simmel, 1968a: 42).

Tragedy of Culture

Simmel introduces the concept of 'tragedy of culture' in order to specify the relationship between subjective and objective culture. He gives a very clear definition of tragic relationships in contrast to 'merely sad or extrinsically destructive relationships': he calls a relationship a tragic one, 'when the destructive forces directed against some being are called forth from the deepest levels of this very being; or when its destruction has been initiated in itself, and forms the logical development of the very structure by which a being has built its own positive form' (Simmel, 1968a: 43). When social destruction is the *necessary* result from the immanent logic of the social unit under analysis itself, then Simmel uses the concept of 'tragic' relationships.[14]

When applying this definition to the field of culture, it becomes obvious what Simmel means when talking about the 'tragedy of culture'. The very idea of culture consists in creating material objects which are meant to be integrated into the subjective sphere of their creators and to be submitted to subsequent generations of individuals. But the very act of cultural creation itself generates a self-destructive potential. In his or her role as cultural receiver the subject becomes the addressee of the destructive effects of cultural objects he has created himself in his role as cultural creator. Not being able, however, to do anything else but be culturally productive and receptive, modern man 'loses itself either in a dead end alley or in an emptiness of its innermost and most individual life' (Simmel, 1968a: 44). It is this situation which Simmel defines as tragedy of culture:

> The situation is tragic: even in its first moments of existence, culture carries something within itself which, as if by an intrinsic fate, is determined to block, to burden, to obscure and divide its innermost purpose, the transition of the soul from its incomplete to its complete state. (Simmel, 1968a: 46)

The third cultural problem of tragedy differs from the problems discussed so far, as the individual's action alternatives in relation to the cultural system seem to have expired. A cultural system which is neither meaningful, nor meaningless to him or her, which he or she cannot assimilate, nor reject, leaves him or her in a situation of blocked activity. In such a state of paralysed action alternatives he or she has neither the energy for revolting or protesting against the cultural system as system, nor for reacting in a deviant, exaggerated way.

Concluding Remarks

Scaff (1990b: 93) has raised the problem whether the following question 'might be taken as the sociology of culture's guide through the maze of modernity': 'How can individuation and all that it suggests (personality, character, the self) be protected against the external, technically mediated, universalizable forms?' After having re-analysed Simmel's contributions to sociology of culture with the help of the analytical frame of reference developed by Archer, we can now agree that this question is of crucial importance for sociology of culture; but at the same time we strongly disagree with Scaff's suggestion to take this question as the sociology of culture's *only* guiding question. On the contrary, we have seen that there are other questions of equal relevance for Simmel and for contemporary sociology of culture. The Archerian analytical perspective has allowed us to discover a more differentiated and even somewhat controversial picture of Simmel as sociologist of culture than has been presented in the literature so far. In addition to the question raised by Scaff of how individuals can be protected against external (objective) forms of culture (Model I), Simmel also raises the opposite question of how objective culture can be protected against the individual's misuse and misunderstanding (Model II). Only when keeping in mind *both* questions of how to protect the individual against the cultural system as 'superpower' *and* of how to protect culture against misuses and misinterpretations from individuals as cultural consumers, we sociologists are prepared for the paradoxes the contemporary cultural scenery confront us with.

Furthermore, we have seen, that Simmel is not only concerned with problems of 'cultivation', that is, with processes of mediating the objective culture into the individual's subjective sphere (subjectification of objective culture), but, vice versa, also with problems of mediating the subjective culture into the sphere of objectified cultural institutions (objectification of subjective culture; Model III). In the long run, the interruption of this double-sided feedback process affects both sides negatively, individuals as receivers of cultural objects *and* cultural institutions. Or, to put it in another way, Simmel is not only concerned about protecting the bourgeois *Kulturmensch*, but also about keeping alive and protecting the existing institutionalized culture, the, as it were, *Kulturerbe*.

We can now understand better that the three problems of culture, 'individualization', 'exaggeration' and 'paralysation', do not contradict each other, but complement and reinforce each other. The more individuals react towards the threat of objective culture with retreatism and cultural deviance ('individualization' and 'exaggeration'), the greater the likelihood of subjective culture and objective culture becoming dissociated ('paralysation'). And vice versa: the more the feedback process between subjective and objective culture is disturbed, the greater the likelihood for deviant cultural behaviour (according to Model II) and rejection of existing cultural forms (according to Model I) to occur. If cultural man, the

Kulturmensch, is paralysed in his action alternatives towards the cultural system, the *Kulturerbe* will wither away and/or become distorted and will as such no longer be able to fulfil the function of 'cultivating' modern man.

Instead of limiting the theoretical and empirical research within the field of sociology and culture on *one* question only, as has been suggested by Scaff, it is proposed here to broaden the scope of future research and to concentrate on the problem of the dynamic interlinkages between the three problems of culture. Only in doing so, could we profit from the legacy of Simmel's theories of culture and contribute creatively to the ongoing 'New Debate on Culture'.

Notes

An earlier version of this article was presented at the XII World Congress of Sociology, Madrid July 1990 to the Working Group on Social Theory, 'The New Debate on Culture' chaired by Margaret Archer.

1. It is worthwhile mentioning that Simmel himself is very well aware of the 'somewhat vague and logically imprecise' implications of this term (Simmel, 1976: 241, note 1). Having defined life as the opposite of form, Simmel would deny its essence if he gave it a precise definition. He explains: 'Life can become conscious of itself only directly, by virtue of its *own dynamism*, not via the stratum of mediating concepts, which coincides with the realm of forms' (Simmel, 1976: 241, my italics).

2. Heinrich Popitz (1987), for example, uses the term 'social subjectivity' in order to conceptualize the double normative requirement implicit in Simmel's notion of individuality.

3. David P. Frisby (1990: 39–55, esp. 53) has argued convincingly that for Simmel there is a nexus between aesthetic perception as a technique of taking distance in everyday life and aesthetic perception as a scientific technique of the sociologist with the help of which he or she distances him- or herself from society as object.

4. Simmel also applies these principles to the process of *creating* art. But as we are only concerned with individuals as art consumers, we can neglect this differentiation.

5. 'The meaning of all stylization is not to give us a sense of the individual rose itself, but to give us an idea of the law of formation [*Bildungsgesetz*] of the rose in the sense of the origin of its form, which may appear in a variety of forms and functions as the integrating generality' (Simmel, 1908: 307).

6. 'The deeper and the more extraordinary the impression we have of a work of art, then generally the less important the question of the style of the work in this impression' (Simmel, 1908: 307).

7. 'The idea that any functional item whatsoever is a work of art in its own right, like Michelangelo's *Moses* or Rembrandt's *Jan Six* is perhaps the most caricaturing misunderstanding of modern individualism' (Simmel, 1908: 310/313).

8. '. . . art and morality, science and purposively formed objects, religion and law, technology and social norms — [are] stations, as it were, through which the

subject has to go in order to gain that special individual value [*Eigenwert*] which is called his culture' (Simmel, 1968a: 30; I have corrected K. Peter Etzkorn's somewhat imprecise translation of the original version: see German original Simmel, 1968b: 120).

9. Levine (1971: xix) summarizes this process as follows: 'Cultivation is the process of developing a state of being in a creature which (1) would not come about naturally, but (2) for which it has a natural propensity, (3) by utilizing objects external to it.'

10. 'Kultur ist der Weg von der geschlossenen Einheit durch die entfaltete Vielheit zur entfalteten Enheit' (Simmel, 1968b: 118).

11. '. . . culture comes into being by a meeting of the two elements, neither of which contain culture by itself: the subjective soul and the objective spiritual product' (Simmel, 1968a: 30).

12. The example Simmel gives is very convincing:

A sunrise which is not seen by any human eyes does not increase the value of this world or make it more sublime, since this objective fact by itself is without relevance to the categories of value. As soon, however, a painter invests his emotion, his sense for form and color and his power of expression, in a picture of this sunrise, then we consider this work an enrichment, increase in the value of existence as a whole. The world seems to us somehow more deserving of its existence, closer to its ultimate meaning, whenever the human soul, the source of all value has expressed itself in something which has become part of the objective world. It does not matter now whether a later soul will redeem the magic value from the canvas and dissolve it in the stream of his own subjective sensations. Both the sunrise in nature and the painting exist as realities. But where the sunrise attains value only if it lives on in individuals, the painting has already absorbed such life and made it into an object; hence our sense of value stops before it as before something definite which has no need of subjectivization. (Simmel, 1968a: 33).

13. 'There is no reason why it [objective culture] should not be multiplied in the direction of the infinite, why not book should be added to book, work of art to work of art, or invention to invention. The form of objectivity as such possesses a boundless capacity for fulfillment' (Simmel, 1968a: 44).

14. I agree with Charles Turner (1989: 520–1) when he emphasizes 'that Simmel is using the term "tragedy" in a technical, and not a normative sense. "The tragedy of culture" is not the expression of a judgement of the modern', but confined to the type of relationship between individuals and their cultural environment.

References

Archer, Margaret S. (1988) *Culture and Agency. The Place of Culture in Social Theory*. Cambridge: Cambridge University Press.

Frisby, David P. (1990) 'Georg Simmel's Concept of Society', pp. 39–55 in Michael Kaern, B.S. Phillips and R.S. Cohen (eds), *Georg Simmel and Contemporary Sociology*. Dordrecht, Boston, London: Kluwer.

Levine, Donald N. (1971) 'Introduction', pp. ix–lxv in *Georg Simmel: On*

Individuality and Social Forms. Selected Writings. Chicago and London: University of Chicago Press.

Nedelmann, Birgitta (1988) 'Aestheticization and Stylization: Two Strategies of Lifestyle Management', pp. 91–110 in Carlo Mongardini and Maria Luisa Maniscalco (eds), *Moderno e Postmoderno: Crisi di Identità e ruolo della sociologia.* Roma: Bulzoni.

Nedelmann, Birgitta (1990) 'Georg Simmel as an Analyst of Autonomous Dynamics: The Merry-Go-Round of Fashion', pp. 243–58 in Michael Kaern, B.S. Phillips and R.S. Cohen (eds), *Georg Simmel and Contemporary Sociology.* Dordrecht, Boston, London: Kluwer.

Popitz, Heinrich (1987) ' Autoritätsbedürfnisse. Der Wandel der sozialen Subjektivität', *Kölner Zeitschrift für Soziologie und Sozialpsychologie* 39: 633–47.

Scaff, Lawrence A. (1990a) 'Simmel's Theory of Culture', pp. 283–96 in Michael Kaern, B.S. Phillips and R.S. Cohen (eds), *Georg Simmel and Contemporary Sociology.* Dordrecht, Boston, London: Kluwer.

Scaff, Lawrence A. (1990b) 'Modernity and the Tasks of a Sociology of Culture', *History of the Human Sciences* 3(1): 85–100.

Simmel, Georg (1908) 'Das Problem des Stiles', *Dekorative Kunst* XI, 7 April: 307–16. A translation of 'The Problem of Style' appears in this issue of *Theory, Culture & Society.*

Simmel, Georg (1968a) 'On the Concept and the Tragedy of Culture', pp. 27–46 in *Georg Simmel. The Conflict in Modern Culture and Other Essays.* Translated and introduced by K. Peter Etzkorn. New York: Teachers' College Press.

Simmel, Georg (1968b) 'Der Begriff und die Tragödie der Kultur', pp. 116–47 in Georg Simmel, *Das individuelle Gesetz.* Edited by Michael Landmann. Frankfurt: Suhrkamp Verlag.

Simmel, Georg (1968c) 'Der Konflikt der modernen Kultur', pp. 148–73 in Georg Simmel, *Das individuelle Gesetz.* Edited by Michael Landmann. Frankfurt: Suhrkamp Verlag.

Simmel, Georg (1976) 'The Conflict of Modern Culture', pp. 223–42 in *Georg Simmel.* Edited and translated by P.A. Lawrence. London: Nelson & Sons.

Simmel, Georg (1982) *The Philosophy of Money.* London, Henley and Boston: Routledge.

Simmel, Georg (1986) 'Die Mode', pp. 38–63 in *Die philosophische Kultur.* Berlin: Wagenbach Verlag.

Turner, Charles (1989) 'Rejoinder. Weber, Simmel and Culture: A Reply to Lawrence Scaff', *The Sociological Review* 37(3): 518–29.

Birgitta Nedelmann teaches Sociology at the University of Mainz, Germany.

Simmel on Social Space

Frank J. Lechner

Space has never been central to sociological thought. To be sure, it has received some scholarly attention in urban sociology (e.g. Suttles, 1968), in the budding sociology of architecture (Ankerl, 1983) and in social geography. In principle, of course, sociologists know that action is spatially situated, that groups and institutions have a 'place'. But it remains fair to say that the significance of space for the discipline at large has been peripheral from the beginning. Among the classical sociologists, only Georg Simmel treated space systematically, but his main contribution was largely ignored. However, this situation may be changing. Recently we have witnessed a certain growth of sociological interest in space, reflected in the work of scholars like Giddens, Harvey and others (for an overview, see Gregory and Urry, 1985). On the other hand, judging from recent interpretive work (for an overview, see Kaern et al., 1990) and the publication of his collected works, Simmel is undergoing a revival as well. These two modest trends will soon intersect with the publication of an English translation of a condensed version of the chapter on space (Ch. 9) in Simmel's *Soziologie* (1958; see Simmel, forthcoming), which should provide a theoretical boost to current research on space while calling renewed attention to this significant but overlooked part of Simmel's sociology. Future debates about and applications of 'Simmel on space' will have to determine how much of a boost it really provides; my purpose here is simply to convey a sense of what Simmel has to offer on this score. Similarly, a thorough critique of the chapter itself will have to await a truly comprehensive interpretation of Simmel's sociological oeuvre as a whole; in this article I only try to locate it in the context of Simmel's larger project.

I suggest that we can interpret Simmel's chapter on space in three compatible ways, each of which is connected to distinct strands in

Theory, Culture & Society (SAGE, London, Newbury Park and New Delhi), Vol. 8 (1991), 195–201

Simmel's work. First, it presents a sociological reinterpretation of a Kantian category. For Simmel, space does not simply denote the abstract (epistemological) possibility of being-together; he emphasizes, rather, that interaction between individuals is usually experienced as the filling of space; the being-together of individuals means that they share space. Second, by examining the various ways in which social relations assume a spatial form Simmel also adds to his project in formal sociology. The usual description of this project as a 'geometry of society' acquires a double meaning here, since this chapter adds to analyses of other 'formal' features of sociation by focusing specifically on how sociation becomes spatially real. Beyond the basic orientation, it shares several characteristics with these other, better known analyses. For example, while it appears as an essayistic set of reflections, it has a clear thematic structure, yet without offering any kind of theoretical closure. But, third, as many Simmel interpreters have emphasized in recent years (cf. Dahme and Rammstedt, 1984), even the seemingly 'formal' parts of Simmel's sociological work contributed to an historically oriented analysis of modernity (cf. Lechner, 1990). This applies to the chapter on space as well. More than a catalogue of social forms-in-space, it offers ideas on the spatial dimension of modern social structures and the modernization of space itself. Thus, as usual in the case of Simmel, the whole is reflected in the parts: the Gestalt of his overall work — which characteristically combines philosophical critique, formal sociology and analysis of modernity (cf. Bevers, 1982) — is evident in each component. In this regard, the chapter on space is exemplary Simmel.

What, then, does Simmel have to say about space? First, he counsels against spatial determinism; space functions as a context for action, but in principle it is only a *wirkungslose Form*. The practically inevitable spatial embeddedness of social configurations should not be confused with the actual causes of social processes. And yet, while he shows how space is in some ways socially formed, he does not treat space as simply a social construct. It retains a reality of its own. Simmel's overall position, then, lies somewhere between spatial determinism and social constructionism. The substance of the chapter serves as an illustration and defence of this position. Disregarding the excursions on the senses and on the stranger inserted in the *Soziologie* (1958), the contents divide into two parts: first, Simmel examines socially relevant aspects of space;

toward the end of the chapter, he considers the effect of social forms on spatial conditions.

The first aspect of space (strictly speaking, an aspect of the way groups treat space) Simmel mentions is exclusivity. The point is that social configurations vary in the extent to which they require exclusive occupation of 'their' space. Nation-states and the Catholic Church represent opposite ends of the spectrum ranging from exclusivity to indifference, with several 'permeable' groupings in between. Even more important from a social point of view is the partitioning of space, since boundaries contribute to the integration, or at least 'centripetality', of a society. Bounded space makes any social order more concrete and intensely experienced. But spatial ordering not only reinforces social order, it also lends greater clarity to conflictual relations. Partitioning thus influences relations within and across boundaries (which can be drawn more or less narrowly). Boundaries themselves, Simmel emphasizes, are 'sociological', not spatial facts. Simmel's third variable is the fixity space offers to social forms. Again, Simmel suggests a spectrum of variations, ranging from configurations that require individuals to be present in a particular place, to configurations that make the actual presence of individuals dispensable. In the former case, the particular places in question will also tend to be more individualized. But fixity can also refer to the extent to which a collectivity depends on a fixed 'point of orientation'. To illustrate possible variations, Simmel contrasts the meaning Rome has for Catholics with that of Jerusalem for Jews. A fourth relevant variable is distance. Being physically near to someone has certain typical consequences, according to Simmel; for example, relations involving such nearness tend to go to emotional extremes and make idealization of the interaction partner harder. Physical distance also has to be carefully managed — it requires tact. And once again, configurations vary in the extent to which they can 'span' distance. Some types of transactions obviously depend on physical proximity, but many more 'objective' social relations lead to indifference to things nearby. Finally, movement through space also has great social significance. For example, high mobility (as in nomadic groups) tends to be associated with low internal differentiation and strong integration; yet when the unity of a collectivity depends on actual movement (if only by the leader), people's consciousness of that unity will be relatively weak.

In the last part of the chapter, Simmel considers the effect of social forms on spatial conditions. First of all, social organization usually requires organization of space as well. More specifically, rational-political forms of organization tend to rely on spatial ordering; people are treated and classified according to location, rather than kinship ties. Domination requires spatial expression as well. The exercise of authority over people, as Simmel says, usually also takes the form of territorial control. A third dimension with spatial implications we might treat under the heading of solidarity. Forms of sociation that have their own 'home' differ from more free-floating associations; the shared place confirms communal bonds, especially when these are somehow insecure. In some societies, but not in most modern ones, membership means being bound to a particular place. Finally, even seemingly empty space can acquire social significance. It may serve as a protective wilderness; it may be up for grabs but potentially seizable; or it may serve as neutral territory in which conflicts may be settled.

Even this skeletal summary, stripped of distinctively Simmelian illustrations and asides, suggests the richness and orginality of Simmel's analysis. At the very least, he makes the case that many forms of sociation cannot be understood without taking into account both their spatial context and their use of space. Clearly, Simmel here adds an important dimension to his work on forms. He may not offer a theory in any conventional sense of the term, but he does outline some powerful heuristics for analysing space in sociological fashion. In working toward a geometry of social forms, he also takes a broader view of space than many contemporary scholars (for exceptions, see again Gregory and Urry, 1985). But with this summary and assessment I do not mean to suggest that Simmel's approach was entirely ahistorical. In fact, the richness of this chapter and much of his other work lies precisely in the interplay, or interpenetration if you will, between the abstract-formal approach and the specific-historical content. In his very method Simmel demonstrates the 'relationism' (always focused on *Wechselwirkungen*) he uses as both epistemological and theoretical guideline. Another kind of interplay evident in his chapter, namely that between micro- and macrodimensions of social life, further relativizes standard interpretations that have portrayed Simmel as a microtheorist. If anything, the emphasis in this chapter is on 'macro' examples. Simmel is especially interested in the role of the state and the spatial dimensions of the modern city, but also refers back to 'parts' of the whole, for example when he discusses the position of minorities in relation to the larger society or the position of the individual in the modern metropolis. He suggests that the modern, objective, 'civilized' way of dealing with space is reflected in a code that structures action at the microlevel, for example in the maintenance of privacy and affective control to preserve 'personal space', as well as at the macrolevel, where the state and the metropolis must treat citizens in a more impersonal, reserved fashion.

These last examples of Simmel's macrosociological interest take us back to one of the things I said above, namely that this chapter also contributes to Simmel's overall analysis of modernity. This is the point of his frequent diachronic comparisons. Throughout the chapter, Simmel also discusses 'modern' social configurations in which space is either controlled in the same way over a large area or made irrelevant. While particularistic forms of solidarity tend to treat space in an exclusivist manner, modern universalistic forms tend to be more open. Institutions with fixed points of orientation must compensate for this (traditional?) spatial constraint if they are to become spatially extensive. The Catholic Church serves as the model for modern institutions with specific centres but a universalistic — social and spatial — thrust; the Jewish diaspora stands for a more abstractly conceived unity without a concrete centre. In Simmel's analysis, a modern society also appears to be 'centreless', to borrow a term from Luhmann. And while sedentariness traditionally had limitations compared with mobility, in modern society even sedentary positions can enjoy the advantages of 'virtual' mobility.

Apart from describing such spatial characteristics of modern societies, Simmel also appears to identify a particular trend in the way modern societies deal with space, namely a trend toward greater abstractness. This process of abstraction is of course familiar in other guises from other parts of Simmel's work. For example, Simmel sees the tragedy of modern culture as the conflict between increasingly abstract objective culture and the flux of life as experienced by individuals. In the *Philosophy of Money* (1990) he treats money as an abstract medium, the pure expression of the value of things as such and thus a pure expression of the form of modern economic exchange, which requires abstraction from individuality and puts a premium on the intellect's capacity for abstraction. The chapter on space is particularly interesting in this regard because Simmel emphasizes that in principle space is one of the most 'concrete' features of social life, one that helps to make social life 'real' in terms of human perception and experience. Yet here, too, Simmel examines forms of sociation in terms of their 'capacity for abstraction'. For example, where actual movement is required for the integration of a social unit, the latter depends on direct contact between actors and thus remains limited. On the other hand, objective (abstract, impersonal) relations may not require similar direct contact and yet create a strong sense of collective unity insofar as they stand over and above the individual. Fixed points of orientation may also limit the potential of an association under modern circumstances; to extrapolate Simmel's argument, the point is to turn their role and the relationship of parts to them into a more abstract one. The paradoxical element is that where, as in the case of the Jewish diaspora, a concrete centre is lacking, unity may initially be weakened but become strong as social relations and the prevalent conception of societal unity become more abstract. Simmel also sees the development from nomadic societies to tribes, cities and modern states in terms of increasing abstraction. In the most 'primitive' case, self, group and environment are hardly differentiated; wandering creates a strong unity; the collectivity must remain exclusive and closely tied within, but distant from the outside world. Although modern states still rely on territorial control and maintain exclusive boundaries, they relate to both their space and their citizens in a much more abstract fashion, treating both territory and inhabitants uniformly, abstracting from the particularities of people and places. Functional relations having to do with the creation of objective culture are most abstract in dealing with association and tend to focus on objective-cultural criteria rather than concrete-spatial considerations, except where the latter fit into a rational scheme (for example, of a company). Modern science can serve as a prototypical case. Purely functional, objectified relations increasingly abstract from space altogether (aided, we should add, by modern technologies). The upshot of the process of abstraction outlined by Simmel is that for many practical purposes we no longer have to be physically present and that concrete spatial settings matter less and less for many transactions — phenomena worthy of further investigation. Indeed, as a result of group expansion and differentiation, society itself becomes increasingly abstract. The paradox of the process of spatial abstraction may well be that we can now be together without sharing space, while we are also always together in the same global space.

Note

This article was written to accompany and introduce the first English translation of Simmel's analysis of space. However, due to space limitations, that lengthy translation could not appear in this issue of *Theory, Culture & Society*. The translation is scheduled for publication in a forthcoming volume on *Simmel on Culture*, edited by David Frisby and Mike Featherstone, which will be part of the *TCS* book series. I would like to thank Omar K. Moore and Roland Robertson for having shared their ideas about Simmel with me.

References

Ankerl, G. (1983) *An Experimental Sociology of Architecture*. The Hague: Mouton.

Bevers, A.M. (1982) *Geometrie van de Samenleving: Filosofie en Sociologie in het Werk van Georg Simmel*. Deventer: Van Loghum Slaterus.

Dahme, H.J. and O. Rammstedt (eds) (1984) *Georg Simmel und die Moderne*. Frankfurt: Suhrkamp.

Gregory, D. and J. Urry (eds) (1985) *Social Relations and Spatial Structures*. New York: St Martin's Press.

Kaern, M., B.S. Phillips and R.S. Cohen (eds) (1990) *Georg Simmel and Contemporary Sociology*. Dordrecht: Kluwer.

Lechner, F.J. (1990) 'Social Differentiation and Modernity: On Simmel's Macrosociology', pp. 155–79 in M. Kaern, B.S. Phillips and R.S. Cohen (eds), *Georg Simmel and Contemporary Sociology*. Dordrecht: Kluwer.

Simmel, G. (1958) *Soziologie: Untersuchungen über die Formen der Vergesellschaftung*. Berlin: Duncker & Humblot.

Simmel. G. (1990) *The Philosophy of Money* (second edition). Translated by T. Bottomore and D. Frisby. London: Routledge.

Simmel, G. (forthcoming) 'The Sociology of Space'. Translated by Mark Ritter, in D. Frisby and M. Featherstone (eds), *Simmel on Culture*. London: Sage.

Suttles, G. (1968) *The Social Order of the Slum: Ethnicity and Territory in the Inner City*. Chicago, IL: University of Chicago Press.

Frank J. Lechner teaches Sociology at Emory University, Atlanta. He has published a number of papers on Sociological Theory and the Sociology of Religion.

DISCOURSE & SOCIETY

Edited by *Teun A. van Dijk*

*A vital new forum for
interdisciplinary research on
language use, discourse and
communication!*

Published quarterly in January, April, July and
October

1515

Women and Objective Culture: Georg Simmel and Marianne Weber

Lieteke van Vucht Tijssen

A Theory of Gender Relations

The transformation of gender relations is one of the core elements of the process of modernization. Although the founding fathers of sociology were well aware of that fact, most of them focused their attention on other aspects. Apart from Spencer, who was a source of inspiration for him in this respect, Simmel was the only one to develop a theory of changing gender relations as an integrated element of a theory of modernization. He published about fifteen essays on this subject between 1890 and 1911, which were republished in Germany in 1985 under the title *Schriften zur Philosophie und Soziologie der Geschlechter*.

Simmel's ideas on gender relations coincided to a large extent with those of many of his contemporaries. However, they also met with criticism, some of it from Marianne Weber. The wife of Max Weber, she was also an intellectual in her own right. Her publications include a number of essays on the problems of women. She discussed Simmel's theories of gender relations in one of these essays, 'Die Frau und die objektive Kultur' (Weber, 1919). In this short article I will present the core of Simmel's ideas on men and women along with Marianne Weber's critique of them. I will also pay attention to the practical consequences that Simmel draws from them and to Marianne Weber's comments on them.

Simmel's Metaphysics of Gender

Simmel develops his sociology of gender relations not only against the background of, but also as an elaboration of, his ideas on the relation between lived experiences and the forms that channel them, as well as on the relation between subjective and objective culture. Simmel at first held that these relations always are full of tension.

Theory, Culture & Society (SAGE, London, Newbury Park and New Delhi), Vol. 8 (1991), 203–218

On the one hand, 'the energies and interests of life are defined and molded by the forms of "objective culture", the world of cultural forms and their artifacts, that have become independent of individual human existence' (Oakes, 1984: 6), on the other hand, life itself transcends these forms time and again (see Weinstein and Weinstein, 1990). By offering possible 'molds' for experience, objective culture provides the instruments for the individual to transform himself into a cultural being, that is into a person. In order to do so the elements of objective culture have to be incorporated in the 'subjective culture': the life of the individual as a cultural being (Oakes, 1984: 7; see also Bevers, 1982: 84–104; van Vucht Tijssen, 1989). Ideally the individual should be able to absorb all the elements of the objective culture in the subjective culture, but the process of modernization has brought about the separation of objective and subjective culture. The range and complexity of objective culture increases to such an extent, that it is no longer possible for an individual to appropriate objective culture as a whole and to integrate the elements into subjective experience. That is a tragedy of modernity.

In his essays on 'Female Culture' and 'The Relative and the Absolute in the Problem of the Sexes' Simmel modifies this point of view. In these essays he argues that the tensions between lived experience and the forms of objective culture, as well as the dissociation of objective and subjective culture have to do with the specific characteristics of the nature of men. The tragedy of modernization is the tragedy of men, not of mankind. It is only because the male way of being in the course of history has acquired the status of the universal way of being, that this has not been noticed before (Simmel, 1984: 102, 103). In order to correct this one-sidedness Simmel thinks it necessary that modern society does justice to the specific characteristics of the female sex as well. Men, he claims, indeed create objective culture. As a consequence all its components, from the great works of art to the forms of government and from scientific theory to labour relations, are completely permeated with male characteristics, male emotions and male intelligence. Besides, objective culture will always depend on these male characteristics for its very survival.

> . . . Our culture is, with a few exceptions, predominantly a male culture. Men have created art and science, trade and business, polity and religion, and as a

result they do not only display a male character, but for their continuation also are dependent upon specific male characteristics. (Simmel, 1985: 161)[1]

The specific characteristics that Simmel ascribes to men are: their ability to put themselves in the service of grand ideals, their capacity to act in a goal-oriented and rational way, and their tendency to specialization and the division of labour (Simmel, 1985: 161–2, also 1919: 256–7). Simmel dwells particularly on the latter characteristic. In his view, men are endowed with the capacity to devote themselves fully to one task and one specific achievement, even if this only appeals to a limited part of their personality. As a result, men are also able to distinguish between their professional activities and their subjective personality. As far as their jobs are concerned, men allow themselves to be guided by the anonymous rules of objective culture, and at the same time they repress their subjective interests and emotions, confining them to the realm of private experience, to prevent them from interfering with their work. It is this male schizophrenia in particular which Simmel sees as the bed-rock of modern culture. Such a complex and differentiated culture can only be created and continued because men are inclined and prepared to specialize and to act in a business-like fashion (Simmel, 1985: 161–2). In other words, modern culture is what it is because men are rational and dissociated, because they are torn apart between subjective and objective culture (Simmel, 1985: 207).

In contrast with the nature of men, Simmel conceives of women's nature as transcending or being beyond the division of objective and subjective culture from which men suffer, and as a consequence also as beyond the frictions between lived experience and the objective forms of life. Women represent a kind of wholeness which men do not experience, which is as important a value as the ones represented by men and their nature (Simmel, 1985: 208, 1919: 264–6). This difference can be discovered in the way in which both sexes handle the sexual relationship. Because of their dualistic nature men involve only part of themselves in it, while for women it is an intrinsic part of their whole existence. As a result:

> For the man there is a sense in which sexuality is something he does. For the woman, it is a mode of being. (Simmel, 1984: 107)

Because of this capacity for differentiation men can be rather sensible to the purely sensual. Female sexuality on the contrary is at the core of the immanent nature of women. Therefore for women sexuality is a far less carnal matter.[2]

The wholeness of female life not only shows itself in the way in which women engage in sexual relationships; it spreads throughout women's whole way of being and expressing themselves. Men continuously strive for the transcendental, they reach out beyond themselves for the empirical realization of ideas. It is precisely because of this pursuit of the absolute, that their lives are divided between the two poles of objective and subjective culture.

> The reaching out, in all they do, for the realm of the supra-personal . . . implies a dualism from the start, a splitting of the unity of life in the form of above and below, of subject and object. . . . (Simmel, 1985: 209)[3]

Men themselves are indeed able to reduce this gap and to find a new harmony, but in order to do so they have to assimilate the whole of objective culture and create a new synthesis. As objective culture becomes more differentiated and proliferated, this task becomes harder and harder (Simmel, 1985: 3, 220–4). Unlike men, women are not naturally inclined to specialization or to the pursuit of objective ideas. Consequently, they are not inwardly torn apart. On the contrary, they achieve in a natural way the inner unity that men can only attain in an indirect manner. Women live their lives as an unbroken whole. A woman therefore, according to Simmel, remains much more self-contained: 'Her world gravitates, to its own distinctive centre' (Simmel, 1984: 111–12).

> Here the dualism, that splits up the roots of life, is lacking. . . . Life is lived and experienced as a value in itself and is meaningfully centred in such a way that even the expression that it is lived as a goal in itself, tears it apart too much. (Simmel 1985: 210)[4]

Because of the specific characteristics of their existence women also are less inclined to rational, that is logical and objective, thinking. Their way of dealing with the world is much more emotional and intuitive. In western culture for a long time this has been a reason to consider women as being inferior to men. Simmel reverses this argument. To him these qualities turn women not into inferior, but into superior beings compared with men. Because of their intuition, they have a better understanding of complex situations and besides they are also better able to cope with ambiguous situations (Simmel, 1985: 43–5, 1919: 284–6). Their greatest quality, however, is the unity of their existence. While men strive to attain objective reality, the existence of women is anchored in life itself. Women therefore are a counterweight to the dissociative tendencies of men (Simmel, 1985: 210ff., 1919: 284-6). Simmel even alleges that precisely in as far as a woman is beyond the distinction to which the man is subjected, she is the more authentic human being (Simmel, 1984: 112).

Simmel's ideas on the difference between women and men in the end are based on a metaphysical argument. Ultimately the superiority of female nature has do with the relationship of her existence to the nature of the cosmos in general (Simmel, 1984: 119). Simmel apparently ascribes two dimensions to the cosmos: that of absolute ideas or forms and that of the forces of life. These two dimensions are also the basic characteristics of human existence.[5] On the level of the cosmos both aspects are fused in an undivided whole. Yet in human life they take two different a priori forms, the male and the female. For reasons that Simmel does not clarify, in the nature of men idea and life get dissociated, while in the nature of women they still are an unbroken whole. This means that women's nature is closer to that of the cosmos as such (Simmel, 1984: 120-30).[6]

On the basis of this presupposition Simmel draws a couple of epistemological and ethical conclusions, which have to do with the intellectual and moral capacities of women. That women do not strive for the empirical realization of ideas and also are less inclined to rational thinking is, against this background, not the result of a deficiency but, on the contrary, of a superior access to the objective. Because life and spirit in female existence have not grown apart, because the life of a woman is grounded in the fundamental as such, women are able to arrive at an immediate existential unity with the ultimate foundations of existence. As a result, contrary to men, women do not need to reason rationally in order to get access to the realm of the absolute (Simmel, 1984: 120).

> As a result, the form of method that is characteristic of all our discursive knowledge is unnecessary and irrelevant for her. (Simmel, 1984: 120)[7]

The same goes for morality. Again because of the unbroken character of their nature, 'morality . . . stems from the innermost instinct of women's nature' (Simmel, 1984: 126). Women therefore are capable more easily than men to reach the state of the 'beautiful soul' (*schöne Seele*), of the inner harmony of their volitional actions which disclose the metaphysical unity of the nature in us and the idea above us.[8] Men also are able to reach this state but only by overcoming their dualistic nature. The path of women is a pre-dualistic one (Simmel, 1984: 122). On the basis of these considerations Simmel concludes that instead of one, there are two a priori forms of life: a male and a female one, each of which represents a privileged access to the cosmos. In this sense both forms transcend the borders of gender and represent in their own way an objective principle.

> In the same way that the man, independent of this relationship, is more than male, so the woman is more than female. This is because she represents the universal fundament that comprehends the sexes substantially or genetically. . . . In the former case, the absolute arises as the trans-sexually objective, which is male. In the latter case as the trans-sexually fundamental, which is female. (Simmel, 1984: 128)

Therefore, in order to attain the universal, mankind needs both a priori forms. Yet one of the problems of modern culture is that it acknowledges only the male principle as the absolute and ignores the female principle. The only remedy to this, according to Simmel, is a fundamental reappraisal of the female a priori form of life. At the same time this also would be the best way to reinforce the position of women in modern society.

Women, Men and Human Nature: The Critique by Marianne Weber

Marianne Weber agrees with Simmel's ideas about modernization and the fissure of objective and subjective culture, but this is as far as she is prepared to go. She does not argue with Simmel about his view on the tragic consequences of this process for modern culture as well as for the lives of men. Instead she emphasizes that participation in objective culture gives men and women the chance to develop their creative capacities and to contribute to something supra-personal and she finds this highly rewarding.

Besides, and this is even more important, she cannot accept the link of objective culture with the so-called male characteristics, that Simmel presupposes. In Weber's view, at this point in his work Simmel turns an empirical judgement on a historical process, in which some positions and characteristics were assigned to men and others to women, into a normative judgement about male and female nature. Marianne Weber considers this confusion of facts and values to be completely inadmissible. Her main objections, however, are not aimed at the form of his argument, but at its content. She argues that Simmel's ideas certainly do differ to a certain extent from those of his predecessors, like Kant, Schleiermacher and Schiller, philosophers who had viewed men as the bearers of humanity and women as no more than a second sex, deriving the meaning of their existence from bearing children and from pleasing and serving men. Those philosophers in other words, measured the value of women's existence with a male yardstick. Furthermore, they supposed that women can only develop their qualities in relation to men (Weber, 1919: 97–100). Simmel differs from them in conceiving femininity as an autonomous phenomenon with its roots in female nature, i.e. independent of men. Simmel also sets a high value on the qualities attributed to women. Marianne Weber admits that he thereby breaks through the magic circle which his predecessors had drawn round men and women, creating room for women to follow their destiny separately from men (Weber, 1919: 102–3). Nevertheless, despite her admiration for Simmel in this respect, she disagrees completely with his ideas about women as such. She begins by pointing out that his perspective does not differ essentially from the ideas held by the earlier philosophers. Although Simmel presents his ideas in a very sublimated form, they still boil down to a projection on to women of the qualities which men themselves find hard to realize (Weber, 1919: 102). Apart from that, she also rejects Simmel's assumption that there are metaphysical differences between men and women. Marianne Weber considers that the logical consequence of accepting Simmel's notion that mankind has split into two entirely different sexes is that the female sex is a mistake of nature. Of course, a lot of women would agree with Simmel's ideas on femininity, but there are also women who would not allow themselves to be confined to the domain of intuition and care, but would very much like to participate in objective culture in the same way as men do. How is this to be understood, and what would the bio-ontological status of these women be? According to Simmel's ideas, they could only be conceived as a kind of third sex. In other words, besides real men and real women there would also be a mutation: female beings with male qualities. Marianne Weber sees in this absurd consequence sufficient reason to reject Simmel's metaphysics of gender.

However, Marianne Weber's essay is not confined to criticizing

Simmel — she also develops a point of view of her own. She does accept the existence of differences between men and women, but she approaches them in a different way. According to her, men and women resemble overlapping circles rather than entirely different beings. True, they do differ in some respects, but they also have a lot of qualities in common. The important thing is to know how much emphasis to put on the differences and how much on the shared qualities. It is clear that Simmel and his predecessors overrate the differences. Marianne Weber herself prefers to draw attention to what men and women have in common, a core of shared capacities which she refers to as 'das allgemein menschlichen' (Weber, 1919: 96, 109, 132):

> Above the idea of specific male qualities there is also the general imperative of being a full human being, which does not simply coincide with them, while this idea also stands above that of specific female qualities. (Weber, 1919: 132)[9]

Starting from this presupposition, Marianne Weber rethinks the relationship of men and women to objective culture. Simmel's identification of objective culture with specific male qualities now becomes untenable. Of course, objective culture will still have some male characteristics, but because men are also human beings, objective culture contains a number of general human qualities at the same time. In other words, rationality, objectivity and orientation toward a goal are not specific male capacities; they are human ones. Women possess them just as men do. Consequently, the criteria for being able to contribute to objective culture are also valid and attainable for women who want to participate in objective culture (Weber, 1919: 111, 126, 130–2). This argument can also be turned the other way round, and this is precisely what Marianne Weber does, although carefully. Her thesis is that men for their part have the capacities and the duty to contribute to the domain of life and care. In principle, men should be allowed and encouraged to develop this part of their personality as well.

> To be a 'real human being' for men also means a richer existence than the male one — a synthesis that a mere male existence would lack. (Weber, 1919: 132)[10]

Apart from rejecting the identification of objective culture with male characteristics, Marianne Weber also criticizes the idea that the domain of women coincides with so-called female ones.

Taking care of people, she argues, is not just a matter of intuition, spontaneity and communication; it also calls for organizational capacities. Moreover, even the running of a household involves objective values and norms that do not necessarily coincide with the personal taste and preferences of the individual, thereby implying that housewives do not always experience their lives as an unbroken whole, but can be subjected to the same tensions between subjective and objective culture as men (Weber, 1919: 112). Marianne Weber does not, however, draw the corollary that the domain of objective culture contains more female characteristics than Simmel assumes. Nevertheless, she makes it perfectly clear that the human qualities, that she refers to, do not only include so-called male qualities, but also a number of 'female' ones.

Women and Objective Culture

Simmel's sociology of gender is intimately linked to his theory about modernization. One of the consequences of this process of division of labour and objectivization of culture is the belittlement of household tasks. Simmel acknowledges that this can result in an increasing demand by (bourgeois) women for participation in other domains of objective culture. This entrance of women in what was traditionally the domain of men, is precisely the reason why he thinks it necessary to reflect on the essence of male and female nature (Simmel, 1985: 170–1). Yet in his essays on gender, Simmel does not restrict himself to the development of a metaphysics of gender. He also pays attention to the more practical question of the desirability of the participation of women in objective culture. The most radical consequence of his own theory, of course, would be that women by nature are not fit for participation in objective culture and should stay where their nature obliges them to belong. To a great extent Simmel indeed adopts this point of view (Simmel, 1985: 173). In the end there are only a few domains in objective culture which Simmel considers as created by or as accessible to women. In order to support his point of view his discusses a number of professions. To him an important precondition for allowing women to enter objective culture is the demand that women should not try to repeat male activities, but that they should make a contribution of their own which is both suited to their specific qualities and capable of introducing new elements into objective culture.

> As we see it, the real problem for culture is: whether the required freedom of women would give rise to new cultural qualities . . . whether they would contribute something *that men can not*. (Simmel, 1985: 163)[11]

The array of professions, Simmel discusses, ranges from factory worker to artist. And indeed women by nature prove to be absolutely unsuited for some of them, such as working in a factory, because these jobs are fragmented and disciplined (Simmel, 1985: 163-4). Women can only contribute to other professions in a limited way. In the world of art, for example, women are not capable of becoming artistic geniuses because they have no need for the pursuit of grand ideas. Instead, it would be better for them to confine themselves to the performing arts, which are indeed suited to their intuitive and communicative capacities (Simmel, 1985: 165-70). More or less the same applies to the sciences. Most of them are not suitable for women, with the exception of history and medicine. These are domains in which women's intuitive capacities can add something that men cannot. Simmel makes no comment on the other professions. The result is therefore rather disappointing. Objective culture does not seem to have much room for women. In fact there is only one real contribution women have made to objective culture and that is the creation of the home as a form of life. To Simmel it is more than a historical accident that women in the process of modernization have claimed the domain of the household, family life and social relations and have turned this realm into their own, it is rather a matter of 'elective affinity'. This is indeed where women can make the best contribution to culture (Simmel, 1985: 170-1, 1919: 284-6). Because they are intuitive, spontaneous and emotional and because their existence springs from and is focused on an undivided subjective existence, women in particular are able to concentrate on the well-being of the people in their immediate surroundings (Simmel, 1985: 173, 272-38, 1919: 262-6). Apart from their contribution in the domain of care, they also play a more indirect role. Besides the home, their most important contribution to objective culture, according to Simmel, is the male soul, but because of the ontological differences between men and women this is rather a secondary one (Simmel, 1919: 288). Besides alleging that women are capable only of contributing new elements to objective culture in a limited way, Simmel also argues that participation in objectivity would destroy the unity of their existence. They would end up just as dissociated as men, and thus would harm their metaphysical nature. If it was up to Simmel, women would clearly concentrate on the roles and domains which allow them to express fully their own form of life. Apart from mother and wife, there is only one role that fits this criteria and that is the role of 'schöne Seele'. The idea is that a woman strips her femininity of all sexual elements and refines and sublimates it in such a way that she radiates pure femininity, rest and harmony (Simmel, 1985: 168–9, 1919: 283–4). Only by fulfilling their nature in these ways, can women avoid the imposition of (male) criteria on their nature and gain independence from men (Simmel, 1984: 99). Thus in the end Simmel leaves the problem with which he started, unsolved. Although the modern household leaves women with a lot of time and energy, Simmel denies them access to most of objective culture and instead refers them back to the home.

In her essay, Marianne Weber also considers the possibilities for women to participate in objective culture. Of course, she disagrees with Simmel. To begin with she is less pessimistic than Simmel about the impact of modernization on the existence of women. She rather welcomes the diminishing of household tasks, because that leaves women with time also to contribute to objective culture and thus to fulfil their calling as human beings. She also thinks it necessary to reflect on the opportunities and hindrances for women to enter the objective culture, but she approaches this problem from a more practical point of view. For example, she considers the question of whether women are suited to sit behind machines or not as academic. In practice those women work because they need an income. It would make no sense to throw them out of work because of their assumed unsuitability. It would be better to create provisions that would allow those women more time to take care of their families and households (Weber, 1919: 122–3). Marianne Weber's ideas on the arts and sciences also differ from Simmel's. The only constrictions that she sees for women in this domain are those of time. In her opinion, a lot of women have just the same need, are just as able as men to devote themselves to grand ideas and to become geniuses. However, as long as they have to take care of their households and families, women simply lack the time to do so (Weber, 1919: 129). As for the role of 'schöne Seele' which Simmel praises so highly, Marianne Weber is again very critical. She points out that the peace that these women seem to radiate is merely a facade which conceals a lot of frustrations and feelings of discontent that men will never suspect. Besides, she thinks that this role does not provide intellectually or artistically gifted women with a meaningful existence. She argues that it is precisely participation in objective culture which would render the existence of these women more harmonious than the cultivation of their femininity (Weber, 1919: 113–14). Yet this does not mean that it will be easy for women to participate in objective culture. When they do so they even will have to face a double dualism instead of the one that men are confronted with. They will not only have to cope with the gap between objective and subjective culture, but they also have to overcome the tension between their calling as a woman and the demands of objective culture (Weber, 1919: 117–18). Although she finds this a difficult task, she is confident that, given time and opportunities, women will be able to cope (Weber, 1919: 119).

Apart from disagreeing with Simmel's practical proposal for the participation of women in objective culture, Marianne Weber also rejects his general presuppositions. She argues that there is no reason to demand extra qualifications and specific contributions from women. As human beings, women are able and entitled to participate in objective culture in precisely the same way as men do. She also sees no reason why they should not be measured with the same yardsticks as men. The way for women to gain autonomy is not to shy away from those criteria, but to live up to them. Marianne Weber acknowledges that, because of the historical disadvantages of women with respect to education and because of her caring tasks, it can take some time before women can stand the test, but to her this is mainly a matter of hard work and patience. In the end women will catch up with men and will be able to meet the same standards (Weber, 1919: 104, 127ff.).[12]

A Continuing Story
Although the controversy between Marianne Weber and Georg Simmel took place more than half a century ago, it is still relevant. Together with, for example Tönnies, Scheler, Mannheim and to a certain extent even Max Weber, Simmel belongs to a sociological tradition that combines the analysis of modernization, with a critical judgement of this process. Amongst them Simmel has a special position. All of them agree that modernization equals rationalization and objectivization at the expense of emotion, love and care and they all look for remedies, but Simmel is the only one who relates the development of modern culture to the domination of men

and who appeals to women to compensate for that.[13] He thus anticipates the ideas of present cultural feminism. Representatives of this current allege too that most of the institutions of modern society are dominated by men and based on male principles and, in addition, they presume that the nature of women is totally different from that of men. Just like Simmel they think it necessary that women provide a counterweight to the alleged one-sidedness of a male-dominated culture. Nevertheless their emancipatory strategy is opposite to the one Simmel develops. In his essay on female culture, Simmel argued with the German feminist movement and in particular with the bourgeois-liberal one. At that time the ideology and strategy of this German movement were very different from those of the women's movement in the rest of Europe and the US. In fact their ideas on the nature of women were rather similar to that of Simmel but also to that of present cultural feminism. At the core of the ideology of the German bourgeois women's movement was the idea that there existed radical differences between men and women, which required different callings for both of them. Of course, women were specialists in the caring tasks and jobs (Evans, 1976; van Vucht Tijssen, 1990: 157-9). Just like present cultural feminism they tried to use this difference as a political weapon to gain access to public life. In their eyes women's nurturing skills did not necessarily confine them to home and children. These also enabled them to contribute to culture and society in general. Moreover, they argued that this contribution was an essential one that would enrich culture in important ways. The practical results of this strategy were very disappointing and in the end the bourgeois women's movement became increasingly timid and conservative (Clemens, 1988: 127-8; van Vucht Tijssen, 1990: 158). Against this background Simmel's critique of these tactics perfectly shows the dangers of overemphasizing the difference between men and women. The propagation of an essentialist view on the differences between men and women probably can raise their social status and their values, but it also makes it easy to exclude women from most parts of objective culture, precisely because of their specific nature. That clearly is not a satisfactory solution. Yet present cultural feminism, by reviving the idea of radical differences, risks running into the same dead end.

Marianne Weber's conception of overlapping circles, might provide the starting-point for avoiding that pitfall. On the one hand, she acknowledges differences between men and women while, on the other hand she presupposes a general human nature which is endowed both with 'male' and 'female' characteristics. In order to become full human beings each sex should have the chance to develop both sides of their personality. Simmel in the end only puts women in a 'gilded cage' next to the 'iron cage' in which men have locked themselves away. Marianne Weber's presuppositions allow her to plead for equal access to objective culture for men and women without denying the importance of the qualities and values developed by women (see also van Vucht Tijssen, 1990). Even today that is a major step forward.

Notes

1. '. . . unsere Kultur ist, mit Aussnahme ganz weniger Provinzen, durchaus männlich. Männer haben die Industrieen und die Kunst, die Wissenschaft und den Handel, die Staatsverwaltung und die Religion geschaffen, und so tragen diese nicht nur objektiv männliche Charakter, sondern verlangen auch zu ihrer immer wiederholten Ausführung spezifische männliche Kräfte' (Simmel, 1985: 161).

2. Simmel indeed also argues that this feminine quality does not vanish with the physical attractiveness of the woman, but in itself remains unchanged (Simmel, 1984: 109–10).

3. 'Das über sichselbst Hinausgreifen in aller Produktion . . . enthält von vornherein einen Dualismus, ein Auseinandergehen des einheitlichen Lebens in die Formen des Oben und Unten, des Subjekts und Objekts . . .' (Simmel, 1985: 43, 220–4).

4. 'Hier fehlt der die Wurzeln der Existenz spaltende Dualismus . . . das Leben wird als ein in sich ruhender Wert gelebt und gefühlt und ist in seinem Sinne nach so in seinen Mittelpunkt gesammelt, dass selbst der Ausdruck, dass es Selbstzweck sei, es noch zu sehr auseinander zieht' (Simmel, 1985: 210).

5. Though it is clear that he distinguishes the dimension of the spirit on the one hand, and a more vitalistic dimension on the other, Simmel is quite unclear about their precise nature. The same type of distinction is elaborated more clearly in the work of Max Scheler who uses the concepts 'Geist' and 'Drang' to designate the two dimensions, therewith subscribing Simmel's remark that men by nature are half angel–half animal (van Vucht Tijssen, 1989: 169 ff.; Simmel, 1984).

6. It should be noted also that Guy Oakes in his otherwise excellent introduction in Simmel's sociology of gender overlooks that this is the ultimate reason for Simmel to value women higher than men (see Oakes, 1984: 3–62).

7. Simmel even compares this female way of 'knowing' with the way in which the great mystics gain access to the cosmos (Simmel, 1984: 128). In her discussion of Simmel's views on female creativity Suzanne Vromen ignores this epistemological argument. She reproaches Simmel for denying women 'the capacity to objectify their existence and to express in external forms their distinctive qualities' (Vromen, 1987: 574). For Simmel, however, this is not a matter of denying women these capacities. Because of their metaphysical nature women do not need to make the same

detour as men in order to get access to the realm of the absolute. This means a real advantage over men.

8. This suggests that women in Simmel's view still would have access to the authentic values that men have sacrificed in the process of modernization.

9. 'Neben der Idee eines spezifisch Männlichen steht so gut die Idee eines allgemeinmenschlichen Soll — des "Vollmenschentums" — das mit jener nicht ohne weiteres zusammenfällt, wie über dem von Mannheit verschiedenen spezifisch Weiblichen' (Weber, 1919: 132).

10. 'Ein "echter Mensch" zu sein bedeutet auch für den Mann reichere Volkommenheit als das Mannsein — eine Synthese von Qualitäten, die der blossen Mannheit fehlen dürfte' (Weber, 1919: 133).

11. 'Das eigentliche Kulturproblem also das wir stellen: ob die erstrebte Freiheit der Frauen neue Kulturqualitäten würde entstehen lassen . . . das sie etwas leisten *was die Männer nicht können*' (Simmel, 1985: 163).

12. In order to support her claim she argues that in the relatively short period that women's right to participation has been acknowledged by society, they have contributed a substantial amount of works to art and science of a reasonable quality (Weber, 1919: 127–8).

13. His pupil Max Scheler for example never thought of identifying the rational with men and the non-rational with women. To him both were human capacities which were developed in a different way by the western and the Asian world. In order to cure the ailments of modernity he therefore did not appeal to women but to Buddhism and Asian culture (van Vucht Tijssen, 1989).

Bibliography

Bevers, A. (1982) *De geometrie van de samenleving. Filosofie en sociologie in het werk van Georg Simmel*. Deventer: van Loghum Slaterus.

Clemens, B. (1988) '*Menschenrechte haben kein Geslecht*'. *Zum Politikverständnis der bürgerlichen Frauenbewegung*. Pfaffenweiler: Centaurus.

Coser, L.A. (1977) 'Georg Simmel's Neglected Contribution to the Sociology of Women', *Signs. Journal of Women in Culture and Society* 2 (4): 869–76.

Dahme, H. (1986) 'Frauen- und Geschlechterfrage bei Herbert Spencer und Georg Simmel', *Kölner Zeitschrift für Soziologie und Sozialpsychologie* 38: 490–509.

Evans, R.J. (1976) *The Feminist Movement in Germany 1894–1933*. London: Sage.

Frisby, D. (1981) *Sociological Impressionism. A Reassessment of Georg Simmel's Social Theory*. London: Heinemann.

Oakes, G. (1984) 'Introduction', to *Georg Simmel: On Women, Sexuality, and Love*. Translated by Guy Oakes. New Haven, CT: Yale University Press.

Scaff, L.A. (1989) *Beyond the Iron Cage*. California: University of California Press.

Simmel, G. (1919) *Philosophische Kultur*. Leipzig: Kroner Verlag.

Simmel, G. (1983) *Schriften zur Soziologie. Eine Auswahl*. Edited by H.J. Dahme and O. Rammsted. Frankfurt a.M.: Suhrkamp.

Simmel. G. (1984) *On Women, Sexuality and Love* (trans. and ed. G. Oakes). New Haven, CT: Yale University Press.

Simmel, G. (1985) *Schriften zur Philosophie und Soziologie der Geslechter*. Edited by H.J. Dahme and K.C. Köhnke. Frankfurt a.M.: Suhrkamp.

van Vucht Tijssen, B.E. (1988) 'De plaats van de vrouw in de moderne cultuur. Marianne Weber contra Georg Simmel', *Sociale wetenschappen* 31 (2): 83–101.

van Vucht Tijssen, Lieteke (1989) *Auf dem Weg zur Relativierung der Vernunft. Eine vergleichende Rekonstruktion der kultur-und wissenssoziologischen Auffassungen Max Schelers und Max Webers.* Berlin: Duncker und Humblot.

van Vucht Tijssen, Lieteke (1990) 'Women between Modernity and Postmodernity' pp. 147–63 in Bryan S. Turner (ed.), *Theories of Modernity and Postmodernity.* London: Sage.

Vromen, S. (1987) 'Georg Simmel and the Cultural Dilemma of Women', *History of European Ideas* 8 (4/5): 563–79.

Weber, Marianne (1919) 'Die Frau und die objektive Kultur', in Marianne Weber, *Frauenfrage und Frauengedanke.* Tübingen: J.C.B. Mohr.

Weinstein, Deena and Michael A. Weinstein (1990) 'Simmel and the Theory of Postmodern Society' pp. 75–87 in Bryan S. Turner (ed.), *Theories of Modernity and Postmodernity.* London: Sage.

Lieteke van Vucht Tijssen teaches Sociology at the State University of Utrecht, the Netherlands.

The War Writings of Georg Simmel

Patrick Watier

My first concern will be Simmel's period in Strasbourg. He published a number of articles about the Great War, and about German attitudes to the conflict in the *Strassburger Post*. Little of this appears in his books. Of additional and particular importance is his text *Die Deutschlands innere Wandlung* (Simmel, 1917b) which he presented at a conference at the Salle de l'Aubette on 7 November 1914.

We must counter an essential misunderstanding with regard to the negative character of Simmel's teachings in the realm of morality. Veil, a contemporary, recalled Simmel's reaction to remarks made about him at the time of the session of the second chamber of the *Landstag* on 26 February 1914: 'it is erroneous to relate philosophical principles to the personalities of those who hold them'. Veil pleaded for the necessary difference of relation between the philosopher and the object of study. Philosophers do not take alleged principles at face value, they question them and make them problematic. He drew out the themes of Simmel's (1910) *Hauptproblem der Philosophie* in order to show the precise operation of a misunderstanding concerning Simmel, and one of the principle objectives of his work was to destroy the course psychologism which was dominant in the domain of ethical problems.

Simmel's War writings return to many of the points made in *The Philosophy of Money* (1990). Sometimes this is just beneath the surface, sometimes it is explicit, as was the case with the Vienna conference on 'The Crisis of Culture'. His positions, however, were always forceful and positive. Indeed, if in *The Philosophy of Money* there is an equilibrium between critical and positive elements (individual liberty counterbalanced by indifference, for example), or an interaction of various themes concerning the money economy, nevertheless, everything is presented as if life could no longer

Theory, Culture & Society (SAGE, London, Newbury Park and New Delhi), Vol. 8 (1991), 219–233

be lived negatively. Mammonism, indifference, cynicism can be left behind, but only by the kind of hard decision which is symbolized by the War.

When it is said that Simmel translated a crisis of social conflict into a cultural question, this is both true and false. It is true because he was critical of the sociocultural state of Germany; he desired a new Germany, and also a Europe which would understand that it could not just be based upon cosmopolitanism and the circulation of money. It is false since his critique rests upon a conception of the money economy and its inexorable development.

Overall, for Simmel, while war is, under a certain aspect, a question of power and of economic interests, it also forces us to address ideological issues.

It is not so much illusions of a new Germany which Simmel's discourse on the War purveys, but their internal theme and the experience upon which they are based which constitute the object of my reflections. Simmel thought the present moment as if with an advance plan for his work on the critique of culture.

Through the War, Simmel could see an analogon, on a grand scale, to something which Weber could only see in pianissimo in modern society: 'a prophetic wind blowing through the great communities and forcing them together'. The fundamental question of the pent up energy in the constitution, consolidation and perpetuation of the social bond is basic to the sociological tradition, and it is this which is in question here.

In *The Elementary Forms of Religious Life*, Durkheim (1979: 611) expressed himself thus: 'The day will come when our societies will experience a new time of creative effervescence in the course of which new ideas will surge forward, and new formulas will emerge to provide a guide for humanity for some time to come.' While, as Aron pointed out, Durkheim only suggested it rather than saying it explicitly, he did seem to think that the religious festivals of the future would be related to critical social and political events, and the example he takes is that of the French revolution: 'This ability of society to set itself up as God, or to create Gods was never more visible than in the first years of the Revolution. At that moment, effectively under the influence of a general enthusiasm, things which were purely secular in nature were transformed into sacred things by public opinion, namely the Nation, Liberty, Reason' (Durkheim, 1979: 306). The historical record, interpreted through Durkheim's vision, does indicate that it was a sentiment of exaltation which aroused the people, perhaps more in Germany than in other countries, at the start of the Great War.

To give some idea of the context, I will refer to certain essayists and novelists: Musil, Canetti, Thomas Mann and his son. Thus Thomas Mann (1968), whose 'Considerations of an Apolitical Man' I consider below, expressed himself through the words of Zeitblom as follows:

> In our Germany, the effect [of the War] was undeniably and pre-eminently enthusiasm, and from a world-stagnation that could go on no longer; as hope for the future, an appeal to duty and manhood, in short as a holiday for heroes. . . . If the war is felt more or less clearly as a general visitation in which the individual . . . thinks of himself as a sacrifice by which the old Adam is put away and from which in unity a new and higher life will be wrested, then our everyday morals are outbid by the abnormal and must be silent. . . . Culture had been free, she had stood at a respectable height; and though she had long been used to a complete absence of relations with the governing power, her younger representatives might see in a great national war, such as now broke out, a means of achieving a form of life in which state and culture might become one. In this we displayed the preoccupation with self which is peculiar to us: our naive egoism finds it unimportant, yes, takes it entirely for granted, that for the sake of our development (and we are always developing) the rest of the world, further on than ourselves and not at all possessed by the dynamic of catastrophe, must shed its blood. (Mann, 1968: 290–1)

Thomas Mann's son wrote in a more measured way: 'In 1914, the German intelligentsia, almost without exception, lined themselves up with the enthusiastic partisans of the war' (K. Mann, 1986: 84). For Elias Canetti, the experience of the War was perhaps the most important thing which determined his passion for the study of masses and crowds; indeed, his fraught experience in Vienna was of almost being lynched when he had the somewhat foolish idea of accompanying the patriotic songs in the vogue language of the day which just happened to be English. Robert Musil (1980) spoke in his journal about these moments of 'great experience'. He was quite clear, if uncritical, that this social intoxication was something which brought God closer, which carried the feeling that it was Goethe who was being defended, and that it reversed the decline of life toward death. For Musil (1980: 419) the willingness to sacrifice one's life was very significant, other interpretations aside. This great mass experience, as Tarde, another misunderstood sociologist, saw very clearly, was hardly something occurring within society in a minor fashion. Perhaps it was ritualized, but it was real. It would be false to try to hide this fact through the representation of society in methodological individualist terms.

The careful analysis and classification of social phenomena may not expect to reveal what the future holds, but at least it should not exclude what is actually happening in the unstable order of societies. If I have brought these matters back to mind, it is in order to understand what seems to be an aberration: the feeling of joy created by a declaration of war. This declaration is located in a context which is also seen as an internal ideological struggle against certain corrupted elements of the social body. Its condemnation is not a simple matter because it made possible a stronger relationship between the individual and the general order.

Simmel's texts on the War, especially 'Deutschlands innere Wandlung' (1917b), are very often seen as falling outside of his oeuvre. This offers a kind of excuse for the excesses of expression to which he would subsequently return, but why did he publish *Der Krieg und die geistigen Entscheidungen* in 1917? I do not think that the question has been addressed properly, and the reason for this is that the real situation has been forgotten, despite apparent references to it. More exactly, what actually does take place in this kind of situation has been forgotten, context is summoned up only for context to be ignored.

Context is, of course, a matter of the greatest interest for sociologists. In order to understand it, they have developed distinctions such as those between the individual and the collective, mechanical and organic solidarity, community and association, calm and effervescence, 'hot' periods and 'cold' periods, and so on. They have then gone on to attribute effects of cohesion to war.

However, Simmel is linked to a particular current, deriving from Nietzsche, in which Germany occupies a special place. In order to illustrate this current, let me quote from Thomas Mann's essay *Considerations of an Apolitical Man*:

So I had the impression that the war, while certainly in one sense a struggle for power and commerce, is — seen from another angle — actually an ideological war which has already been drawn onto a purely spiritual plane, as if the German spirit had already been instilled with a profound distaste (as Nietzsche would have put it) for modernity, the West, and the dialectics of Enlightenment and civilisation, as if in Kant himself the spirit of German society, in all its conservative, constructive and organisational aspects, had been aroused against Occidental nihilism. (Mann, 1975: 153)

It is not a question of forgetting the economic 'causes', nor of sublimating them now that the essential struggle has become spiritual rather than material. But Marxism, as ultimately a form of economism, can at best only see a sort of auto-mystification here, an opiate for the times. Questions of consciousness and cohesion have quite properly their own tradition, and, what is more, a crucial role to play in the understanding of contemporary representations. We should remember that when ideas are taken to be true, they are real in their consequences. If we wish to understand a situation, we cannot suppress those elements which the actors involved regard as essential.

Durkheim's text *Germany Above All* (1915) may not be a major work, but it does display as clearly as anywhere else his pedagogic vocation to instruct humankind. What is more, the analysis therein of the social group is a carbon copy of the demonstration in *Suicide*. Let me simply cite some chapter headings: 'The Conduct of Germany during the War Derives from a Certain Mentality', 'The Facts of the War Explained by This Mentality', 'The Morbid Character of This Mentality'. We can see here something which was revealed by Dumont, relating to the different value systems of the French and the German nations:

> The Germans present themselves, and try to impose themselves, as superior by virtue of being German; while the French seem only to postulate the superiority of a universalist culture and naively identify with it to the point of taking themselves to be its founders. Finally, beyond their immediate opposition, the universalism of the one and the pan-germanism of the other serve a similar function: both express an *aporia* of nationhood, which is at once a collection of individuals and a collective individual. Both translate into some sort of reality the difficult task of modern ideology to provide an adequate image of (intra- and inter-) social life. (Dumont, 1979: 248-9)

Simmel tries to understand what is unfolding in front of his eyes, and I think that this is how we should understand his 1917 publication on war and spiritual division. Further than this, however, he felt himself to be one among many, and he knew from this standpoint, although in a practical and not a theoretical way, that he was part of a whole. But as soon as he recognized himself as part of that movement, he was no longer able to remain neutral. As Musil puts it:

In 1914, men were literally bored to death, and then how the war did sparkle in front of their very eyes, with the promise of adventure and the lure of unknown shores. This is why perfectly ordinary people were turned towards a religious experience, and immured themselves in a unifying development. A way of life which was at best only tolerated lay in pieces; the way forward was, God knows, unclear; it was even possible to imagine a transcendence of selfishness, with all that would imply. (Musil, 1984: 342)

What Durkheim described, in *The Elementary Forms of Religious Life*, as the moment of effervescence had arrived: 'a jolt of unsuspected power seized modern society and threw it into the war'. It was, as he put it in *Germany Above All* a moment of 'intense public life'. There was no longer a question of where one belonged: conflicts of interest were forgotten in order to defend an idea, a symbol, an emblem. This drunkenness would result in a hangover which would last for four terrible years.

The War also served to highlight the relation between the individual and society, which as Nisbet (1966) reminds us was one of the major themes of the founders of sociology. Everything comes back, in one way or another, to the same basic issue: in Simmel's terms, the relation between individualization, the emancipation of communities, traditional relationships and the possibility of a totality which might encompass the particularities which in themselves aspire to be part of a whole. While sociologists understand theoretically that the social has some influence, that collective movements can lead individuals to abandon themselves, that this social ecstasy can be recreated and deepened, that routine social bonds can become intense, all of this is happening here in front of their eyes, and Simmel is trying to make sense of it, to find the form which will put all of these things into some sort of order, but facing at the same time the absence of a determinate form for the modern world.

These great themes occur in Simmel's (1914, 1917b) two texts, 'Bergson and German Cynicism' and 'Germany's Inner Transformation'. As we will see, the fact that these two texts appeared almost together, implies a close connection between their contents, and the choice that they pose is 'to reconstruct a life in a new atmosphere and on new hypotheses, or, if this is beyond us, to return into indecision and survive it' (Simmel, 1917b).

What is most important in this internal dilemma is a new feeling of being together, a coming together of the individual and the whole nation. Simmel's introduction of these thoughts into the situation accords the group its own cohesion and conscience. In some way the situation comes to confirm a particular theory. That theory is that in the existence of the individual only a small part which is truly individual exists. In times of calm this part comes to the fore, since at such times all that matters are the things which differentiate people in terms of their interest and practical activities. The common foundations, however, appear in times of trouble and shock. At that time the almost spatial separation between the common and the singular disappears. The singular enters into the whole and knows itself responsible for all, and life becomes imbued with significance, for each thought and feeling is attached to a supra-individual totality.

Treating the remarks made to Bergson by the *Petit Parisien*, which criticized the German's cynical and barbaric behaviour, Simmel presented the readers of the *Strassburger Post* with the thread of his argument in 'Deutschlands innere Wandlung' that it was precisely a break with cynicism which had brought the War into being.

If we go back a little earlier, we find that miscomprehension abounds. Bergson and Durkheim both condemned the invasion of Belgium as a cynical disregard for treaties. Simmel, however, shows that this view is inadequate, and that, at another level, German actions themselves amounted to a critique of cynicism. In other words, neither Bergson nor Durkheim really understood the German situation. What they did not understand was that 'German existence had been thrown into the crucible, and that this was the strongest influence upon events even in the first moments of conflict, and, furthermore, this reforging was felt more and more strongly as the political and military dangers grew greater' (*Strassburger Post*, 14 November 1914).

For Simmel, the main issues were defined ideologically. With the War, individual and class self-interest was transcended. Previously such self-regard had held any notion of the whole to be chimerical. At the same time, the War saw the disappearance of the pleasure-based aestheticization of existence. Simmel wrote, 'German life has been cleansed of cynicism. No longer is it a question of "Après nous, le deluge" ' (*Strassburger Post*, 14 November 1914).

In general, the freedom which the world seemed to have gained was useless, since it was rooted in cynicism and nonchalance. Thus, the cultural reign of a generalized equivalence of axiologically vacuous signs, values, objects and ideas comes clearly into focus.

However, now that there might be an obligation to behave decently, a crucial moment of transformation may be found. It seems to me, then, that the content of Simmel's discourse on the Great War shows how Simmel refused to make a calculated decision, to say yes or no. Rather, he allowed himself to be totally overcome by the War, the War as the only conflict to take hold of everything in order to submit all to its uniquely sovereign task of transforming life, a life which needed direction, which needed a new context, which needed to become something other.

Simmel's critique of this mode of life is not unconnected to Nietzsche's *Untimely Meditations* and to his way of affirming the present as the place of an 'absolute situation' which would no longer permit either compromise or understanding on the part of an enfeebled historical consciousness. The force of comprehension may, then, be replaced by the comprehension of force. The War was the occasion when the problem of knowledge had to give way to the problem of life, and 'patriotic' enthusiasm signalled that life had so changed that one could be confident of creating something new. Nietzsche's writings pose the problem of the significance of living historically. For Simmel, we are situated at that point where our conscience knows that we are truly witnessing history (*dass wir wirklich Geschichte erleben*), but that it is not only history that makes us.

Simmel's cultural critique, as contained especially in his book on *Schopenhauer and Nietzsche* (1907) is central to his writings on Germany and the Great War. He writes:

> It is in the state of culture that the need to see one ultimate end of life first makes itself felt. It is born from the disquiet into which we are forced by the feeling of being taken hold of by something indirect and provisional . . . the extended development of a series of means and ends, turns life into a technical problem and puts us in the impossible situation of needing to know at every moment what the final link in the series is going to be. (Simmel, 1912: 2-3)

Responding to this text like an echo, we find a passage from Rodin expressing the spirit of modernity as without any point of reference, and which is no longer 'an oscillation between melancholy and intoxication, or cowardice and courage, or madness and disbelief — each of these positions existing substantially in their own right — but a simultaneity of positive and negative rather than an alternation between them'.

The War in this sense placed the individual in an absolute

situation where balance could be a possibility. Logically, this would seem to indicate, although Simmel does not take this view, that affirmation would be as good as refusal. He writes,

> I must put forward the fact that most of us are only now living in what we might call an absolute situation. All the situations and circumstances in which we found ourselves in the past had something relative about them, deliberations between the more and the less seemed to be the order of the day. None of this poses a problem now, since we are faced with an absolute decision. We no longer have the quantitative dilemma as to whether or when we must either make a sacrifice or a compromise. (Simmel, 1917b: 20)

A letter to Gundolf, although merely a small item in the *Strass-burger Post* of 7 April 1918, leads us to think that for Simmel there had been a misunderstanding about what he meant and about what the War meant for him. Discussing the vote on War Loans, he insists on the fact that they are not to be considered as a patriotic sacrifice, but as a matter of pure duty, lest one be reduced to the same status as parasites reliant on the enterprise of others for all means of existence, without which death from starvation would follow. He insists, then, that the War was about much more than patriotism. It may be difficult to understand, but the foreign enemy was once the catalyst that enabled the German economy to realize itself as a unity for the first time, and now it is the means by which a unity is being achieved on, let us say, the spiritual plane.

The question of this agreement to the War can be compre-hended in relation to this experience whereby the individual can only recover a sense of belonging to a totality by being overwhelmed by it. Simmel is supported here by something which was also theo-rized by Durkheim in *Germany Above All*, when he remarked that, 'German mentality anticipated the birth of a new order, of a new Germany achieved through the mobilisation of a collective will, at a moment when time would be utterly disrupted. This anticipation is aimed above all at the state of war. For it is at this point that public life is most intense.'

These two sociologists find themselves in conjunction, for in his theory of conflict, Simmel equally emphasizes that only the War is able in some sense to bring everything together and absorb it all, so that individual personalities are no longer disjointed but integrated and absolutely absorbed. Are these reflections on the War so very different from the so-called 'sacred sociology' of Roger Caillois (1939)? I think not. It is a question of the utmost controversy, the War as a place of antagonism; the frantic search for self takes place amidst the diversity of the world at its most intense time.

Simmel sees contemporary events through the lens of his cultural critique, and it is perhaps necessary to ask in more detail how that contemporary period is related to that theory and especially to the major theme of the conception of individuality. Two texts published during the Strasbourg period mark a sliding of conception from a qualitative notion of individuality as human type, to a conceptualization, no longer in terms of quantity/quality but geographical, even geopolitical: a Latin individuality, a romance individuality, and a Gothic, Germanic individuality. I am thinking here of the conceptions of individuality in painting found in his book, *Rembrandt* (1916); and in the text, as often happens with Simmel, immediately preceding it.

The reviews in the *Strassburger Post* of the work on Rembrandt recognize Simmel's desire to produce a new philosophy of Germanic art. He wished to try and explain the absence of a bridge between the individual and the general which characterizes the German character. Art and philosophy allowed him to focus on this aspect more precisely. In the case of the specific difference between France and Germany, the idea of revenge forms a focus for France and provides a sense of purpose. Germany, on the other hand, to the extent that mammonism had the upper hand, found itself without a consistent purpose. We have, then, two experiences of individuality. Briefly, partial individuality abstracted from a whole, which is to say a romance individuality of a rational kind, will be opposed to another experience where the individual in itself is more fundamental, more extreme, more centred on itself, more tragic. This latter form of individuality is too self-obsessed to ever be an integral part of its surroundings like, for example, the characters in a Balzac novel. Without going so far as to say that the Germans are more individualist than any others, there is a tonality and depth of individuality there which is disconnected from the collectivity. It is this depth which makes the Latin mode of individuality so light by contrast.

If the War was so important as a crucible in which another form of life as much as another Germany was being forged, it is because Germany did not possess, in the same way as the romance countries, a bridge between the individual and the general. It was enthusiasm for the War which allowed the individual to feel responsible for the whole.

For Simmel the central cultural question remains that of the relation between individual and society. This seems to me to be clear from the texts on Rembrandt, Individualism (1968) and *The Fundamental Question of Sociology* (1917a). In the first two, the question will undergo a shift, since the distinction between quantitative and qualitative notions of individuality comes to be not entirely successfully superimposed by that between romance and Germanic individuality.

Simmel's War writings have been described by Gassen (in Böhringer and Grunder, 1976) as hardly credible today, and this may be right if we take Germany today as our reference point. The risk of all prophecy is that it will be confounded by the facts. But these texts remain important for the history of ideas, as well as to provide a better grasp of Simmel's social philosophy. I do not think that they constitute a fourth phase of Simmel's thought, as Landmann (Gassen and Landmann, 1958) has suggested. They are texts which draw upon Simmel's reflections on the commodity begun with *The Philosophy of Money*. As against *Grundfragen der Soziologie* (1917a), they are situated in the philosophical domain, which is limited to two sides, as Simmel sees it: on the one side there is the level of 'conditions, basic concepts, and the presuppositions of research' and, on the other side, the level of interpretation of observed facts which seeks to connect them to a vision of the social ensemble. The latter depends, much more than epistemology or sociology, on 'visions of the world, ultimate convictions that are beyond proof, and an individual and partisan evaluation'.

All this allows me to follow some of Gassen's pointers in regard to the various currents present in Simmel's social philosophy, but equally to look for the beginnings of a response to the question of why the classics are actually seen as classic, and to avoid the tautological response that they are because they are.

The texts we have been discussing exemplify, albeit indirectly, Simmel's 'method': he observes and reacts to events, integrating them into a theoretical complex which crystallizes a little at a time. Thus, what we see in Simmel's discussion of enthusiasm for the War, is an exploration of — in the strict etymological sense of the term — ecstasy, an ecstasy that he takes full account of in presenting his cultural critique, and of which he is simultaneously one of its theoreticians and also one of its ramifications.

In Simmel's work, we can see themes which anticipate not only existentialism and expressionism but also, as Landmann (Böhringer and Grunder, 1976: 10) has pointed out, a communitarian ideology and even, going further, the ideology of totalitarianism. It is not certain whether we are, as Dumont (1979) has suggested, outside of the matrix which has produced these effects, totalitarianism, for example, being centrally characterized by the subordination of the individual to the needs of the collective. However, research into Germany's past allows us to advance a valuable hypothesis which is situated between the familiar modern individual and an individuality which is new and other, whose realization is not certain but which may deliver us from the antinomies of the modern mind. If we follow Deleuze's interpretation of Nietzche, the *Übermensch* is this other, between God and ourselves. Modernity created us, but the modern individual is only a construction, its substance crying out to be reconfigured within a new relation between form and content, where one passes from one temporary form to a new form which will be capable of being ordered, arranged and of integrating differently the relations, so central for Simmel, between the part and whole. The death of man in this sense only astonishes the French.

The mode of thought represented by Simmel, all things considered, is not so very different from Foucault. The theories of both evince a vitalism: life resists the forces of compromise and education, and strains towards an unequivocal direction. Above all, there is the notion of the legal individual which is not unconnected to the notion of style of life, just as Foucault must depend on a notion of 'man' in order to find another relationship to ourselves and others.

Why are the sociological classics seen as such? It is because they are consciously connected to historical upheaval and they did not refuse to address, from the viewpoint of sociological practice, the moral and existential issues raised by the way the world was moving. The classics are classic because these questions remain; in effect, Simmel's new man has not arrived, but the question posed by him retains its full force. They are classic because the social bond gives rise, as Aron (1972) has said, to basic questions that must not be abandoned just because the methodological and epistemological methods available to treat them have not yet been provided. They are classic because, in their openness to general questions, they provide ideal types of possible responses which are not just those borrowed from the societies they examine. And they are classic because they do not take the ideology of modern societies to be unquestionable; human experience, the content and the form it can take are not reduced to the do-it-yourself techniques of methodological individualism.

They were sociologists, certainly, but also historians, philosophers and anthropologists. It is hardly astonishing then that it is the College of Sociology in France between 1937 and 1939 and, above all, Roger Caillois, who represent this theme of foundational violence. For it is at once the experience of ecstasy, the religious experience, the shifting relation between people and the feeling of liberation that results from this, that Simmel tells us about.

Simmel does not reduce the War to its spiritual dimension. He simply sees a blind alley in the cultural antagonisms of the epoch. The effervescence of beginning which should not be denied is like the promise of another link, another relation between form and content: the birth of a new form of life.

In a letter to Marianne Weber in August 1914, Simmel writes:

What is unique at this moment is that, finally and for all time, the needs of the day and the needs of the Idea have become as one. We can only say this experimentally, as a matter of intuition or, better still, as something that emerges from practical experience. When Lukács did not feel this experience, he couldn't be shown it. That is why he speaks of militarism all the time. But for us it is more a question of liberation from militarism. The abiding characteristic of militarism in peacetime is its self-conceit, and liberation would strip this away to produce a form and a means for the total exaltation of life.

Simmel saw hope as something to be shared, and this points to a recurrent phenomenon within societies, which even the reductive philosophy of rational consensus produced by Habermas has to face. War is a total social fact, and the quest for *ekstasis* remains an option for the modern individual. Roger Caillois (1939) described the paroxysmic condition of the modern world in 1939 in terms which virtually mirror those used by Simmel to describe the Great War: '[War] is the total phenomenon which arouses the people and transforms them completely, in terrible contrast with the calm flow of peacetime. It is the phase of extreme tension in the collective life, a great coming together of multitudes and their endeavours.'

But what appears just as clearly in the letter to Marianne Weber is that for once the tragedy of culture can be avoided. For once, the idea and the reality would not be like two mismatching pieces cut from the same cloth. The eternal conflict between life and form would seem to have found a resolution: to love what is, necessarily, for it is the very reality of the idea, and to hate what is, necessarily, for as reality it cannot be the idea.

The interpretation offered here differs from that of David Frisby (1981), who compares Simmel and Ulrich (The Man Without Qualities). Now I would like to compare Simmel and Musil; but above all, the 'Yes' to the war should not be taken as the position of an aesthete whose aestheticism is bound to fail, rather it should be seen as a religious experience which mirrors Musil's own account. Simmel did not seek to find things that were not there, he knew and said that it is necessary to defend this latter view against other interpretations. However, our moral condemnation of war may prevent us from seeing all sides. If the causes are purely spiritual, the description of the mode of life is a way to the — shall we say — psychological conditions, whose understanding is necessary if we are to make any sense of acquiescence to war.

There is, then, for Simmel, ultimately no contradiction. It is only when a form seeks to establish its reign over the entire world, at the expense of all other forms, that it becomes a dogma. The money form and mammonism are critical in this conception, as was the historical materialism of *The Problems of the Philosophy of History* (Simmel, 1977). When a form assumes an absolute character, this is different from the absolute moment in the present which Simmel describes, and which forces one fatal response.

Simmel's War writings give witness to the moment when the play of the diverse forms which serve to order reality give way to a single form which brings all content into the same arena of meaning. We find here, crystallized, the social philosophy of German idealism which Stern (1961) called *The Politics of Cultural Despair*.

Translated by Roy Boyne.

References

Aron, R., M. Weber and R. Polanyi (1972) *Etudes Politiques*. Paris: Gallimard.
Böhringer, H. and K. Grunder (eds) (1976) *Asthetik und Soziologie. Um die Jahrhundertwende: Georg Simmel*. Frankfurt: V. Klosterman.
Caillois, R. (1939) *L'Homme et le sacré*. Paris: Gallimard.

Canetti, E. (1980) *Histoire d'une Vie*. Paris: Plon.

Dumont, L. (1979) 'Le peuple et la nation chez Herder et Fichte', *Libre* 6.

Durkheim, E. (1979) *Les formes elementaires de la vie religieuse*. Paris: PUF.

Frisby, D. (1981) *Sociological Impressionism. A Reassessment of Georg Simmel's Sociology*. London: Heinemann.

Gassen, K. and M. Landmann, (eds) (1958) *Buch des Dankes an Georg Simmel*. Berlin: Duncker & Humblot.

Mann, K. (1986) *Le Tournant*. Paris: Seuil.

Mann, Thomas (1975) *Considerations d'un apolitique*. Paris: Grasset.

Mann, Thomas (1968) *Doctor Faustus*. Penguin: Harmondsworth.

Musil, R. (1968) *The Man Without Qualities*. London.

Musil, R. (1980) *Journaux I*. Paris: Seuil.

Musil, R. (1984) *Essais*. Paris: Seuil.

Nisbet, R. (1966) *The Sociological Tradition*. London: Heinemann.

Rammstedt, O. and P. Watier (1991) *Georg Simmel et les Sciences Humaines*. Paris: Meridiens Klinksieck.

Simmel, Georg (1907) *Schopenhauer und Nietzsche*. Leipzig. (English translation by University of Massachusetts Press, 1987.)

Simmel, Georg (1908) *Soziologie*. Berlin.

Simmel, Georg (1910) *Hauptprobleme der Philosophie*. Leipzig.

Simmel, Georg (1912) *Melanges de Philosophie Relativiste*. Paris: Alcan.

Simmel, Georg (1916) *Rembrandt: Ein kunstphilosophische Versuch*. Leipzig.

Simmel, Georg (1917a) *Grundfragen der Soziologie*. Berlin: Göschen.

Simmel, Georg (1917b) 'Deutschlands innere Wandlung', in *Der Krieg und die geistigen Entscheidungen*. Munich/Leipzig: Duncker & Humblot.

Simmel, Georg (1968) *Das individuelle Gesetz*. Edited by M. Landmann. Frankfurt: Suhrkamp.

Simmel, Georg (1977) *The Problems of the Philosophy of History*. New York: Free Press.

Simmel, Georg (1990) *The Philosophy of Money* (second edition). London: Routledge.

Stern, F. (1961) *The Politics of Cultural Despair*. Berkeley: California University Press.

Patrick Waltier is Maitre de Conferences of Sociology at the University of Strasbourg, France.

Time & Society

Edited by Barbara Adam

A major new journal

Time & Society answers the urgent need for an international journal that will bring together the innovative work that is currently being undertaken in this area.

Interdisciplinary

Time & Society will be interdisciplinary, focusing on views of time drawn from a number of academic disciplines and subject areas including:

- education
- psychology
- business studies

- sociology
- anthropology
- history

- methodology
- geography
- philosophy

- organization studies
- social policy
- women's studies

Time & Society is essential reading for anyone interested in the subject of temporality whatever their discipline. In every issue there will be articles, reviews of the latest publications and scholarly comment on all aspects of social time.

The journal will be published three times a year, starting January 1992.

Bibliographical Note on Simmel's Works in Translation

David Frisby

To 1918

Simmel's work in English translation commenced in 1893 (Simmel, 1893: 490–507) with a brief extract from his *Einleitung in die Moralwissenschaft*, the second volume of which had appeared in the same year. Of greater importance was the translation of his essay 'The Problem of Sociology' (Simmel, 1895: 412–23) in the *Annals of the American Academy of Political and Social Science* (a journal which published sociological work until *The American Journal of Sociology* became securely established). Simmel's essay on sociology was considered by the author himself to be 'the most fruitful one that I have written'. Its English translation contained an important supplementary note defending Simmel's conception of sociology. As the result of Albion W. Small's interest in Simmel's sociology, *The American Journal of Sociology* from 1896 to 1910 carried a series of translations of Simmel's essays and extracts from his works, the majority being future chapters of his *Soziologie* (Simmel, 1908) and actually translated by Small himself. They include: 'Superiority and Subordination as Subject-matter for Sociology' (Simmel, 1896: 467–89, 392–415), 'The Persistence of Social Group' (Simmel, 1897/98: 662–98, 829–36, 35–50), 'A Chapter in the Philosophy of Value' (Simmel, 1899/1900: 577–603), 'The Number of Members as Determining the Sociological Form of the Group' (Simmel, 1902/3: 1–46, 158–96), 'The Sociology of Conflict' (Simmel, 1903/4: 490–525, 672–89, 798–811), 'A Contribution to the Sociology of Religion' (Simmel, 1905/6a: 359–76), 'The Sociology of Secrecy and of the Secret Societies' (Simmel, 1905/6b: 441–98), 'The Problem of Sociology' (Simmel, 1909/10: 289–320), and 'How Is Society Possible?' (Simmel, 1910: 372–91). In addition, two other essays appeared in English during Simmel's lifetime: the first,

Theory, Culture & Society (SAGE, London, Newbury Park and New Delhi), Vol. 8 (1991), 235–241

'Tendencies in German Life and Thought Since 1870' (Simmel, 1902: 93–111, 166–84) appeared in a New York journal, *International Monthly*, whose sociological advisory board comprised Franklin Giddings (Columbia), Gabriele Tarde (Paris), J.S. Mackenzie (Cardiff) and Georg Simmel (Berlin). This provocative essay only appeared in English and was not published in German until 1990. The second essay 'Fashion' (Simmel, 1904: 130–55) appeared in English translation prior to its German version in 1905. It was published in *International Quarterly*, the sequel to *International Monthly* with the same sociology advisory board.

During Simmel's lifetime, it is instructive to compare the extent of translations of his works. Although not complete, still the most valuable initial source is the bibliography by Kurt Gassen — who had studied with Simmel (Gassen and Landmann, 1958: 338–44). In the United States, it was largely Small's initiative at Chicago which established Simmel as the most translated German sociologist in this period. In addition, Small published reviews of Simmel's work in *The American Journal of Sociology*. In France in the 1890s, the influence of Durkheim's student *and* admirer of Simmel's work, Celestin Bouglé was in part responsible for the reception of his work in France. A collection of Simmel's essays appeared in 1912 (Simmel, 1912) with an introduction by the author. In Italy, only 'The Problem of Sociology' appeared in translation (Simmel, 1899); in Spain, a wartime translation of *Schopenhauer and Nietzsche* appeared (Simmel, 1915); in Holland, Simmel's study of religion appeared in Dutch (Simmel, 1909); in Denmark a wartime essay on individualism (Simmel, 1917a). The fact that Simmel had a large number of students from Eastern Europe, including Kistiakowski (Kistiakowski, 1899) and Thon — who wrote on the state of German sociology for *The American Journal of Sociology* in the 1890s (Thon, 1896/7) — is reflected in the extent of early translations. In Poland, three of Simmel's works appeared in book form: *The Problems of the Philosophy of History*, *The Philosophy of Money* and 'The Self-preservation of the Social Group' between 1902 and 1904. The largest number of translations — over twenty articles, extracts and books (*The Problems of the Philosophy of History*, translation of the 1892 version, and *Religion*) divided almost equally between Simmel's philosophical and sociological studies — appeared in Russian by the time of Simmel's death in 1918.

Post-Simmel

The post-First World War period saw the continuation of translations of Simmel's works into Russian (to 1928), Polish and more extensively into Spanish, both in Spain and Argentina (including *Soziologie* in 1939). Of interest, are the translations which appeared in the important cultural journal founded by Ortega y Gasset in 1923, *Rivista de Occidente*. In the United States, between the two world wars, the impetus for translations of Simmel's work lay solely within the Chicago school, either in Park and Burgess's introductory textbook (and Park had been a student of Simmel's) (Park and Burgess, 1921: 322-7, 343-56, 356-61, 552-3) or in translations circulating within the Chicago sociology department. Until his death in 1926, Albion Small continued to make reference to Simmel's work and even to detect signs of the development of 'post-Simmelism'. However, such signs were not reflected in further translations of Simmel's works which only commenced two decades later in 1949 (Simmel, 1949: 254-61) with Everett Hughes's translation of 'The Sociology of Sociability' (Hughes was a student of Park).

The 1950s saw the first new wave of interest in Simmel's sociology, stimulated most significantly by Kurt Wolff's edited collection *The Sociology of Georg Simmel* (Wolff, 1950). Publication of these translations, drawn largely from *Soziologie*, stimulated several empirical studies of Simmel's social theory. Wolff's volume contains the following (unless otherwise indicated, all extracts are from *Soziologie*): *Grundfragen der Soziologie* (1917b) (Fundamental Problems of Sociology); 'The Quantitative Determinateness of the Group'; 'Superordination and Subordination'; 'Note on Out-Voting'; 'The Secret and the Secret Society'; 'The Negative Character of Collective Behavior', 'Note on Adornment'; 'Note on Written Communication'; 'Note on the Negativity of Collective Modes and Behavior'; 'Faithfulness and Gratitude'; 'The Stranger'; 'The Metropolis and Mental Life' (1902 lecture). Aside from the occasional reprint of earlier translations in edited collections, *Conflict and the Web of Group Affiliations* (Simmel, 1955) with a foreword by Everett Hughes brought together two further important essays from Simmel's *Soziologie* translated respectively by Kurt Wolff and Reinhard Bendix.

At the hundredth anniversary of Simmel's birth, Kurt Wolff (Wolff, 1959) assembled a commemorative volume which contained essays on various aspects of his work as well as further translations.

The latter comprise: 'The Adventure'; 'The Ruin'; 'The Handle', 'The Aesthetic Significance of the Face'; 'On the Nature of Philosophy'; 'The Problem of Sociology'; 'How Is Society Possible?' (the last two essays are from Simmel's *Soziologie*). In the same year, Simmel's *Die Religion* appeared in English translation as *Sociology of Religion* (Simmel, 1959).

Almost a decade later in 1968, Peter Etzkorn edited a valuable translated collection of Simmel's essays on culture and aesthetics (Simmel, 1968a) which contains the following: 'The Conflict in Modern Culture'; 'On the Concept and Tragedy of Culture'; 'Sociological Aesthetics'; 'On Aesthetic Quantities'; 'On the Third Dimension in Art'; 'Psychological and Ethnological Studies of Music'; 'The Dramatic Actor'; 'A Chapter in the Philosophy of Value'.

Two further translations of Simmel's essays also appeared during this decade: 'The Poor', (Simmel, 1965) — from *Soziologie* — and 'A Review of Social Medicine' (Simmel, 1968b: 331–4). A valuable collection of extracts from Simmel's works which once more made his work more accessible to students was that edited by Donald Levine in 1971, *On Individuality and Social Forms* (Simmel, 1971), which contained a valuable introduction, new translations as well as extracts from works already available. Levine's collection with a useful introduction, contains the following (unless otherwise stated, from *Soziologie*); 'How Is History Possible?' (brief extract from *Problems of the Philosophy of History*); 'How is Society Possible?'; 'The Problem of Sociology'; 'Exchange' (from *The Philosophy of Money*); 'Conflict'; 'Domination'; 'Sociability' (see Simmel, 1949); 'The Stranger'; 'The Poor'; 'The Miser and the Spendthrift' (from *The Philosophy of Money*); 'The Adventurer' (see Simmel, 1959); 'The Nobility'; 'Freedom and the Individual' (posthumous); 'Subjective Culture' (from 'Vom Wesen der Kultur', 1908); 'Eros, Platonic and Modern' (from Simmel, 1923); 'Group Expansion and the Development of Individuality'; 'Fashion' (Simmel, 1904); 'The Metropolis and Mental Life' (1902 lecture); 'Subordination and Personal Fulfillment'; 'Social Forms and Inner Needs'; 'The Transcendent Character of Life' (Simmel, 1918b); 'The Conflict in Modern Culture' (see Simmel, 1968a).

A further collection of Simmel's writings, edited by Peter Lawrence, usefully containing both previously untranslated material and retranslated works, appeared in 1976 as *Georg Simmel: Sociologist and European* (Lawrence, 1976). It contained the following: 'The Field of Sociology' (see Wolff, 1950); 'Sociability' (see

Wolff, 1950); 'The Intersection of Social Spheres' (from Simmel, 1890); 'Differentiation and the Principle of Saving Energy' (from Simmel, 1890); 'Conflict' (see Simmel, 1955); 'Individual Freedom' (from *The Philosophy of Money*); 'The Style of Life' (from *The Philosophy of Money*); 'The Conflict of Modern Culture' (Simmel, 1918a); 'The Meaning of Culture' (1908 essay), 'The Future of Our Culture' (1909 essay note); 'The Crisis of Culture' (Simmel, 1917c); 'The Idea of Europe' (Simmel, 1917). In the following year, a complete translation of one of Simmel's books, *The Problems of the Philosophy of History* (Simmel, 1977), with an introduction by Guy Oakes appeared. The translation is of the second edition of 1905, the first edition of 1892 being to a great extent a different work. In 1978 another complete Simmel text appeared in translation, *The Philosophy of Money* (Simmel, 1978, 1990), by Tom Bottomore and David Frisby, with an introduction by the latter. An enlarged edition appeared in 1990. A second translated collection by Guy Oakes, with a valuable introduction, appeared in 1980 under the title *Essays on Interpretation in Social Science* (Simmel, 1980). Its contents supplement and extend Oakes's earlier translation since they comprise the following essays: 'On the Nature of Historical Understanding', 'The Problem of Historical Time', 'The Constitutive Concepts of History' and 'On the History of Philosophy'. Oakes also translated some of Simmel's essays related to women and love in *On Women, Sexuality and Love* (Simmel, 1984) which, together with a stimulating introduction by Oakes, contain the essays 'Female Culture', 'The Relative and the Absolute in the Problem of the Sexes', 'Flirtation', and 'On Love (a fragment)'. A further complete translation of a Simmel volume appeared in 1986, *Schopenhauer and Nietzsche* (Simmel, 1986) translated with an introduction by Helmut Loiskandl, Deena Weinstein and Michael Weinstein.

The last decade has seen a marked renewal of interest in Simmel's work which is manifested, in part, by translations of his works — for instance, in Italy, notably, of *On Social Differentiation*, *The Philosophy of Money* and *Sociology*, in France of *The Problems of the Philosophy of History*, *The Philosophy of Money* and other texts. Since 1989, under the general editorship of Otthein Rammstedt (Bielefeld), the first volumes of a projected series of twenty-four of the critical German edition of Simmel's works have begun to appear. It is to be hoped that this development, and the increasing attention given to Simmel's work, will stimulate further English translations.

References

Gassen, K. and M. Landmann (eds) (1958) *Buch des Dankes an Georg Simmel*. Berlin: Duncker & Humblot.

Kistiakowski, T. (1899) *Gesellschaft und Einzelwesen*. Berlin: Liebmann.

Lawrence, P. (1976) *Georg Simmel Sociologist and European*. Translated by D.E. Jenkinson et al, with an introduction by P.A. Lawrence. Sunbury, Mddx: Nelson; New York: Barnes & Noble.

Levine, D.N., B.C. Ellwood and E. Gorman (1976) 'Simmel's Influence on American Sociology', in H. Böhringer and K. Gründer (eds), *Ästhetik und Soziologie um die Jahrhundertswende: Georg Simmel*. Frankfurt: Klostermann.

Park, R.E. and E.W. Burgess (1921) *Introduction to the Science of Sociology*. Chicago: University of Chicago Press.

Simmel, G. (1890) *Über sociale Differenzierung*. Leipzig: Duncker & Humblot.

Simmel, G. (1893) 'Moral Deficiencies as Determining Intellectual Functions', *International Journal of Ethics* 3.

Simmel, G. (1895) 'The Problem of Sociology', *Annals of the American Academy of Political Science* 6.

Simmel, G. (1896) 'Superiority and Subordination as Subject-Matter of Sociology', *The American Journal of Sociology* 2(2).

Simmel, G. (1897/98) 'The Persistence of Social Groups', *American Journal of Sociology* 3(4).

Simmel, G. (1899) 'Il problema della sociologia', *Riforma sociale* 6.

Simmel, G. (1899/1900) 'A Chapter in the Philosophy of Value', *The American Journal of Sociology* 5.

Simmel, G. (1902) 'Tendencies in German Life and Thought Since 1870', *International Monthly* 5.

Simmel, G. (1902/3) 'The Number of Members as Determining the Sociological Form of the Group', *The American Journal of Sociology* 8.

Simmel, G. (1903/4) 'The Sociology of Conflict', *The American Journal of Sociology* 9.

Simmel, G. (1904) 'Fashion', *International Quarterly* 10.

Simmel, G. (1905/6a) 'A Contribution to The Sociology of Religion', *The American Journal of Sociology* 11.

Simmel, G. (1905/6b) 'The Sociology of Secrecy and of the Secret Societies', *The American Journal of Sociology* 11.

Simmel, G. (1908) *Soziologie*. Leipzig: Duncker & Humblot.

Simmel, G. (1909) *De godsdienst*. Amsterdam: Cohen.

Simmel, G. (1909/10) 'The Problem of Sociology', *The American Journal of Sociology* 15.

Simmel, G. (1910) 'How Is Society Possible?', *The American Journal of Sociology* 16.

Simmel, G. (1912) *Mélanges de philosophie relativiste*. Paris: Alcan.

Simmel, G. (1915) *Schopenhauer y Nietzsche*. Madrid: Beltrán.

Simmel, G. (1917a) 'Individualismus Formen', *Spectator*, 28 January.

Simmel, G. (1917b) *Grundfragen der Soziologie*. Berlin/Leipzig: Göschen.

Simmel, G. (1917c) *Der Krieg und die geistigen Entscheidungen*. Munich/Leipzig: Duncker & Humblot.

Simmel, G. (1918a) *Der Konflikt der modernen Kultur*. Munich/Leipzig: Duncker & Humblot.

Simmel, G. (1918b) *Lebensanschauung*. Munich/Leipzig: Duncker & Humblot.

Simmel, G. (1922) *Zur Philosophie der Kunst*. Potsdam: Kiepenheuer.

Simmel, G. (1923) *Fragmente und Aufsätze*. Edited with an afterword by ·G. Kantorowicz. Munich: Drei Masken Verlag.

Simmel, G. (1949) 'The Sociology of Sociability', *The American Journal of Sociology* 55.

Simmel, G. (1955) *Conflict and the Web of Group Affiliations*. Glencoe, IL: Free Press.

Simmel, G. (1959) *Sociology of Religion*. Translated by C. Rosenthal and introduced by F. Gross. New York: Philosophical Library.

Simmel, G. (1965) 'The Poor', *Social Problems* 13(2).

Simmel, G. (1968a) *The Conflict in Modern Culture and Other Essays*. Translated and introduced by K.P. Etzkorn. New York: The Teachers' College Press.

Simmel, G. (1968b) 'A Review of Social Medicine', *Social Forces*, 47(3).

Simmel, G. (1971) *On Individuality and Social Forms*. Edited and introduced by D.N. Levine. Chicago: University of Chicago Press.

Simmel, G. (1977) *The Problems of the Philosophy of History*. Translated and edited by G. Oakes. New York: Free Press.

Simmel, G. (1978) *The Philosophy of Money* (second, enlarged edition, 1990). Translated by T.B. Bottomore and D. Frisby and introduced by D. Frisby. London/Boston: Routledge.

Simmel, G. (1980) *Essays on Interpretation in Social Science*. Translated and introduced by G. Oakes. Totowa, NJ: Rowman & Littlefield; Manchester: Manchester University Press.

Simmel, G. (1984) *On Women Sexuality and Love*. Translated and introduced by G. Oakes. New Haven/London: Yale University Press.

Simmel, G. (1986) *Schopenhauer and Nietzsche*. Translated and introduced by H. Loiskandl, D. Weinstein and M. Weinstein. Amherst: University of Massachusetts Press.

Thon, O. (1896/7) 'The Present Status of Sociology in Germany', *The American Journal of Sociology* 2.

Wolff, K.H. (1950) *The Sociology of Georg Simmel*. Translated and introduced, except 'Metropolis and Mental Life', by K.H. Wolff. Glencoe, IL: Free Press.

Wolff, K.H. (ed.) (1959) *Georg Simmel 1858-1918*. Columbus: Ohio State University Press. Reprinted in 1965 as K.H. Wolff (ed.), *Essays On Sociology, Philosophy and Aesthetics*. New York: Harper & Row.

Book Reviews

Rembrandt. Ein kunstphilosophischer Versuch
by Georg Simmel
Munich: Matthes & Seitz, 1985, pp. xxxi + 205.
Reviewed by Bryan S. Turner

Donald Levine (1989) has recalled that the late Max Horkheimer, while Visiting Professor at Chicago University in the mid-1950s, once observed 'Ach ja! Simmel is der einzige Soziologe, den man heute noch lesen kann' (Simmel is the only sociologist whom one can still read with profit). Despite this widely shared sentiment, it is now almost universally agreed that Simmel is the most neglected 'founding father' of sociology. While there have been some important translations of Simmel's work in recent years (such as *The Philosophy of Money* in 1978), Simmel's later studies in art history and the philosophy of culture have been almost completely ignored. Simmel published the short essay *Kant and Goethe* in 1906 and *Rembrandt* appeared in 1916. His *Rembrandtstudien* were published posthumously in 1953, to be followed in 1957 by *Brücke und Tür*. Of course, while the study of Kant and Goethe is no more than an essay, *Rembrandt* is a major study.

Whether or not this 'significant aesthetic dimension' (Frisby, 1984: 26) represented a distinctive reorientation of Simmel's work away from sociology to aesthetics has been much debated. It is more reasonable to argue that the interest in aesthetics was a continuous aspect of Simmel's work. For example, he had written a *Rezension* in June 1890 on the problems of individualism and the aristocratic tendency in culture which anticipated later discussions relating to Nietzsche's moral standpoint. *Rembrandt* illustrates many of the perennial concerns of Simmelian sociology.

There are many themes in his analysis of Rembrandt, which reflect the principal components of his work as a whole. For many commentators, these final publications are, for example, an important feature of Simmel's commitment to *Lebensphilosophie*. Like *The Philosophy of Money*, the study of Rembrandt is an enquiry into how creative genius becomes locked into the form of classical art. The section on religious art in *Rembrandt* also illustrates Simmel's complex view of the relationship between form and content, where an artistic form can be shaped by many different processes and where artistic content can assume multiple forms.

Rembrandt is as a result an aspect of Simmel's final intellectual development which has unfortunately received remarkably little attention. There is apparently a Japanese translation which was undertaken by K. Onishi, Professor of Aesthetics at Tokyo University (Shimmei, 1959: 204), but it has been neglected in Anglo-American commentaries on Simmel. In this beautiful, modern and generously illustrated edition by Matthes and Seitz, there is a valuable introduction by Beat Wyss, which places Simmel's study of Rembrandt within the wider context of contemporary art history, especially in the framework of Heinrich Wölfflin's *Kunstgeschichtliche Grundbegriffe* (1915) and Wilhelm Worringer's *Abstraktion und Einfühlung* (1908). Within this context, it is important to recall that (the quintessential Dutch artist) Rembrandt had been '(re)discovered' by French art historians in the middle of the nineteenth century, and appropriated by the Berlin art world in the 1880s. The main paradigm for understanding Rembrandt at the time was consequently in terms of a North/South polarity. Rembrandt was caught between the thrust of southern baroque emotionality and northern Gothic rationality, between southern empathy (*Einfühlung*) and northern rationalism in the form of *Abstraktion*. This northern mentality was the product of medieval Christianity, which eventually produced a predominantly abstract orientation; the South received the legacy of the ancient world, Greek rationality, Renaissance and baroque. According to Wyss's introduction Simmel transformed these traditional artistic categories into a sociological enquiry which addressed three issues: the problem of style, the nature of classicism and the issue of modernity. It might be more accurate to believe that Rembrandt's studies were a perfect illustration of Simmel's concept of the tragedy of culture which was an organizing principle of his entire oeuvre.

Simmel's *Rembrandt* is divided into three major sections. The first division deals with subjectivity and individuality in the portrait and the self-portrait. The middle section addresses the history of individuality, character and death in western art, while the final major section examines objective and subjective religion, religious art and artistic creativity. These topics, of course, also appear in his other studies in the sociology of religion, and in his many reflections on the individual and sociation.

Although it is possible to interpret Simmel's later interest in the philosophy of culture as a departure from the early work on social differentiation, money or moral science, *Rembrandt* can be read as a further elaboration of the 'tragedy of culture' theme. For example, one aspect of the study is a reflection on the paradoxical interweaving of death and life in art. Rembrandt's portraits show perfectly this immanence of death in the midst of life. Although the 'Vanitas painting' was a common genre within bourgeois art in the seventeenth century, Rembrandt, influenced, not only by traditional Christian perspectives, but also by Caravaggio and northern baroque transformed this artistic form into a universally powerful statement of death-in-life. The intensity and honesty of Rembrandt's haunting self-portraits also allowed Simmel a further opportunity to reflect upon the notions of character, personality, singleness (*Einzelheit*), individuality and uniqueness (*Einzigkeit*) in relation to the development of western culture. For Simmel, the greater the work of art, the less the importance of style, because a major work of art is an address to humanity as such, not an address to the artistic community.

In conclusion, this splendid analysis of the artistic representation of subjectivity by Simmel should play a much more significant role, not only in the evaluation of the nature of Simmel's sociology, but in the sociological interpretation of modern aesthetics, individuality and culture. In short, *Rembrandt* is a model of how to do cultural sociology.

References

Frisby, D. (1984) *Georg Simmel*. London: Tavistock.

Levine, D. (1989) 'Simmel as a Resource for Sociological Metatheory', *Theory and Society* 7(2): 161–74.

Shimmei, M. (1959) 'Georg Simmel's Influence on Japanese Thought', pp. 201–15 in K.H. Wolff (ed.), *Essays on Sociology, Philosophy and Aesthetics*. New York: Harper Torchbooks.

Simmel, G. (1906) *Kant und Goethe*. Berlin: Marquardt.

Simmel, G. (1957) *Brücke und Tür. Essays des philosophen zur Geshichte, Religion, Kunst und Gesellschaft*. Stuttgart: Koehler.

Simmel, G. (1978) *The Philosophy of Money* (second edition, 1990). London: Routledge.

Wölfflin, H. (1915) *Kunstgeschichtliche Grundbegriffe. Das Problem der Stilentwicklung in der neueren Kunst*. Munchen: Bruckmann.

Worringer, W. (1908) *Abstraktion und Einfuhlung. Ein Beitrag zur Stilpsychologie*. Munchen.

Bryan S. Turner is Professor of Sociology, University of Essex, UK.

The Philosophy of Money (second edition)
by Georg Simmel
Edited by David Frisby
London: Routledge, 1990, pp. xli + 537.
Reviewed by R.J. Holton

This is the first complete English translation of the revised 1907 edition of Simmel's classic, first published in 1900. In this later edition, Simmel provided further general arguments on value theory going beyond his earlier formulations, while also offering additional elaboration of other themes in the original book. The significance of these changes is discussed by David Frisby in a useful afterword on 'the constitution of the text'.

The importance of this second, enlarged edition of *The Philosophy of Money* is not so much any newly accessible material by Simmel, as the new preface by Frisby. This picks up and develops further a number of issues discussed in his introduction to the original English edition. Here Frisby dealt with the reception of Simmel by his critics, examined the impact of key thinkers on Simmel's work and traced the subsequent influence of Simmel on more recent work. Frisby also raised the uncertain status of Simmel's study of money as a classic text. This was explained in part by Simmel's anti-systematic pantheistic and impressionistic intellectual idiom. This rejected formal academic discourse, together with the core questions of disciplines such as philosophy and economics.

In his new preface Frisby comments in more depth on some critiques of Simmel, identified but not pursued very far in the earlier introduction. Most interesting perhaps is the contribution of Durkheim. He argued that the abstract symbolic characteristics Simmel attributed to money cannot exert a profound influence on moral life simply by virtue of their symbolic nature. What is of decisive importance for Durkheim is the presence or absence of regulatory procedures and rules affecting the operation of money within economic life. This contrast between Simmel and Durkheim brings to the surface a central conflict over theories of sociality and sociation. Whereas Simmel emphasizes the tragedy of the division between objective culture and subjective culture mediated by money, Durkheim offers an integrated theory of sociality based upon the socialization and indeed sacralization of the individual.

Frisby also adds to earlier accounts of the reception of Simmel's work with new commentaries on reviews by George Herbert Mead, Carl Menger (the Austrian neo-classical economist) and the Göttingen economist, Wilhelm Lexis. One area of common interest among them is the inadequate nature of Simmel's discussion of the theory of value. In the 1900 edition of *The Philosophy of Money*, Simmel had attempted a critique of objectivist theories of value, such as the Marxist labour theory of value. Simmel did not, however, regard this as entirely successful. New passages, translated into English for the first time in this enlarged edition, indicate an attempt to retain both subjective and objective aspects of value, while somehow transcending them within the act of exchange. Exchange is crucial for sociation, according to Simmel, because it 'raises the specific object and its significance for the individual above its singularity, not into the sphere of abstraction, but with that of lived interaction' (p. 110). Frisby also comments more extensively in the new preface on the influence of Nietzsche on Simmel's value theory through such notions as the transformation of all valuation, the levelling of values and aesthetic value sensibility.

There are many other interesting issues sketched out in Frisby's brief commentary. These include the significance of Simmel's analysis of the position of women, the comparison of Simmel and Keynes on money and the beginnings of an empirical research agenda around Simmel's theory of money within the recent work of Viviana Zelizer. Frisby also notes the affinity between Simmel's discussions of the symbolic significance of money, the autonomization and the aesthetic mode of experience, on the one hand, and current theories of postmodernism, on the other.

There are many reasons therefore for welcoming this new edition of Simmel's enigmatic but influential classic. Meanwhile, Frisby himself continues to apply the highest standards of erudition to Simmel scholarship.

R.J. Holton teaches Sociology at Flinders University of South Australia.

Fragments of Modernity
by David Frisby
Oxford: Polity Press, 1985, £8.95 pbk.
Reviewed by Roy Boyne

David Frisby's investigation of Simmel, Kracauer and Benjamin has been around for some time now, although it has only comparatively recently been available in paperback. The book is an unpretentious guide to three cognate approaches to aesthetic modernity. These writers were more than adequately acquainted with Marxist and other approaches which sought to subsume all of social experience under one conceptual system, but they are presented here as each concerned more with the transient and ephemeral aspects of society. As Frisby puts it:

> In their different ways, Simmel, Kracauer, and Benjamin were all concerned with the new modes of the perception and experience of social and historical existence set in train by the upheaval of capitalism. Their central concern was the discontinuous experience of time, space and causality as transitory, fleeting and fortuitous or arbitrary . . . (p. 4)

Although Baudelaire's invention of the concept of modernity, and his account of it in terms of a dialectic between transient novelty and immutable eternity was a basic influence upon all three of Frisby's subjects, it was apparently not intended that this book would advance a thoroughgoing critique of Baudelaire. Interestingly enough, Benjamin himself saw the need for such a critique, noticing how inconsistent Baudelaire had been in his treatment of antiquity, at times ignoring it and at other times treating it as a paradigm of value. Benjamin did not admire Baudelaire's theory of modern art; he said, quite explicitly, that it lacked profundity. Perhaps he meant that it lacked a certain specificity, that Baudelaire's description of the modern painter as someone who depicts the 'passing moment and all the suggestions of eternity that it contains' is mere rhetoric, at least as far as the question of eternity is concerned. We have to move forward from Baudelaire to Monet to find a realization in art of what the specific relation between transience and eternity might look like. The critical reception of Monet's fifteen 'Poplars' paintings, shown together in a way that no landscape painter had ever done before, was to be located precisely between the transience of decoration and the eternal values of nature.

Marx, of course, had a particular grasp of the connection between the essential and the inessential, and Frisby details, briefly, how Marx understood the surface phenomena of modern society:

> If the mystified world of commodity exchange did create the impression of a fleeting, transitory, arbitrary and indifferent constellation of social relationships, the mere experiencing of these relations did not open up the possibility for the realisation of the transitory nature of capitalist society as a whole. . . . The dialectic of modernity remained hidden by vulgar political economy and remained hidden to the participants in the 'bewitched world' of capitalist relations. (p. 27)

Whilst Marx and Baudelaire can be connected through the mechanism of a Hegelian dialectic of essentiality and inessentiality, it is rather harder to link Nietzsche to modernity in this way. Nietzsche is placed in apposition to Marx as part of a critical symptomatology of modernity. This is achieved through a particular interpretation of Nietzsche's doctrine of eternal recurrence: the contradictory monotony of ever-changing commodity production is evidence that our society is incapable of eternal newness. While, in one sense, this reading of Nietzsche by Benjamin is certainly sustainable, in another sense it misses the point that Nietzsche's *Beyond Good and Evil*, for example, is a critique of the very idea of society, and that *Zarathustra* aspires to think the human condition in absolutely genuine singularity.

There is, of course, a lively debate over whether Nietzsche can be claimed for modernism or for postmodernism. In much the same way, Turner and Stauth have claimed Simmel to be first sociologist of postmodernity in contradistinction to Frisby's claim that Simmel is the first sociologist of modernity. Whatever side one prefers, it is clear that Simmel was influenced by Nietzsche's longing for an authentically original auto-creative subject, and that Simmel's reaction to the fragmentary experience of life was for the subject to create its own existential synthesis. A certain obstinacy of mind or megalomania of vision, however, is needed if all of social life is to be treated as arbitrary, and Simmel had neither. He was aware that certain events just cannot be treated as mere transience — the Great War, for example, which he referred to as the 'absolute situation'; he was alive to the way that human creations can expand beyond their utility into realms of heedless autonomy; and he knew, as much as any other sociologist who has ever lived, a great deal about the quasimathematical limitations upon innovation in forms of social interaction. Such full appreciation of so many countervailing factors and considerations deprives Simmelian *Kulturtheorie* of that clarity of vision which is founded, as Paul de Man might have said, on blindness.

Siegfried Kracauer's best known work is on the cinema. In this field, he has a certain reputation as a realist. In his *Theory of Film*, he argues that film can act as a mirror to reality, and he hints therefore that film can deliver us from the distortions of an over-fetishized, hyper-scientized, and mega-technologized society. Film can do this through its capacity, as mirror, to be honest. We did not need the experience of *Robocop* of *Total Recall* to instruct us that Kracauer's virtually absolutist vision of the inherent properties of the film medium is somewhat flawed. What, however, are we to make of his vision of modern society? There is also a prior question: why should we bother ourselves with Kracauer's vision of society anyway? David Frisby's answer to the latter question is provided in the title of the chapter on Kracauer: 'Exemplary Instances'. That answer is further elaborated by Walter Benjamin's statement that Kracauer was,

A rag-picker early in the dawn, who with his stick spikes the snatches of speeches and scraps of conversation in order to throw them into his cart.

It is striking that *Fragments of Modernity* follows its three subject figures by refusing to postulate a basic theme or an organizing framework. The question of the metropolis arises over and over again in the book, but one could not say that it is its organizing theme. The Paris–Berlin axis continually reappears, but there are very significant parts of the text which do not appear to connect to this corridor at all. In the end, what Frisby has done is to present three instances of showhouse modernism without pandering to the inauthentic desires of the audience or to the dubious techniques of the distraction factory.

Roy Boyne teaches Sociology at Newcastle Polytechnic.

The Modern Stranger: On Language and Membership
by Lesley D. Harman
Berlin: Mouton de Gruyter, 1988.
Reviewed by Bryan S. Turner

In this slim but excellent study of the sociology of the stranger, Harman addresses three distinctive tasks. The first is to explore the theoretical impact of Georg Simmel's essay on the stranger (1971) from his *Soziologie: Untersuchen uber die Formen der Vergesellschaftung* of 1908 on twentieth-century social thought. The second is to contrast the German and American cultures of strangeness, and finally Harman attempts to develop a new typology of the stranger which is more in tune with the nature of contemporary social relationships. The result is a systematic tour through the multiplicity of perspectives on the nature of social memberships, but the linking theme in his analysis is that of nostalgia. Whereas the stranger of nineteenth-century sociology was the isolated traveller who had crossed the boundary between traditional *gemienschaft* and cosmopolitan *gesellschaft*, the diversity and complexity of modern urban life has produced global estrangement. 'Strangeness is no longer a temporary condition to be overcome, but a way of life' (Harman, 1988: 44). Whereas the stranger was the exception in Simmel's world, today the stranger is the rule. Simmel's stranger was the archetypal Jewish trader. While he did not make roots in the local community, the interaction between insiders and strangers defines the geographical and cultural coordinates of group membership. The stranger is spatially close to those from whom he is culturally remote. While the stranger is detached from the group, he is also drawn into it by interaction, and it is this very detachment which gives the stranger an objective insight into the social workings of the inside group. Simmel's stranger is thus defined along two axial dimensions: remoteness/proximity and detachment/involvement.

Simmel's essay raised issues which became a persistent feature of the American sociology of urban space. The essay was translated by Robert E. Park and Ernest W. Burgess in 1924, and it was consequently given a definite place within the Chicago tradition. As Harman points out, however, there were important differences between the American and German versions of the problem of the stranger. Whereas German theorists like Simmel and Schutz (1944) were interested in the phenomenology of being a stranger, the Chicago sociologists were interested in the impact of the stranger on the host community. The Chicago pragmatists turned the German question (what is it like to be a stranger?) into an American issue (how can we make them like us?). The consequence of this domestication did, however, produce a remarkably robust literature: Park's 'marginal man', Siu's 'the sojourner', Wood's 'the stranger', Reisman's 'the lonely crowd' and Lofland's 'world of strangers'. These studies were the product of twentieth-century migration, urbanism and the creation of a multicultural America. In this context, American sociology was based on the question: how is a society of strangers possible?

There is of course a relationship between Simmel's notion of the stranger (*der Fremde*) and Marxist ideas of alienation as estrangement (*entfremdung*). Various commentators on modern society have taken the idea of the stranger as indicative of a deeper problem in human ontology. The problem of the stranger relates to the more general issue of whether 'man' (in the sense adopted by Arnold Gehlen) can be at home in the world. For a variety of philosophical anthropologists (Plessner,

Gehlen, Uexkull, Buitendijk and Kellner) building on an idea in Nietzsche that 'man' is a 'not-yet-finished creature', human beings who are biologically homeless are necessarily estranged from and in the world. The cultural roots of this idea are deep; for example, the central theme in Christian soteriology is that 'man' is in the world but not of it. Harman is correct to detect in this tradition a fundamental nostalgia for a Home which will bring an end to the stranger. Thus, Fromm's 'escape from freedom', Berger's 'homeless mind', Packard's 'a nation of strangers' and Riesman's 'other-directed man' establishes a traditional ideal of home from which all forms of modern life must be a Fall.

Harman therefore argues that we need new means of conceptualizing strangeness in the modern world, because Simmel's framework is now historically remote and the nostalgic vision of a world free of strangers is a myth which is potentially dangerous. Taking a theoretical lead from Donald Levine (1979), Harman argues that home is a movable feast, a suitcase that one carries around and which can be opened up at will. The modern stranger is like an anthropologist who has to be sensitive to and sympathetic towards new, complex and alien codes of behaviour. The modern stranger, suitcase in hand, adjusts rapidly without nostalgia and without regrets to each new habitus. This modality of cultural nomadism implies a new type of self whose authenticity is found precisely in the act of (successful) communication: 'the self has *become* the looking-glass' (Harman, 1988: 151). The transition from the Simmelian stranger-as-itinerant to the stranger-as-looking-glass self is in fact the social transition from the modern to the postmodern.

References

Levine, D.N. (1979) 'Simmel at a Distance: On the History and Systematics of the Sociology of the Stranger', pp. 21–36 in William Shack and Elliott Skinner (eds), *Strangers in African Societies*. Berkeley: University of California Press.

Park, R.E. and E.W. Burgess (1924) *Introduction to the Science of Sociology*. Chicago: University of Chicago Press.

Schutz, A. (1944) 'The Stranger: An Essay in Social Psychology', *American Journal of Sociology* 49(6): 499–507.

Simmel, G. (1971) 'The Stranger', pp. 143–9 in Donald N. Levine (ed.), *On Individuality and Social Forms*. Chicago: University of Chicago Press.

Bryan S. Turner is Professor of Sociology, University of Essex, England.

*Aufsätze 1887–1890. Über sociale Differenzierung. Die Probleme
der Geschichtsphilosophie*
by Georg Simmel, edited by Heinz-Jürgen Dahme
Gesamtausgabe Band 2.
Frankfurt am Main: Suhrkamp, 1989, pp. 434, DM 48 hbk;
DM 24 pbk.

Einleitung in die Moralwissenschaft
by Georg Simmel, edited by Klaus Christian Köhnke
Gesamtausgabe Band 3.
Frankfurt am Main: Suhrkamp, 1989, pp. 461, DM 48 hbk;
DM 26 pbk.

Philosophie des Geldes
by Georg Simmel, edited by David Frisby and Klaus Christian
Köhnke
Gesamtausgabe Band 6.
Frankfurt am Main: Suhrkamp, 1989, pp. 788, DM 74 hbk;
DM 28 pbk.
Reviewed by William Outhwaite

These three volumes are the first to be published in Suhrkamp's massive *Georg Simmel Gesamtausgabe*, edited by the eminent sociologist Otthein Rammstedt. The whole edition is planned to run to twenty-four volumes, coming out at the rate of two a year, so even without delays this heroic project will not be complete until well past the *fin de siècle*, and it may well run into the centenary of Simmel's death in 1918. It seems clear, however, that Simmel's time has come at last; neglected until recently in both the English- and, more surprisingly, the German-speaking world, his works are now selling at a healthy rate, and this edition, reasonably priced even for potential readers outside the Deutschemark zone, should make a major contribution.

The edition is chronologically ordered, partly because, as the blurb delicately puts it, most of Simmel's work cannot be unambiguously assigned to particular disciplines such as philosophy, sociology or aesthetics. These three volumes come from the first of the three periods which the editor identifies in Simmel's work: 1879–1900, 1901–8 and 1909–18. The early essays in Volume 2 are a characteristic example of the range of Simmel's work, covering pessimism, an essay on 'socioethical' issues which ranges from ancient Greece to Indian pessimism and Russian nihilism, a newspaper article on Michaelangelo's poetry, an essay on the psychology (*sic*) of money, delivered to the economist Gustav Schmoller's seminar and published in his yearbook, another on the psychology of women and finally an article on 'Moltke as a Stylist', written for a special number of the *Berliner Tageblatt* to mark the General's ninetieth birthday. The bulk of the volume includes two book-length works: 'On Social Differentiation', in which Simmel presents, among other things, a first version of his conception of an epistemology of social science, and the first edition of his 'Problems of the

Philosophy of History', substantially different from the expanded editions of 1905 and 1907.

Volume 3 is devoted to the first volume of Simmel's 'Introduction to Moral Philosophy' and a short reply to a review. Volume 6 contains the complete text of 'The Philosophy of Money'. All three volumes contain the minimal editorial apparatus, including useful lists of variations in the texts from one edition to another. All in all, a bold and admirable venture.

William Outhwaite teaches sociology at the University of Sussex, Brighton, England.